Jacki Lyden is a senior correspondent for National Public Radio and an expert on the Middle East. When not on the road, she lives in New York. *Daughter of the Queen of Sheba* has been optioned for film by Windrush Productions.

DAUGHTER OF THE QUEEN OF SHEBA

....

JACKI LYDEN

A FEW WORDS

This book was written first and foremost for my mother and my family, without whose reminiscences I could not have created it. But in the end the memories are mine, colored or pitted, perfect or imperfect, as best as I could recollect. It is the past as only I see it. My mother was unsparing in allowing me access to her records, and I have been unsparing, I suppose, not only in recreating her here, but in sharing memories with the world I know she does not always share herself. For all these reasons, I've changed many place names and proper names. However those closest to me regard this work, it is my tale, and a living reflection of the world we once shared together.

A *Virago* Book

Published by Virago Press 1999

Copyright © Jacki Lyden 1997
This edition Copyright © Jacki Lyden 1999

The moral right of the author has been asserted

A CIP catalogue record for this book is available from the British Library

ISBN 1 86049 653 9

Typeset by Palimpsest Book Production Limited
Polmont, Stirlingshire
Printed and bound in Great Britain by
Clays Ltd, St Ives plc

Virago Press
A Division of
Little, Brown and Company (UK)
Brettenham House
Lancaster Place
London WC2E 7EN

for my family

ACKNOWLEDGMENTS

This book depended on so many kind friends at odd intervals that it seems a miracle to have completed it. To name everyone who spoke an encouraging word would take pages, and yet I needed those words and am grateful for them. I would like to thank first of all Molly Daniels and the Clothesline Writers Workshop at the University of Chicago, as well as the William Benton Fellowship and its directors. Also the Writing Program at Skidmore College and the tutelage of David Rieff. I am deeply indebted to the writers Beverly Donofrio and Alex Kotlowitz, who kept congruent with me through many adventures and who, in Bev's case, led me to countless moments of revelation, as well as to the world's best and most indefatigable agent, Gail Hochman. I am grateful to her beyond anything I can put on the page. I would also like to thank the Ragdale and Yaddo foundations for their timely, indispensable retreats. And Natoinal Public Radio, and Bill Buzenberg and Barbara Rehm, for almost everything, lo these many, many years. In Canada, David and Grecia Kendall provided refuge, along with the denizens of Draper Street in Toronto, including Sally Glanville. And Amy Marcus, for Ward's Island, our readings, and her extraordinary friendship. In Ireland, thank you always to Ellie Lyden, who defines grace. And farther abroad, from the Gulf War and Baghdad to beyond, Nora Boustany, Hillary Mackenzie,

Geraldine Brooks, Tony Horowitz. Also in Iraq, I owe large thanks to Isho Yousif. From the Albourz Mountains and Tehran to Toronto, I am grateful always to Ramin Dedashtian and his loving companionship. And in Los Angeles, to Renee Montagne and Patricia Neighmond, colleagues and shelterers extraordinaire. Also to Jeffrey Shore for his wisdom and strength. He put me back together again.

Janet Silver at Houghton Mifflin is simply the editor of one's dreams, brilliantly talented. Her work on this book saved it from many swerves. And she was spectacularly assisted by Jayne Yaffe, my manuscript editor.

Finally, my thanks to Yair Reiner, for the joy he brings each day. And for reading that last line.

Failing to fetch me at first keep encouraged.
Missing me one place search another
I stop somewhere waiting for you

—Walt Whitman, *Leaves of Grass*

DAUGHTER OF

THE QUEEN

OF SHEBA

OH, MISS AMERICA, YOU ARE SO BEAUTIFUL TO ME

THE QUEEN OF SHEBA appeared one pallid afternoon about a week after my mother's return from the hospital. I came home from school to an unnaturally quiet house. My sisters were off somewhere with my grandmother, who had taken over the task of picking them up from school and sometimes took them on errands or to her house to give my mother a break. My mother was home alone, sitting at the smooth ranch oak kitchen table, staring out our second-story window at Lac La Jolie. Trees rimmed the hard darkness of the lake's edge, like dirt in an old bottle. Their branches moaned in the wind. It was starting to snow, and the remaining day was a natural fugue for November. My mother had taken the belt off her shirtwaist dress and was running it absently through her hands. I hugged her but felt uneasy, and asked if she was all right. She said yes in a distant and small voice. Not satisfied with her response, I sat with her awhile, then went to my room to change clothes. I curled up on my bed for a moment, intending to go back and jolly my mother up. I liked to do that. I had a talent for it. I would make her a treasure hunt. She found those amusing. Each clue would be a flower, something exotic to me like a hyacinth or a bird of paradise. I touched the flowers in my bedspread. My mother had painted my room lavender and hung lavender drapes. It was the first room of my own, a peace offering for having to live in my stepfather's house. In my room, I was allowed to stack as many books as I liked. I was reading one about both the Mayans and the Aztecs. The latter worshipped the goddess of the moon in the creamy light that fractured among the dark ziggurats of the Mexican plains. It was my Other Cultures period. I was dancing somewhere with the feathered hordes, holding a spray of quetzal plumes, when there was a knock on my door. Then the door opened and a vision stood there.

'I am the Queen of Sheba,' my mother announced to me in a regal voice. She had taken the silky yellow sheets from her voluptuous bed and twisted them around and around her torso like a toga, leaving one shoulder, as white as a gardenia, bare except for her bra strap. She'd used her eye pencil on her arms – the same one with which she lined the upper and lower inner lids of her eyes – and drawn hieroglyphics. The sheets around her were hooked together with heirloom antique pins from Austria. Her long auburn hair was swept up and crowned with an old tiara that we girls had played with as little children, pretending to be lost princesses. She looked at me solemnly.

'I am the Queen of Sheba,' she murmured confidentially, 'and I bequeath to each of my three daughters a country. To you, Jacki, the oldest, Mesopotamia. To your sister Kate, Thebes. To my youngest daughter, Sarah, who is nine, Carthage.' My mother moved her shoulders from side to side in the dreamy undulation of a tribal dance and twirled her fingers in the air, as if she wrought from it the great gift of an enchantment. Then she silently mouthed an incantation and blew me a kiss, backed up, pulled the door shut, and was gone.

I was alone in the house with her, but she might have been on another continent. I could not follow her. For a long while I lay still as I imagined a captive might lay on an Aztec altar. Then

I went to phone my grandmother at her bungalow. She didn't believe me for a moment, she said. Then she told me not to tell anyone and to stay in my bedroom until she arrived. My mother's bedroom door remained shut for almost an hour. Sheba was a vision, and she vanished that same afternoon in the twilight.

Christ Jesus had appeared to her as a white octopus, luminescent in the darkness, deep in the middle of the night in our small town of Menomenee, Wisconsin. It was 1966. I was twelve. My mother was young and beautiful, married to a man who didn't appreciate her nighttime disquisitions with 'Reverend Lord.' 'Jesus said, "Take my hand,"' my mother explained to me a quarter century later. My mother's hand was open like a bisque cup, all porcelain, and Christ Jesus' fingers were tentacles entangled around her palm. 'He said, 'Dolores, you are destined to do great things.' He said, "Dolores, I will exalt you through a thousand contests of the soul and the summits of all mountains and always be with you."' Well, someone had to be. Her conversation with Jesus was hardly a non sequitur. And everything happened to us after that.

My stepfather was the one in charge, not God. He was a doctor in our provident town and owned a small hospital and clinic, which treated half the populace, who granted him authority over their lives and paid him not only with cash but barter trade – buckets of blueberries, cartons of tomatoes, picked by hands smelling of motor oil. We lived above the clinic, on a fragment of a lush old farm overlooking Lac La Jolie. Having money walled us in, I thought. It afforded my stepfather a manner of universal disdain, accented by his height and his dark, ungraying hair, which was slicked back by brilliantine into a shining crest like Clark Gable's. To the people in our town, my stepfather was Richard Cory in the poem by Edward Arlington Robinson. He glittered when he walked.

The day after my mother had her first vision, without saying anything to anyone, he drove her in his banana yellow Cadillac to Wagner's Hospital. Wagner's was an old mansion that had been turned into a home for the mentally ill on an estate at the edge of town, beneath heavy and towering pines. I knew about Wagner's. The fate of unfortunate people was decided there, a fate reflected in the spectral light that shined through the pine bows surrounding it. I had heard that there were souls snaking in the branches. The shagged-off bark looked like the whorls of fingerprints, as if the trees had been touched by ghost escapees who cast hunched shadows on Wagner's long, circular drive. I could imagine my stepfather striding through the trees at Wagner's, parting the shadows like so much velvet drapery at daybreak. 'Nervous breakdown,' he announced to the receiving nurse at Wagner's, and my mother was small and mute beside him, more like a pretty child than a wife. He signed her in to one of the locked wards, and that was all we knew.

I came home from school to find my mother's mother standing like a rag bundler in my mother's kitchen. My grandmother always looked like that, like a woman born to physical labor, the Irish fishwife who trundled wheelbarrows full of mollusks, or dug kelp into the garden on her knees. Yet she loved drama, she had an almost operatic feeling for it. And so my grandmother was crying, inhaling her tears in a stagestruck manner, her embroidered sighs sailing like hankies somewhere down to me. She was keening, heaving, and intoning the names of Jesus and Mary and Joseph and all the saints. I wasn't praying; I was calculating. I compared the void of my mother's absence with the volume of my grandmother's sobs. I thought my mother was dead, that my stepfather had finally killed her and hidden her under the deep pine-needle carpet at Wagner's. Or that he had left her sequestered there forever in an old room with worn velvet brocade on the walls, until she joined the other ghosts. Of course, he hadn't killed her. But if she couldn't be perfect, she might as well be dead. Cracked crystal always gets thrown out, after all, no matter how cherished it once may have been.

Nervous breakdown. I wrote the words in my diary on October 1, 1966. I was a diarist from the time I could write, and I wrote on anything I could find: drug company calendars discarded by my stepfather, church envelopes, manila folders and shirt cardboards, autograph books, and my white plastic Girl Scout Diary with its gold trefoil and lock. I imagined my mother's nervous breakdown was like a maypole unraveling, reversing the centrifugal force, the streamers of her mind spinning backward in one grand rush. Perhaps that's how the mind loosened, with a snap, a fluttering sound, its images in tatters.

It was my grandmother who used the word *breakdown* first. 'Your mother's in the nuthouse,' she said that very first afternoon, tears winking over her face. 'Nervous breakdown. Like a car brakes is gone. No control. She's tired, her nerves is shot, she needs a rest. She dassn't know who she is.' My grandmother was a peasant and a rebel. She had the thickness of tallow in her voice, and she rubbed animal fat onto her red knuckles and face when she skinned beaver or mink. I loved her almost as much as I loved my mother. She believed in lies, or as we called them in the Irish tradition, stories, the more elaborate the better, and if stories had been gemstones then my grandmother would have offered to me the Hope diamond and the Jewel of Jamshid, the greatest star in Persia, because there was no story too great to offer her daughter or granddaughter. Which is why we almost never believed her. But I believed her that afternoon. Nervous breakdown meant nothing to her unless it meant a heart attack of the spirit. And I was grateful to her. Had Mabel, my grandmother, not come to stay with us – my two younger sisters and me – then we would have had to stay alone in that house with my stepfather. Then I might have been tempted to crush his brain with the piece of petrified stone I kept above my bed. Or I might have run away and joined the rodeo, a secret I often shared with my grandmother but did not effect until some years later. But how could I run away? Kate and Sarah and I and Mabel and my mother, Dolores, names like the rays on the compass. They were the world of visible magnetic force, and I could no more abandon them than rearrange the continents. My mother learned, however, that when the old geography became too painfully familiar she did not have to abandon it. She invented a country of her own.

Often that October when she picked us up from school in my mother's station wagon, my grandmother would drive my younger sisters and me past Wagner's Hospital, which was across the road from the silvery Lake Ipesong. Firs circled it like a feather collar. Many times we stopped, pretending to pick milk-weed pods or cattails or count geese on Ipesong, as we secretly cast hard glances up at the broad lawns of the sanitarium. We children had hunters' eyes for our mother. I could see a few patients wandering the greens, searching for croquet balls lost in another century, their gestures full of sticky lassitude, as if it were hot summer and not autumn. I never saw my mother, even though I felt her eyes upon me. I looked in vain at the vaulted windows for a lock of auburn hair under the Gothic eaves, or for a hand with red-painted moons. It was as if she were behind a harem's scrim, and she did not appear. Fall moved from soft to brittle days. From the lawn at Wagner's, I collected some of the vestigial leaves of autumn to look at them under the microscope in the junior high science room. The veins, their nervous system, were traceable, dissectible. In the leaf world, all was in order.

Nervous breakdown: the words locked in my diary. Nervous breakdown meant my mother slackened and sank, where before she was perpetual movement and our lives were the synthesis of that movement. Those were the days of my great religiosity: Bible classes, Communion classes, supplicant prayers. I pictured my mother's form caught in a pillar of light, as was the kneeling Mary Magdalene's on the flyleaf of my Bible, forever keeping watch in the Garden of Gethsemane. My mother would be sculpted and frozen solid, encased by the Gethsemane moonlight, she and Mary Magdalene on their knees together. Just as I was getting used to this image, my stepfather brought her home.

As my mother came up the front walk toward us, she looked to me like a fawn I'd seen penned on a farm, its nose sniffing the air. Like the fawn, she held her head at an odd angle, as if invisible antlers weighed it down. Or perhaps she was listening for faraway music. A lambency lit her eyes: on, off, there, here. You could see the filament glow and fade. But she said, 'Oh, kids, I missed you so,' and we cried, 'Oh, Mom, we missed you too!' and she had yards of hugs for all of us, holding my youngest sister close until she writhed in her arms. She planted kisses. She baked cookies for us. It was years before I knew that my stepfather had checked her out against all advice and prescribed her medication himself from that time on, upping the Haldol on his own scrip. I saw the scrawls and the bottles lined up in our medicine cabinet. 'To Pretty Face for Peace of Mind.' 'To Dolly Girl for a Weak Heart.' Nembutal, Valium, kisses from the 1960s.

I have been watching warily for the Queen of Sheba ever since, but never so hard as when my mother slips off into the caverns where the past and present and future are etched together. You could say that my life as her daughter, the life of my imagination, began with my mother's visions. My sisters and I took them for our texts. Her madness was our narrative line. I am trying to decipher that line still, for its power and meaning over our past. Many years later, as an adult, I longed to be sent to find things out in places of great secrets, loving most the places that were the farthest and strangest and hard. When I finally reached Mesopotamia as a journalist in the curse-filled days before the Gulf War, when Saddam Hussein had vowed to burn up half the earth and dance on crushed skulls and drink the blood of American pilots (but could not in fact properly air-condition his hotels), secrets were the main currency. In those long afternoons in Iraq, where men were held hostage as human shields, I drank cocktails in the shelters of embassies and private clubs and thought of the misery and lust on the faces of those who could not leave the heavy glaze of their confinement. I traveled. I was free. To interview the hostages, I could put on a dress with patterns of green leaves and fruit. I could dress with the care of an ancient queen. I could trace my toe in the red dust of Saddam's false Babylon, a grotesquerie not worthy of my mother's imagination. I could wander Baghdad with the secret police, the Muhabarat, trailing along in bored pursuit.

I remember peeling a date, so at ease, cleaning it and chewing, and buying postage stamps of Saddam Hussein at a kiosk, beneath the signs of Babylon that pictured Saddam as the direct descendant of Nebuchadnezzar, his fantasy. I was thinking of Sheba. She was my conqueror. She was at my back, always, her hand on my spine, pushing me before I woke each morning, pushing me even to Iraq as I waited for a war to begin, pushing me or I would not be writing this down. A veil slips from Sheba, and underneath I see . . . wind through the date palms, an eddy of limbs dancing. Her fingernails are like the crescents of moon that adorn the mosques of all believers.

For just like that, our lives had a way of falling prey to her guile, as my mother herself fell, a slippage, a breath, nothing very great, no time to look back, to grab each other's hands. Just my mother turning around to say, 'I must be dreaming,' and our lives fell away at a touch, mine with hers – throughout my life as a college student, girlfriend, journalist in Belfast or Baghdad, Chicago or London, the life that paralleled her life as a cocktail waitress, a hotel clerk, a model. Reality fell in waves with unreality, commingling, and washed out to sea. But I could never re-create myself as completely as my mother had. Returning from an assignment, I would fly home to Menomenee, Wisconsin, to discover my mother in a new guise: a millionairess or a coronated duchess, a CEO patenting great inventions, a racehorse owner. Once I found her intent on tracing some trajectory of her brain, using the kitchen knife as a quill on Kate's ribs. Kate's arms, thank God, were too strong for her.

When I was growing up, my mother's bouts of madness usually lasted a few months and then melted away like ice in the spring. But before she was dragged back to her ordinary life, after the forcible administration of drugs to her bloodstream as she writhed under leather restraints, something monstrous showed itself beneath the rind of ice. Let us call it desire. I am not suggesting that my mother went mad because she felt, as a beautiful woman, that she deserved more. Yet unanswered longing and betrayal leave their scars. Men have played some savage parts in her life, have failed to come to her rescue. For myself I would like a cross between Albert Einstein and a Canadian Mountie. But we manage to save ourselves in the end. Everyone does.

For me, my mother's deliriums were like the tides created by the moon, growing in force as I grew older and pulling me after them, with a precise gravity, pulling me ineluctably from whatever bank I clung to, no place too far. My grandmother and sisters felt these nethertides too, and every time they summoned me I went home. No one seemed to be able to corner my mother without me, and I couldn't stay away. The women in my family learned to relay the signals, beginning in earnest when I went away to college. My grandmother would call me at all hours of the day and night to say that my mother had deposited a basket of kittens at a car dealership in lieu of payment, or purchased a carload of lingerie, or legally changed her name so that it somehow matched the name of a department store. Dolores Gimbels of Gimbels Schuster.

'She's ashamed a' the name I gave her,' my grandmother said, sobbing. 'She dassn't want to be reminded a' me! Like I'm not even her ma!' Oh so true, Grandma, so true, your muskrat soup, your tacky flypaper trailing over the kitchen sink, your worn, crepey slippers that flap as they shuffle on the stairs. I mentally turned over the several last names that my mother had acquired over the years – real name changes, phony ones, temporary pet names from books or songs – and thought of how we all called one another by our first names now, my grandmother, mother, and I. More like sisters that way, as Mabel, Dolores, and Jack. A boy pulled Dolores onto his lap when she visited me at a college party, both of them flirtatious. She was past forty. Bruce, I said, meet Dolores. Mom, I said, meet Bruce. His momentary recoil, then his change of heart! He pulled her to him, his face lusty as if it didn't matter what age she was! Meet any nice mothers, Bruce? his friends teased him later. Is that your sister? people would say, looking at my mother and then at me. Yes, I would answer, convincing them easily, feeling the truth to be private knowledge. She was at such moments not my mother but the essence of womanhood, drawing on some fount beyond age.

As the years passed and I entered my twenties in Chicago, Mabel, my grandmother, would call deep into the night and sigh down the phone line. Sometimes she left the line open even if I was nearly silent, my head buried between pillow and phone, the cord coiled between the night's hangover and perhaps a lover in the bed, hummocked and sleeping beneath my sheets. I lay awake listening to my grandmother, her sibilant hisses like a membrane webbing us together. As I lay still I could hear her smoking. I could see the smoke rings in the air. My grandmother lived only eight miles from my mother, in a bungalow on Lake Puckawasay. My grandmother's house was always damp and musty from the lake's decaying presence. Mildew flowers bloomed on her furniture. It was easy to picture my grandmother, sitting up suddenly at night in her cheap tin bed, her gray hair spiked and twisted like a poppet's. The flannel collar she wrapped around her arthritic neck would be slipping down. Her puckered fingers, red and rough with bleach, would poke at the collar. 'Can'tcha come up, Jack?' she'd say into the phone, her hoarse insistence rousing me. Her voice was rustic, a peasant's voice, a linguistic hand-me-down left behind by the Swedes and the Germans and the Irish-speaking to one another over plows and stone fences in the late 1800s. 'I dassn't know what t' do. I'm sweatin' bullets. Can'tcha come up, Jack, can'tcha come up?'

I would sigh, and then inhale, smelling the clouds of Woolworth's talcum powder that floated in her bedroom where she was forever dabbing it on her broad, hot feet. She said, 'Can'tcha come up?'

On the morning of a particularly blinding hangover in 1979, with the trace of someone – the Mexican waiter who poured the flaming blue aquavit – outlined onto the sheets and my head thrumming like a tuning fork, Mabel called and croaked, 'Your mother's dead.' It was a Sunday in December, 10:45 A.M. exactly. The quivering pain in my head exploded.

I looked outside at a dog barking on the street, its breath a blot of cloud. How could this dumb creature be alive and not my mother? I remembered that fraternity party, 1973, six years before. She'd worn a sweater dress the color of French vanilla, a thread trailing from the hem in a smudge. I had watched her leap up, the thread tracing an arc of energy. She could not be dead. 'How?' I asked Mabel. 'Car accident,' she wailed. 'Smashup on the highway. Just her.' She was dead, and immediately the thought followed that I wanted her gone. I felt the most sickening sort of relief, entering that gyre of the forbidden. To be rid of her felt like a simultaneous blessing and curse.

On that snowy December Sunday in Wisconsin, a small woman

in beautiful clothes had parked her soon-to-be-repossessed late-model sports car amid the crowds of Christmas shoppers at a mall, clutching her faux fox collar around her neck to avoid detection. Slipping inside a phone booth. Faking a terrible Bavarian accent. 'Hello, iss this Mabel Palkovic? Hef you got a Dolores Taylor there? Oh no? That's kass we hef her, dead on the highway, smashed like hickory nuts, a terrible car accident.'

Then the poseur, also known as Mom in schadenfreude dialect, told my grandmother to order a funeral wreath. 'Such a shame, too young to die, yah?' I couldn't believe that my grandmother had fallen for this, even though she fell for everything, a fibber's courtesy. It took me not five minutes to check with Wisconsin highway authorities. Hickory nuts were the tip-off. We three girls had flattened them with our father, with big stones, on the shores of Lake Puckawasay, fishing the mild nutmeat out with bent nails and scattering the shells in the water.

But my mother *was* missing on that December Sunday: vision, essence, and corporeal self. That night I did the first radio show of my life, pretending to talk to that 'one special person out there,' as the veteran disc jockey whom I adored advised me to do. For him, that one special person was a lonely salesman hopefully selecting a shirt for his Saturday-night date, a new mother rocking a tearful baby with one hand as she tuned the knob to the Doobie Brothers with the other. And my one special person was my mother, Dolores, missing in action, faking her own death, torching the tame moment, a different fantasy with every succeeding hour. I fantasized that she could hear me, my debut on the air of this Chicago FM station, WKQX. I am talking to you, Mom, I thought. Goddamit. Listen to me for once. Wherever you are, this is me, your daughter, speaking. My voice on the radio at last! Damn, damn, damn. Give yourself up. Or I will – what? Manacle you to my side? Put you in a pumpkin shell, a closet, a hospital ward?

I was an invisible denizen of the radio band that Sunday night, talking as if I knew what I was talking about, talking on an absurd late-night public affairs show, talking about the gold standard and how it was a hedge against inflation and trouble in the Middle East, the region of unstable tribes. I was twenty-six years old and knew nothing of gold or OPEC or the tribal scores settled among Arab nations. Talking, hearing myself chatter. I would never own any gold. *Dhahab*, in Arabic. 'You're listening to "Backtalk" on WKQX, Chicago. A gazette for the informed listener, every Sunday night.' Do I sound as ridiculous as I feel foolish? Mother, might that be you? Are you laughing at me? Can'tcha come up, Jack? Can'tcha come up? I'll manacle you to my side.

The show finished at midnight. 'Good night, Chicago. Hope you've enjoyed it as much as I have.' But you can't know what I know, Chicago, now can you? I flew to the car and behind the wheel, with Jack Daniel's as my co-pilot. In those days I thought absolutely nothing of speeding up to a hundred miles an hour. I thought that's what highways and odometers were for. So did my grandmother. My foot was welded to the pedal, and I shouted over Willie Nelson on the radio, singing, 'Mama, don't let your babies grow up to be cowboys,' the tollbooths just a smear behind my eyes, the odometer jagging upward like the fuel gauge on a juggernaut. Snow slanted into the headlights and there was nothing more to see in the middle of that black December night on a highway in the Midwest, except the cornstalks frozen in the headlight's beam, snow draped over them like the altar scarves on crucifixes.

My brain, stirred by the loss of sleep and ancient agitations, rolled out images of my mother as vivid as the sunrise over Lake Puckawasay: my mother in her Menomenee Legion Band marching uniform, 1958; my mother in her gold brocade dress, second wedding, 1960; my mother in her afternoon-tea outfit of houndstooth check with matching cape, 1970. That would be for the Lac La Jolie Golf Club Women's Auxiliary. And after 1975: my mother in her sales clerk's apron, her waitress's dirndl, her flat-soled shoes laced up and her elegant costumes of decades past pushed to the back of the closet like discarded circus finery.

My mother was the one who showed me how to pull my hair into a French twist. She was auburn-haired, like me, a petite woman. She had perfectly even teeth in a bright runway smile and huge, startling brown eyes. What transformed her beauty was her belief in it, and her belief in its protection. She romanced trouble; it was a gold bar, a bar of *dhahab*, that she gave to me as a hedge against boredom. She believed in risk. She taught me to say, on a day when the high school seniors dressed like characters from old movies (God, how innocent that seems now . . .), 'When you get an eyeful, fill your pocket.' I said it a hundred times to everyone, a phrase lost on me but not, apparently, on the high school principal, who asked me about it later, red-faced in the privacy of his office. My mother.

I pulled off the highway at two A.M. My mother, now divorced from my stepfather, was living in a bald suburban development then, so new and raw that it smelled of the cow manure pasture it had once been, even in winter. Her home was as dark as Calvary. I crept into the house delicately, listening, letting the door swing open and calling out to her. She could be dangerous in the dark. 'Mom,' I shouted at the door. 'Are you here? Answer me if you are!' I stayed there, trembling. When I was little I used to sing to my mother, 'I love you a bushel and a peck, a hug around the neck.' I hummed it now in my head, past the dark, past the blue demons I was sure lined the hall. I sang loudly, making the notes dance toward the basement and up the stairs. A hundred bushels and a thousand pecks, I do, I do.

That's when I realized that the house smelled awful, a smell of dead fish. I snapped on the lights. Dizzy. A mistake. It was a house party for an acid trip, the Mad Hatter's tea party, and I felt as if I had drunk the Red Queen's dram. My mother had taken reality away with her and turned it inside out like a glove.

The Christmas tree had been spray-painted gold and stuck in a bucket of plaster of paris. The spoon she had used to mix the plaster was stuck in the bucket too, like an ice cream scoop frozen into a dish of vanilla. The dead and gilded tree leaned over at a drunken angle, like a cocktail parasol in a shot glass, and when I gave the tree a tap, the brittle needles prattled onto the carpet. Starlights twinkled in what scraggly limbs remained. The crackling, shrunken branches of the tree were festooned with dog biscuits and expensive, lacy bras, and a baby bracelet that I recognized as belonging to one of my sisters. A pair of gold panties dangled from one branch. I breathed slowly, listening to more needles patter into the booming silence. This was my mother's Christmas tree, a gold shrunken skeleton, wearing panties. On the walls, my mother had stuck large drawings, diminishing the living room. There were giant praying hands and an Infant of Prague, the Catholic icon of childlike confidence, at least that's who I thought this crowned baby was, a pudgy blue fist clutching a real-life rosary tacked onto the wall with nails. In the basement rec room, my mother had set up brightly colored directors' chairs, strewn around the green carpet like a day at the beach, their backs painted with whatever catch phrases had jolted into her head: 'Once is never enough' and 'Take what you need' and 'Girls just want to have fun.' They had a gay, Annette-meets-Frankie quality, as my mother herself did when she was well.

The smell like a rotting catch of mackerel came from the dining room. My mother had laid on an elaborate and careful party, betraying days of manic effort: radishes carved with tiny faces and spelling out the word *love* on a silver tray, steak tartare decorated with whipped cream and tiny plastic ballerinas on swizzle sticks, dancing merrily: oysters on platters with paper

feet cut from magazines; and clams with pink feather fluffs. I
checked the Christmas place cards, little angels bearing names.
Lord Jesus the Christ, of course, was at the head of the table,
and there was Mary Baker Eddy, the Christian Scientist founder
who was always a portent of my mother's insanity. Harvey the
Six-Foot Pooka had a place of honor. ('You can't see him,' it said
on his card, 'but he's here! Shake Paws with Harvey!') And there
was a card for my sister Sarah, announcing that she was now the
CEO and treasurer of my mother's new business, Ant Trap Zap,
designed to lure ants into old bottle caps and electrocute them.
'They die as they fry,' my mother's curly handwriting crowed. And
there was a card for Alfred, another potential problem. Alfred
really existed. A wealthy local brewmeister who'd decamped to
Menomenee County from Milwaukee, Alfred had no idea who
my mother was, despite the fact that he was her secret lover. And
yet I had come to think of *him* as an interloper on *our* peace.
When my mother was ill, she sent Alfred things, all sorts of
things. The sheriff once called to tell me that he'd picked up a
roomful of such stuff from Alfred, who was mulling over whether
to file some sort of lawsuit. I tried to imagine his mystified face as
he received a pack of silk G-strings with a note from my mother.
'From your Secret Admirer, Zippity Doo-Dah! And I know you
can fill these up! Zip, Zip!'

I picked up a polished silver butter knife. Every piece of the
Eternally Yours silver pattern had been tied with a pink bow.
Every bit of crystal sparkled. And yet no one would raise a
glass to my mother to offer her Christmas cheer. On the table
and growing stale, indeed, petrified, were platters and platters
of cheeses and sausages, accompanied now by an odorous whiff
of my mother's famous sour cream dip, coagulated and turning
spotty. In the middle of the table was a black cast-iron cherub,
lying on its back, all fat belly, its legs splayed and a pickle placed
between them in unmistakable suggestion. A slip of pink paper

in the cherub's mouth said 'Ha!' Ha, yourself, I thought. We'll see who has the last ha! I plucked the pickle and ate it.

Then I picked up one of my mother's homemade cookies, the lumpy brown joke cookies that she'd baked before, containing whiskey or chile oil or anchovies, even soap. They were a variant on a game we used to play in Girl Scouts when we'd have to eat bits of mystery food wrapped in foil and placed in a paper bag. A relay race followed. Failure to eat the mystery morsel meant that you had to drop out. Once my mother wrapped a clam like a candy kiss. The first person to eat an anchovy cookie and throw up lost.

I moved slowly up the stairs to Dolores's bedroom. Her white twin beds looked hard, even virginal, as though they belonged in a convent. A crucifix hung over the one she used, on the left. Neat stacks of paper lay on the spread of the other bed. She'd been busy. Mania eats up slumber, grabs at repose and shakes the body awake for dances, for plots, for a carousel of tales that spin on the mind's gimbals. Sleep was ravaged, but sometimes my mother did fall into a kind of trance, a numbness showing a half-drawn eyelid, the white showing beneath the pleated pink like blank paper lying in a drawer. Her room was strewn with notes and diagrams that I hoped would be the clues to her netherworld – fictitious family trees showing her to be the daughter of Mary Baker Eddy, divine instructions, Bible verses torn and glued with cutouts from the newspaper crosswords. SEE. CRETE. ALFRED IS THE SON OF GOD DIVINE.

Her hands were always busy trying to translate her brain. 'Fantastic,' she would say, staring at the horizon like the Sphinx, and jot something down. Months of manic jottings. Reams of paper. The prosaic and humdrum modes of life were her alchemy. She could make rituals out of pencil and ink.

On the mirror over the low bureau something caught my eye. At first I thought it was another Infant of Prague diorama. But no, it was I, the Infant of Dolores. A baby picture of me and of my two sisters, our heads cut out, pasted to the mirror with fruit stickers, pineapples and bananas, from Dole. We were like seraphim, with crayon wings drawn around our disembodied heads and magenta lipstick applied to our lips. Our mouths were bleeding, open wounds, demented. Above our decapitated trio, my mother had written in more lipstick, 'I like myself. Thank you, God. Tra-La!' But what of your children? I wanted to know.

When my mother was sick, the connection between us could not be contained in a simple word like *love* or *hate*. In her illness her children were a manic memory, boiled in a manic brain. And yet the energy of her mania was no different from the energy that kept her up all night, superior to all other mothers, making us costumes for special occasions and inventing games to play with our friends. Now she had fled from me. And why not? She knew I was trying to trap her, waiting for her to make a false move. Waiting to slam her into what we both sometimes called the bin, the nuthouse, the funny farm, the Good Ship Lollapalooza. Lock the lunatics away, you think, and they will do no permanent damage to themselves or others. The damage grows inside, though, where you can only sense what is unseen, spreading like moss, or a spiked vine creeping over the brain and flaring down to the tongue.

I longed to know my mother's secret language when she went mad. I yearned to know its passwords and frames of reference. In the last and most desperate stages of mania, my mother's speech falls to pure sound. A guttural like Urdu, rhythmic and completely foreign. Often I can make out words, but they have no context. At such times I cannot help but go a little crazy myself. I talk to the ghosts, to the people in our lives thirty years ago, to two small girls in long grass. I mean I talk to my mother and to me. I ask us why we cannot grow up, what has happened to make the past so vexing for us both. I torture myself that she is suffering now for all the longings then, longings I helped inflict in my child life. I have become obsessed with finding her in a chiaroscuro world where, despite every art of intimacy that I have ever learned, I am in high seas. She is lost. And I cannot follow.

Yet I want to follow. For our journey, I want a map, compass, and sextant, I want a dictionary with all the common usage and formal tongues of speech in her vocabulary. I want the langue d'oc and the langue du pays, the romance and the common languette of her invented diction. I want to meet all of the people she will be meeting on her descent, as I go with her, a journalist to the last. Do I need anything in this world but notebook and pen, tape recorder and microphone? I have crossed the world dozens of times with no more than that. I am a searcher. I collect the potsherds of evidence. I take names. I want to know more about these impostors and pretenders, and what they think they are doing there dancing with my mother. Isn't it unseemly for her to do the hula, dancing the shape of stars to music I can't hear? And if any of her unseen partners gets fresh with her or hurts her in any way, I want to punch his lights out. Most of all, I want these creatures to be kind to my mother, not to disappoint. They must make up now for what was denied to her then.

In her well life, Dolores might say, 'Jack, come look!' Come look at the albino squirrel! Come look at the great blue heron! He's a walking stick over the water, a minuet bird in the shallows of Lake Puckawasay, performing this parsed motion just for us. Dolores kneels on the sidewalk outside my grandmother's bungalow. 'Look how the moss rose has grown again here by the pathway where I've pulled it up a thousand times!' Yesterday there was nothing but a skin of earth. Now come and look at the tenacious world blooming in her hands. And then my mother might, in a moment, a breath, slip off, growing strange gently at first and then with force, a tidal pull. It was an immanent act I could not see, the creeping voices lushly filling her, whispering, until in mere hours she was a lunatic standing stock-still at the bottom of the stairs and chattering, 'I must be dreaming. I am getting a message in my curling iron. Is God trying to tell me something? Is he unhappy with me?' Sometimes she would write such questions on cards, with illustrations, and tape them to her mirror. Or she'd stare, seeing the inhabitants of Lilliput, perhaps, or the other unhealed ghosts she'd meet in those transcendent grottoes.

On that December night with the gilded Christmas tree dying downstairs, I sat at my mother's dressing table, no room for anything in my mother's mirror but myself. I pasted a roll of pink raspberry stickers to each of my fingers, like a manicure, a roll of raspberry fingernails extended one by one to wave at my image. Her room. At first I could not sense it, but the longer I sat before the mirror I felt her stare sear me. Felt it grow hotter, and start to scar, and mutate into a kind of howl in my head. Something greater than fear clutched at my throat, and I could feel my mother embracing me, invisible, pressing my arms from behind, her flesh on mine. Once, she had attacked Kate and me in a local restaurant, although, to be fair, Kate and I had seized her by the shoulders and tried to pull her bodily past the dessert cart. She was wearing nothing but a black bra underneath a peekaboosheer blouse and a matching miniskirt. She was trying to entice. She would have succeeded. She would not come home with us. It was late. Kate and I charged. Diners gawked as the three of us wrestled over a sofa and a lamp, gouging and scratching, red grooves on our arms, a bite mark on my shoulder, blood under all our fingernails. I felt those wounds again, felt their outlines, and heard her terrible chambered laugh as I was smothered by rich skin and mussed hair and orchid perfume. She was there, pushing the air from my lungs, my mother as Durga leering in my body, and in the force of her lust I'd be obliterated. I ran from the bedroom and the house, leaving the lights on, breathing breaths I told myself were my own to breathe, no one else's, running to the car and jacking it into reverse and roaring for the haven of my grandmother's house.

It was almost dawn, and Mabel would be up waiting for me. Often at dawn, no matter how much she'd drunk the night before, Mabel would bake bread. I wanted to touch the roughness of her baking boards and touch the flour to my forehead as if it were Ash Wednesday. I rolled down the car window. The snow was still falling, cloaking all that was raging and burning, like the secret trembling in my head and the mother inside me. I wanted the car to fill with snow, to drive headlong into it, one hundred thousand miles an hour. Swathed in snow, wrapped around us like a beautiful winding sheet, the car and I would dive down – and then no more thought. But I saw that I was already at Lake Puckawasay, which was as still as a chapel.

Much later that morning, my sister Kate arrived at my grand-mother's and listened while I described our mother's house. 'I have a hunch Dolores tried to go to Las Vegas,' Kate said. Kate lived nearest of all to my mother, but was not considered the arbiter of my mother's destiny. She had at that time just moved back from a commune in Oregon, where she'd run naked and eaten wild plants and roots and renamed herself 'Ka.' Ka had acquired a sun tattoo the size of a grapefruit on her belly.

'If you hold up a piece of cucumber, Jack, you can see the sun particles in it,' she'd once said, doing so and squinting at it with one eye. Another time, as we were quietly riding our horses in the woods, she declared, 'The reason I am so subservient to men is that in my previous life I was a geisha.'

But I loved Kate. I felt responsible for her, as I did for Sarah too, but Kate and I were closer in age, thirteen months apart. When Kate was small, she had been so shy that if a stranger looked at her, she'd close her eyes and stop breathing, huffing only in little gasps like a cornered animal. I have a memory of her fist in mine when she was a kindergartner, too frightened to ask the counterman for the root beer barrels and lemon drops behind his glass case. Kate closed her eyes against the world, mute. I'm six and she's five. Sunlight sluices over her as she stands amid the tin pails and bridles of the general store, her feet making not a sound on the floorboards. Sssh! Jack, someone might hear us! Tiptoe quietly.

And then, one day, Kate turned thirteen. Her biceps balanced her on the parallel bars, her legs scissored the gymnasium air, and Kate was a star. Cheerleading, acrobatics, tumbling. The muscles corded over her. And then the jumbled kinetics of teenage years, the hoodlums on the fringe, a boy who died of alcohol poisoning as he froze sleeping in his car. Kate's best girlfriend and three others perished in a boozy prom-night car wreck. A canyon opened in my sister. Kate swallowed pills. After high school, Kate became Ka. Layer by layer and year by year, she'd given up her shyness for an amalgamation of white witchcraft, Taoist philosophy, Rosicrucian prayer and study, vegetarianism, and whatever else she found interesting. She was brilliantly good with the tarot, she had the gift. She had her own visions. These were her defenses against my mother.

'She's been talking about Las Vegas for a while now,' Kate repeated in a focused, un-Ka-like way.

I explained to my sister that I hadn't done my usual thorough investigation at our mother's house. 'I had a panic attack in her bedroom. I dreamed she was devouring me, and I wasn't even asleep. I ran out of there like there was some nighthawk at my heels.'

'You saw the forces of darkness itself,' Kate said, being Ka again.

'I saw myself,' I said. Going crazy. My mother had been completely well until the age of thirty-four. My secret, fathomless fear was that I would reach that age and follow suit. I had less than a decade to go.

I called the airport. It was closed by the descending blizzard, and that was some comfort. I sat down heavily. I was the oldest, stiffest twenty-six-year-old in human history, chastened by the limits of my mortality. My mother could fly, she had wings that stretched to the Strait of Magellan. I had braggadocio that said, 'Only I can save her.' But I did not know how.

'I saw how she decorated the tree,' said Kate, who'd visited my mother earlier that week. 'It's a real doozer.' She grinned.

'A doozer for a schmoozer,' I said. 'There're some interesting food items on that dining room table too. By the way, have you seen your baby bracelet recently?'

I mulled over the Las Vegas notion. Of all the poses my mother adopted, none frightened me more for her safety than that of a certain feigned raciness. In her real life, my mother was flirtatious in a sort of Doris Day style, but an utter pot of milk on the follow-through. In her mentally ill life, she was outrageous, a cocktease, an imaginary mistress and feather-boa operator. I could just imagine her telling a blackjack dealer at Circus Circus, after she'd bet the house and lost, that Alfred of Milwaukee brewing fame would soon show up to pay the tab. Cleavage from here to South America. Say she picked up someone, a farm implement dealer from Wichita, his face a smile like a half-pulled zipper. He would regard her as booty, a crazy slot machine for combine salesmen. I saw her make an escape, talons over his eyes. When ill, she had the strength of several men. She might say that she had a Mafioso boyfriend coming over to break his thumbs. In her mind, it was just possible. Bones would be broken, or worse. I sat and thought of the headlines in the *Menomenee Herald*. 'Local Woman Terrorizes Las Vegas Casino.' 'Six-Foot Pookas Nibble on Mob Bosses.' The fear was bunching up again in my throat, buttoning itself in.

My grandmother interrupted my line of thinking. She came trundling up the unfinished stairs of her dank basement with a basket of laundry, in her stained pinafore and baggy anklets as resigned as a charwoman, an elderly scullery wench in servitude to my enchanted mother. Mabel's dark green glasses, lenses the color of smoky forest glades, were askew, always a sign of alarm and rattled thoughts. Mabel looked as blanched as I felt, the rheumatism collar around her neck reeking of Ben-Gay. She took another step and emerged from the darkness, dropping the laundry basket, and her hands darted over the kitchen basin like crazed water spiders, going for her pills.

'So,' she said, sitting down heavily. She spilled a mess of socks into her apron, Molly Malone and her oyster shells. She took her teeth out of her mouth and put them back in. 'We dassn't know where she is. She ain't called. Kate calls and thinks she dead. Then *she* calls and *says* she's dead. Then *you* call and she ain't dead. I feel like a truck backed over me seven times. So who's goin' over to clean up your mother's house? Or are you just goin' to leave it like that?' Kate and I got ready. Mabel had been ready for hours. Bake bread, drink a little whiskey, and go. That was Mabel. All her life she'd lived for thrills, and my mother gave her plenty of them. And not cheap ones, either.

In the end I did not want my grandmother to see Dolores's house until Kate and I had cleaned up as much as possible. There are things that even seventy-eight-year-old mothers do not need to see or know about their daughters. The lingerie came down from the tree, except for the topmost pair of panties. We found them gaily defiant, like our mother at her best. I collected all of my mother's scribblings ('God is love.' 'Keep your hearts and minds filled with truth.' 'Wisdom is the principal thing, therefore get wisdom,' Proverbs 4:7) and put them into my keepsake box, where I saved all evidence of my mother's mental health. The torturous food was swept into garbage bags. We aired out the dining room and kitchen. I dutifully called the sheriff to say that

Dolores was missing, hoping the phony car accident might rouse some interest, but clearly he was not going to look for her on a snowy Christmas Eve day unless I came up with a scenario of immediate danger. The sheriff knew my mother and had come to admire her never-say-die lunacy. His own mother was 'that way,' he once confided to me. Bought a condominium in Florida with a second mortgage no one knew about. She had other delusions of grandeur too, once going to the beauty parlor asking to look like Jean Harlow! Charged the equivalent of her life savings on her credit card. Once they got 'that way,' you had to sit back and see if they didn't wander off buck naked. If Dolores *really* stabbed someone, he might come. Meanwhile, lock up the knives. He said I was to call him when things got really bad, 'You know, if she comes home and is kind of aggressive.'

So like tribal villagers trying to appease a distant god, Kate and I prepared the foods for Christmas that my mother would have made had she been well and home. I thought of our household arts, begun in a Betty Crocker cookbook for children in the 1950s, standing on a chair, my mother whipping icing as we made igloo cakes and painted-face cookies. Now, I suggested to Kate, we might put our snacks on some kind of pedestal outside the house and see if Dolores were lured by our offerings of midwestern savories, oyster stew, Swedish meatballs, Mexican dip (which I am sure no Mexican has ever heard of), and spritz cookies squeezed to look like camels and hearts and one with blue sugar spelling out Dolores. Dolores Come Home. I made one that said, 'Surrender, Dolores.' I saved a few of the joke cookies to see if anyone would notice. Kate and I made rum punch and waited for Sarah to come home from law school. 'Surprise,' I hooted at Sarah when she walked in the door. 'Who can identify the owner of the Christmas panties?'

'A masterpiece,' said Sarah, dropping her suitcase and looking around in total amazement. She knew my mother was gone.

'Mabel called and put Mom on the phone a couple nights ago. She was crying hysterically about this party no one came to. I was trying to get ready for my torts final.' She really never forgave Dolores for her poor grades that year. But then, I told Sarah, she needed to roll better with the punches.

Sarah was twenty-three, smart, and in her first year of law school. She believed, wrongly, that law was a career that would be free from surprises. Wildly caustic, willfully sensible, she had walled herself in against my mother, who kept poking through the chinks. I shall have none of this, Sarah insisted to herself, annihilating our mother in her head, plotting her own life like a graph, with flowcharts, balances, and columns carried forward into personal dividends. 'You see, I just want to know this week precisely what I'll be doing next week at the same time,' Sarah once said to me earnestly. Sarah would separate the wheat from the chaff, the loonies from the bin, and become a lawyer, intent on a world full of order and things that matched. My mother knew this, even when unwell, and nailed Sarah neatly, once leaving a red satin bustier on the doorstep of Sarah's apartment in Milwaukee. Often, my mother had some legal work she thought Sarah should do on behalf of her many lawsuits, which my mother neatly wrote out on yellow legal pads and delivered at dawn. My mother had learned law as a legal secretary. Sarah admired my mother's logical briefs even as she fortified herself against Dolores, not always successfully. Once, when Sarah was in junior high school and Dolores was sick, Sarah wandered into the best clothing shop in Menomenee and pilfered everything she could get her hands on, grown-up stuff that she could never have worn. 'I couldn't help it, Jack,' she explained to me when I went to fetch her after the store manager's summons. 'The clothes were just flying onto my body, Jack.' She was fourteen then.

'Can't you do something?' Sarah said to me now. 'I feel like her life is consuming mine. I study torts, and she calls up and says she's suing the town of Menomenee for towing her car when she left it on the sidewalk. I've got a nuisance complaint filed by Vinter's Toy Store last month because she's left Lurex G-strings on their shelves. Or she calls up and tells me to sue her plastic surgeon because her ears aren't on straight, one is an inch higher or lower than the other. Or she tells me that now that she's admitted her Mafia connections I should write some Mafia guy named Frank Parmenetti because she's going to inherit his money. She'd like to have it now in small bills tied with garters. Blue ones. Do you think we should get some kind of restraining order so I can study?'

'Gee,' I said. 'I'm sorry you're so inconvenienced. Study harder, and when you get to be a lawyer, we can keep it all in the family. I'll write an exposé, Kate can tackle her, and you can defend her.' I suppose this has come true, if not in that order. But I had no good answers for Sarah then. The law of Wisconsin which governed our lives stated that not until my mother became an absolute 'threat to the life of herself or others' could we commit her. And so each time we waited and agonized, watching as her money drained away, commiting acts that would have mortified her had she been well. We tried to compile evidence, planning for the moment when she was a significant threat but not so significant that someone was hurt, or hurt only mildly. Which was a trick for us in itself.

We celebrated Christmas by christening the tree 'Alfred,' by putting more rum in our eggnog, and then having an extra glass before midnight Mass. Mabel had extras of extras and fell asleep in a chair. We put all Dolores's favorite Christmas records on the stereo, hamming it up on lines like 'She sees you when you're sleeping, she knows when you're awake' or 'I saw Mommy kissing Santa Claus!' Every time someone bumped the sofa or jumped onto the stairs, needles flew from the tree so that before long the bare branches held one pair of panties like the Lambda Chi flagpole. Hard to acknowledge, hard to believe that she was not home with us, she who so loved celebration, who would drive thirty miles out of her way to get the right Christmas ornament. We had teetered before, a matriarchal family on a rubber raft in roiling water, but Christmas was the Eucharist of faith over chance. We had without fail always spent it together. Now she was out there somewhere in the snow, a delusional night thing. I entertained myself with fantasies of her scrunched in the plastic chair of a soup kitchen. More likely she was at the Ritz-Carlton in Chicago, eating off silver chafing dishes and taking calls on her pink toy telephone from her broker, who was helping her buy Majorca. She'd believe both that it was for sale and that she could buy it.

On Christmas morning, the front door flung open with an 'I'm here!' And she was. Exultant reverberations as we yodeled, whooped 'I knew it.' Running, cursing the pine needles pricking through our socks. My mother's head appeared first, covered with a little black felt flapper's cloche bristling with rhinestones. She peered around the door like a child. 'It's me,' she shouted, in gleeful certainty. 'I've been gone exactly four days, four hours, and four minutes! Whoever thought I was dead, raise your right hands!'

An elf, she hopped into the room making a star turn into the assemblage, delighted at her own entrance. She looked a bit like Liza Minnelli about to appear at the Kit Kat Klub. She had on a new pink velvet quilted jacket and slinky black leather pants, and she walked with a stage strut. She was thin, terribly thin, and her eyes were piercingly bright. Perhaps the rhinestones on her hat were glinting in her eyes.

'Did you miss me?' she trilled. 'Hey, girls, how do you like the house? Isn't it a superdoozer? Where's the party? Were you worried? I hope you had some fun while I was gone at least. It's *wild*, isn't it,' she said, spinning her arms out and talking as if to birds or house pets, in singsong. 'I brought the crazy house to us this time, girls, so I don't have to go there. La-di-da. Who made the *kruns kuchen* for breakfast? Don't tell me Mabel did. With lard instead of butter, I bet! Or squirrel fat. Dee-lish-ee-oso. Hey, Mabel, did Frank Sinatra call? I talked to him yesterday. Gosh, I've been so busy I've been almost out of my mind.' She slapped her thighs at that joke, and her laugh, vaulted and shrill, made me want to pop her one right in the kisser.

'This is my party house, girls, and you were all invited,' my mother sang. 'Only none of my friends came because I haven't got any friends. Not one in the whole wide world on the planet Earth,' she said, more slowly. 'And I worked so hard, hours and hours and hours. And then I cried and cried.' Her jaw quavered and tears rimmed her eyes. This is the isolation of the lunatic. Can you hear those syllables in the distance where her language fractures and returns to you? Words are breaking on a barrier reef. She is the guest of honor at the party where no one will honor her, she has sunk below the surface and cannot understand the speech of those who are in the world above her. She is an exile, and when I look at her crying, I suffer her sense of solipsism, an iris of pain, opening and shutting.

My mother's demented world had but one real being, herself, and even we children were shadows, touching her sometimes just enough for her to feel the pain that delusion embalmed. At such times, the mania slipped away for a moment and the truth of her existence left her shocked and reeling.

'Am I dreaming?' she'd say, in horror. 'What is happening to me? Why can't I wake up?' Then she'd slip off again.

'But anyway,' my mother continued, brightening, 'you wouldn't believe how well my new business is going. International demand. I'm a millionaire already,' she bragged, fanning out business cards she had undoubtedly collected in hotel lobbies and bars. I winced. Ever since her divorce from my stepfather six years before, my mother had been trying hard to invest her alimony wisely. But she was on a first-name basis with guys called Earl or Champ, guys whose names belonged on dog collars, who would tell her things like, 'Dolores, are we not having fun? Isn't this life on the edge? I've got a limited real estate partnership here in a shopping mall in Omaha, and, Dolores, before it melts like butter in July, invest. You could make a killing.' My mother studied their brochures, the butter melted, the reports of dividends were always good, and she bought. But what the Earls and Champs didn't see was how she spent her daytime hours – waiting tables, punching clocks, long drudging shifts with cloddish bosses just out of trade school who thought of an older woman employee as a piece of furniture. She'd been a night hotel clerk; a Mary Kay lady; a waitress in a theme restaurant, made to wear an abbreviated train conductor's outfit when she was past forty. This was not the life she'd dreamed of as a doctor's wife. And yet my mother tried hard to embrace her freedom. She had a million schemes for making money. In the late seventies she'd been a diet counselor at a weight loss clinic, but as the mania deepened had told a client that she looked like a walrus. The management laid her off. 'And I bet that the gal did look like a hippo too,' my grandmother had said loyally. 'Everyone's envious of your mother's cute figure.'

Ah, well, to hell with it all, I thought. My mother pranced about the room like little Gloria Vanderbilt, happy at last. Oblivion has its comforts, and the miracle of plastic belied our penury that Christmas morning. A cornucopia of gifts and packages spilled from my mother's arms, rainbow colors, bows in the shapes of animals. She was Mother Christmas, and I prayed that I'd be able to find the receipts so I could take everything back to the stores. There was a Mont Blanc pen for my former stepfather, and a silver humidor from Dunhill of London for Alfred, complete with hand-rolled cigars that smelled as if you'd light them in a penthouse, thickly sweet and redolent of secrets. There were pinky finger signet rings, gold-plated, for my sisters and me, each of our first initials lovingly entwined with the last initial in Alfred's name.

JP. KP. SP. The rings winked at me from their boxes, salaciously suggesting, Isn't this a gas? She was flat broke and because she'd had these useless rings engraved, there'd be no refund! I forgot to play along.

'Can these go back?' I demanded loudly.

'Go back where, Jack?' my mother asked. 'They're gifts from Alfred, who probably got them in Switzerland on one of his travels. We've set a date – the wedding's in June. I do hope you'll all be able to take time out from your busy schedules to attend. I want us all to be such *good* friends. Mabel, you can be the flower girl!' she said to my grandmother, plunking a sticky bow on her gray wicket of hair.

'And, Jack, you give the toast and butter!' my mother continued merrily. My grandmother swiveled her beribboned head toward my mother. After Mabel had reported my mother's delusions to me, she seemed to believe that she had no right to intervene, a belief my mother shared. Or maybe like the rest of us, Mabel couldn't wait to see what would happen next. Raise the curtain on the next act.

It was Christmas. Easy enough to pour the coffee and don gifts of gold underwear over our blue jeans, ask Dolores the name of the hotel she intended to buy on St Kitts. Easy enough to listen to my mother gabble about how she and Alfred the imaginary lover would honeymoon in Tahiti while Alfred the Christmas tree shed more needles and Mabel bit into one of the anchovy cookies.

'Ain't so bad,' she said, wiping her hand on her mouth.

'Thanks,' said Dolores, truly pleased. And then my mother swooned onto the sofa. I thought of Lear, the moors, the raveled sleeve of care knitted up by sleep. If sleep knits up care, then lunatics are in sleeveless chemises. My mothers eyes were like paint on a macabre mask, her penciled eyebrows like thunderbolts. Her lips moved. From her mouth came the fetid breath of someone whose body has begun to starve and feed on itself for nutrition. The skin sank below her cheekbones. I bent down and traced them with my fingers; they stuck out like small cliffs. Such good cheekbones, elemental ridges of rock. Combs in her hair, hair falling out from vitamin loss. I methodically went through her wallet, confiscating keys and credit cards and collecting receipts – good thing she was such a meticulous saver, I'd have no trouble returning most of the things – and found her tab from the only seriously expensive hotel in Milwaukee. No decent food, no drink, just desserts and manicures. And a plane ticket, one way to Las Vegas dated two days before, when the airport had been closed. Bless the snow.

That evening, I toted up the damage of the past several months. The knife feint at my sister in November. Then there was my mother's faked car accident and her suicidal feelings just before she disappeared. Several ugly welts puckered the car. A good enough case to phone the county sheriff and mental hospital, to punch through the recorded messages to the incoming notetaker who would start the slow, desultory relay to fetch my mother. I made the call the next morning, the day after Christmas, idly snapping through the place cards for her imaginary party as if it were a full playing deck. My fingers searched for the Red Queen. I took the cards with her name and my name, hers with a flower and mine with a maple leaf. I have kept them along with so many other things as souvenirs, an assortment of ephemera.

By noon, a patrol car was outside the door. A deputy sheriff and a heavyset matron knocked on the door like undertakers. They were the plague wardens, bring out your dead. My mother sat primly on a stiff-backed chair beneath several just finished oil crayon pictures of imaginary rendezvous with Alfred. Alfred's face looked like a child's drawing of a turkey. And as always, there were several pictures of a dark-haired, dark-eyed woman. Who, I've never known. Dolores herself? Me, Mabel, Mary Baker

Eddy? Deidre of the Sorrows, crying from a distant Irish shore, the captive taken against her will? My mother had taped the pictures on the wall. She looked at the sheriff's deputy, turning a full-wattage smile on him. Lipstick, like bits of velvet, stuck to her teeth.

'My girls make up double whoppers sometimes,' she told the deputy, grimacing at him, meaning it to be fetching. 'Do you have children? You know how they invent? Well, my daughters are geniuses. I invented them, you know, my three little geniuses. And especially this big genius here.' She shot me a look from the abattoir in her head.

The deputy, with his laconic face, moved closer to her.

'Hey, Scrooge, ya big lug, why don'tcha get a little Christmas spirit, for crying out loud?' My mother tried to pin a battery-operated Santa on the deputy, a Santa whose nose blinked when you pulled his chain. 'I hope your wife likes it, buster,' she said to him in Deidre's voice, deep and low. Then an octave higher: 'Why don't you wear it to the bin? Maybe you'll get a better room if they think you're good for a few laughs.'

But the matron had my mother upstairs packing in no time. I would have thought her job the most unenviable in the world, except perhaps that it afforded her the pleasure of locking up pretentious kooks like my mother. This woman had a fullback's stance of alertness, and she wore a uniform that my mother described as dead-leaf brown. 'You ought to brighten up with some electric pastels,' my mother continued. 'I'm a couture dress designer and a diet counselor. I could help you, even in your whalelike condition. You could wear hot pants and get the man you love!'

So we got my mother ready. She packed her drawings of Alfred, her Bible with the pages painted over and religious medals sewn to the cover, and the Mary Baker Eddy reader with bobby pins marking the good phrases. She also insisted on taking her enormous topaz cocktail ring, which I correctly predicted someone would steal (surely not the matron?), and a large spray bottle of Estée Lauder's White Linen. She had on that morning a large, ebony crucifix with a silver Christ from our trip to Mexico in 1964, which she wore around her waist like a monk. Around her head, she tied a scarf, harem style, so that you could see nothing but her eyes. 'I don't want any television cameras,' my mother said.

For a moment I actually believed I'd see reporters out in the snow, St Bernards with Leicas. My mother submitted to handcuffs with a theatrical flourish. I felt as if I were sending an errant child to reform school for the crime of stealing a few apples. I knew the county hospital. It did not practice the subtler arts of the mental health profession – we could not afford them. Then there was my mother's resistance to consider. She would not voluntarily sign herself in anywhere. She distrusted all doctors, denied she was ill, until we came to rely on the most medieval of methods to shackle her back to sanity. Her fierce resistance complicated a proper diagnosis for decades. I think of restraints, straitjackets, endless notes, and my childlike mother. She was sitting up very straight in the patrol car, as though no child with such bearing could possibly be guilty of the crimes she was accused of. From the rear, she looked perhaps twelve, the age I had been the first time she made such a journey. Now it was I who was locking my mother up, and I wasn't even going along for the ride.

The notetakers write in a flat hand and with flatter judgment, making pronouncements about the patients as they are checked in. 'Patient admitted 12:10 pm, Dec. 26th, 1979. Patient's personal belongings include one topaz evening ring, a solitaire, one painted Bible, six hair combs, a Christian Science prayer book, various perfume vials and drawings.' A few good evening clothes, in case the hospital served cocktails. 'Patient, an undernourished 49-year-old female, says attendant has face like a badger and should bury it,' the notes say. 'Patient says she is member of the Milwaukee Mafia and will carry out pistol-whipping on all who wear masks over prying eyes.'

I want them selfishly, all her words, all these utterances that would seem so Lewis Carroll if only they belonged to him and not my mother. And yet I admire her pride. Her words are jumbled with Haldol and thickened with Thorazine. Her hallucinations gurgle into my ears, chugging through the surf of antipsychotic drugs. Her brain is a bubbling Molotov cocktail. When it explodes, my mother raves. After one hospitalization, she swears that she is put into a small, closed-front rubber room with only a drain in the floor for her bodily functions and a stinking mattress. 'They beat me,' she wrote. 'They called their 'treatment' stupid craft projects.' She spent thousands unsuccessfully suing after that stay. Whatever the hospital care, however broad or clumsy in its approach, however overprescribed and inept the treatment, I seldom asked questions. I would tell myself that as long as she was locked away, she could sink no further, that we had all been in danger, that our faces were targets in her eyes and that there had been no other choice. Better to dose and even overdose and restrain her, and we'd pick up the pieces later. But on reading the reports from scattered handfuls of hospitalizations, from the consistent thrum of horror in my mother's reminiscences, I've come to realize that the torment begins as the sanity returns. In her delusions, my mother fancied above all else that she had dignity and power. She could fly beyond mortal realms to inhabit all the shining positions of influence that she lacked in the real world. In the hospital, layer upon layer of delusions were peeled back to reveal the designs of human vagary. To be only human caused fear, and doubt and mortality, and the dead weight of having run out of dreams.

That night, after my mother had been taken to the hospital, I had the nightmare I have so often waked from as though someone had just walked through my heart, as if it were a jungle. My mother is lying at the bottom of a great deep well near crumbling Mayan ruins that could be those of Chichén Itzá in the Yucatán. She is lying where a high priest has thrown her. I see her submerged in clear green luminescent water, her hands outstretched like the carving of a little Madonna, beseeching. My mother is about twelve, and like me at that age she has long hair, so long that it weaves with the current and is as alive and sinuous as she is dead. Her waxen corpse looks nothing like either of us but portrays us both. When I dream this dream I know that I must save the girl, my mother, though she is already plainly dead, perhaps never even born, a pink fetus in a bell jar. Her eyes are closed and her skin is as translucent as an opal, and on the whole of her pale, milky body she wears only a necklace of heavy silver icons. I see the coral organs of her liver and heart sliding away underneath her crystalline skin. I am aware that if I can bring this girl to the surface of the water, then she will wake. I dive down toward the girl; I know she is my own flesh. I touch her ivory skin but can get no grip. I see the organs float like herbs in jars of oil. She is her own reliquary. My hands slip on wax skin; I can't move her. She is the weight of ages, a bone of the earth, a root from below. I awake, covered in sweat, head tossing on the pillow. I am awake, but in the darkness she lies at the bottom of the deep shining green well, faintly smiling and immortal. I am at the surface, peering down at her. My talisman.

My mother was released after more than a month in the Menomenee County Hospital in late January 1980. I had no time to pay proper attention to her treatment. I was busy with the radio show seven days a week. Mabel said the hospital people reported that Dolores was no longer raving. And she wasn't. She was as docile as an altar girl in her servitude, whacked out on a chalice full of antipsychotics. We'd arranged to meet in Gimbels department store, where she had a new job in Junior Separates. She was desperate to get work to begin paying off the debts of illness and as usual had taken anything she could get. Before she saw me, I spotted her by the clothing racks. Her face was dead and white; the Thorazine had bloated her by a couple dozen pounds. Her flesh looked as if she'd been preserved in formaldehyde. Her swollen ankles called to mind my grandmother's, puffing out over flat soles. A customer was berating my mother, who waddled and lowered her head. She was not a queen but a beast of burden. She had turned old.

'Christ,' the customer bitched to my mother. 'Can't you read the sizes? What country are you from? Do I look like I wear a size eight?' My mother was staring at the horrible clothing, clothing so ugly I knew she hated touching it. She was scratching absently at a nonexistent itch. She moved slowly to another rack, trying to find the customer's right size, her own bearings, the entrance where she'd come in. Trying to find out who she was. And it struck me as a more disturbing sight than when she had been ill.

'I can't find your size,' my mother said thickly to the customer. 'I can't find anything.'

'Hey, Mom,' I said, stepping in. 'Closing time.' I glared at the young customer. Test me, test my ardor, I wanted to say to her. I wanted her to know that my fingers could gouge her eyes out, my teeth could puncture her throat. The customer turned and slunk away through the racks. The next weekend, my mother swallowed every pill in the house. Ah, but she made sure I was on the phone with her as she did, her voice trailing off like the echo of a cannon shot. I frantically called the paramedics, who came and took her away and pumped her stomach as I sped up again from Chicago. The regular hospital this time. Suicide attempt, Dalmane overdose. My mother leaps and I catch. No one will if I don't. No one will save her. I longed, for the thousandth time, to re-create life as something other than this daughter and this mother.

FISHING ON LAKE *P*UCKAWASAY

MY SISTERS AND I grew up like boys on Lake Puckawasay. My father took us fishing from the time we could walk. At dawn we dug in the moist earth of the garden for night crawlers, loose bits of dirt running through our hands, still a world without shoes in the summertime, grass and mud between our toes. Life itself seemed tangible, full of pores, the friable earth sifting through our small hands in our part of Wisconsin, saturated in black soil. Dank hosts, crumbled in the darkness before God. Each dawn, mist hung over the fields behind our house like drifting nets that caught the birdsong and the lowing of cows as they poked their noses under the barbwire fence of the farm that bordered our property. The cows, with wet muzzles and a sweet-grass breath, were always after our garden. The land sloped from the farm on the horizon to the fields, down to our back yard, rolling and lowering onto Lake Puckawasay, which ran along the opposite side of our road. We were sinking, my mother said, down into our earthly lives. She had been sinking for a while now, ever since her marriage in 1950.

One of the first stories I remember hearing from my mother was how she'd lived in a basement until she was a teenager. 'I could see the feet going past me at night,' she'd begin. 'Shoes, all kinds. People walking as I lay in bed. When I got to be a teenager, traces of ash from the street dotted my cold cream as I lay on my pillow.'

Mabel had no patience for hard times. 'You always ate,' she'd hiss. Mabel cooked kidneys in the basement. The smell of fried urine made my mother wretch. My mother dreamed of college, got brilliant 99s and 100s on her report cards, was so shy that she had few friends. 'It's your looks,' Mabel told her. 'Pretty girls don't have friends.' Nor did they have educations; her perfect test scores were put away in a drawer for decades until I found them. 'I thought about college,' she said. 'But I knew better than to ask my father, and I didn't know who else to ask. The principal?' The day after her graduation, my grandfather found her a job in a bakery.

But before graduation her parents did scrape together a sweet sixteen party, and she invited an older boy she knew slightly, Patrick Lyden, to be her escort. He was nicer than the other young men, she'd tell us girls, not rough. The party was at the Knights of Columbus Hall on Vliet Street in Milwaukee. She had six attendants, all of them wearing fuchsia satin dresses they had made themselves. Patrick Lyden looked earnest in a white dinner jacket. I know these things because I have a framed photograph of them at the party on my dresser. I look at it, and I think, From these two people am I created, yet my mother said she was never in love with my father a day in her life, though she wished him well. They are quite beautiful, the pair of them, all dark eyes and hair. My father is holding my mother's hand. Looking at them, I want to cry, 'Stop! Stop! You will bring each other tragedy and nothing but misery. One of you will go crazy and the other will suffer in silence forever!' But my mother could not avoid the marriage, her father had decreed it. Patrick Lyden went off to join the paratroopers in the victory forces over Japan. They floated like feathers over the earth. He wrote letters of gratitude to my mother for not sending him a Dear John note. She winced and wrote on. When Patrick returned from Japan, he stepped off the plane and my mother searched out another man's face, styling it to her memory, not recognizing my father. He was both her disappointment and her inevitability, a man at the edge of the crowd in uniform. Always in her mind a man at the edge of the crowd.

'I was buried alive after that marriage,' my mother would say. 'Really dead out there in the country.' She pined for city rhythms, for its shopkeepers and cinemas and cheer. I can remember her describing roller-skating on a sidewalk in Milwaukee before I had ever tried it, the look on her face as she renavigated the sidewalk cracks she'd leapt over as a girl. To her, birdsong on the shores of Lake Puckawasay was a dirge. Her father had been shot through the heart in a bar holdup, a rare thing in 1950. Now she and Patrick lived in the little house that her father had been building as a retirement cottage, thirty miles out from Milwaukee. The house had no entrance facing the road, but edged toward the world like a shy schoolgirl. The door was on the side, opposite the neighbors, and the Jimineys could watch our every move through the picture window. It was a house adjacent to fields – burrs, Scotch thistle, marshmallow, timothy grass. The foot sank through the lawns; darling tiny toads crawled up a child's ankle. Swampy land no one else wanted but workmen on the line at the Milwaukee breweries. Some were G.I.s who threw their deeds for a dollar into the chips of a poker game after their shifts had ended. Even older were the asphalt fishing shacks on the road, like rotting teeth amid the neater white bungalows. Other homes looked more like boat wrecks.

At first my mother tried to make the best of being stuck in the fields like a radish, living on a lane of shacks. She covered the sofa and chairs in gay jungle-print fabrics and put green ceramic panthers on the mantel. Outside, the elderly men on our lane congregated, sharing memories of the fields and factories near Kiev or Tirana or Gdansk. They sat around in card games on lethargic afternoons, leaning against the shacks that eventually became permanent homes with the addition of a little more tar paper, a little more asphalt. They said things like 'Deal me once!' and 'What's your name, little girl?' and, to one another, 'An old bohunk like you dassn't smell so good.' The sweat came through their clothes until they reminded me of oily sausages wrapped in butcher paper. Sometimes they took their teeth out to show me, strings of saliva like dew gleaming on their dentures. Mabel, astonished to find herself a widow at fifty, amazed my mother by marrying one of these gnomes, Louie from Czechoslovakia. She moved into his bungalow on Lake Puckawasay and didn't leave until she died thirty-four years later. My mother wrinkled her nose and said now that her father was dead, my grandmother was turning into a fishwife.

To amuse us on long afternoons when we heard the cowbells tinkling through her bedroom window, my mother staged fashion shows. My mother had been a runway model at Gimbels for three seasons between the time of her marriage and my arrival. I could listen for hours to my mother's tales of parading in costume while ladies lunched on petits fours and miniature sandwiches, filling in order blanks with doll-sized pencils. My sisters and I would pull on white cotton gloves and our Easter hats and play the part of the ladies as our mother twirled on the living room carpet. We dipped our crayons into notebooks, pretending we could write. Dolores modeled sundresses, capris, and sheaths she'd sewn herself, on a runway we made by laying boards over building blocks. 'And then, girls,' my mother recounted, 'I would pivot and turn, like this.' A quick pointing of the toe and a twist on the balls of her feet. 'Can you do that?' I was six, Kate was five, Sarah only three. 'Pivot and turn!' we shrieked. 'Pivot and turn!'

My mother let us raid her hope chest, a huge cedar trunk at

the foot of her bed containing, among other things, her wedding trousseau. We put on her dainty slippers and satin wedding gown and veil, which we tried to avoid trampling on the stairs up to the attic playroom, the fifteen-foot-long train flowing like gallons of the thickest cream. My mother had paid the photographer extra to make her wedding picture look like an oil painting, and the satin of her dress had the luster of baby teeth. That was how it was. Even when she had almost no money, she had the kind of style that got people to look twice.

'Pivot and turn!' we screamed. 'Good!' sang my mother. She was not like the other mothers on our road. She painted her fingernails as red as crayons, redder – as red as a cluster of scarlet tulips. And her toes, too. She wore pedal pushers and stiletto heels, and shaved her arched calves with a pink General Electric razor, a concupiscent thing. We leaned against the bathroom door and begged to be allowed in to help her shave her legs and hook the eyelet at the back of her neck. Always, before she went out in the afternoon or evening, my mother chose a purse that matched her blouse, dumping tubes of lipstick and mascara from one to another. When you get an eyeful, fill your pocket.

My mother's vanity was blond wood with a half-moon of mirror, big enough to accommodate her reflection and the reflection of her three little girls. We'd hand her her gilt brush and attend her, gazing up as she let us guide the brush through her long auburn hair, which fell in thick waves down her back. Outside, the cows grazed in the fields, but inside the room was chartreuse and maroon and rows and rows of bottles lined her vanity. A tall, amethyst decanter. A slim black Chanel No. 5 bottle, like Marilyn Monroe, my mother's favorite actress, no doubt had. And there was a crystal atomizer with a gold silken sphere attached by a tube. I picked it up to squeeze it, anointing us with Youth Dew. My mother contemplated our reflection with huge, steady eyes. She had a mantra.

'Always remember,' she often said to us solemnly, 'that *you* are the most beautiful woman in the room,' and in her case it was true. I knew it as the gilt brush glided through her hair, as her hands pushed tortoiseshell combs into the auburn mass to hold it up. Men doted on my mother, rushed to pull out her chair or bring her a cocktail she'd refuse, all to linger for just one moment in her eyes. To look at my mother was to know purity and energy. She believed. But we had to be ready. Finding me slumped in a chair, sounding out the words in a book, my mother would say, 'Do something!' and snap her fingers. Do something wonderful, she meant. Do something gorgeous, and do it with style. It seemed a worthy mantra then for all of life.

The vanity was a hallowed place of thought and imagination for my mother and sisters and me – a place of costume and escape, a sorceress's ball, a witch's teacup. We could enchant ourselves there. If my mother braided her long hair, pinned it up, then tied a scarf into a bow on her crown, and donned long hoop earrings, she emerged as Carmen Miranda. 'Now there was a character, even if she wasn't pretty,' my mother said. Carmen Miranda meant South of the Border, a place of señoritas and mantillas and high cactus, where women in long dresses danced to marimba music. My mother, the timpanist in the Menomenee Legion Band, owned a pair of red maracas. She shook them as she sang the Chiquita Banana jingle. 'I'm Chiquita Banana, and I come to say, Bananas like to ripen in a certain way.'

Her dreams infused mine in front of the vanity, protean dreams with a hypnotic beat, like an oracle leaning down to say, 'Whatever there is, is *out* there. It's not here. Not here.' Dream songs, lullabies, soothing and deceptive. How often I have hummed them to myself, waiting in a palace anteroom or at a border checkpoint, waiting to put questions to an Arab king or British prime minister, waiting for the man described as a terrorist or the woman described . . . how? How is the woman described?

Often she never is. I hear them ululating. I wait and wait and find myself humming the Chiquita Banana riff as I travel the long hot highways of the Levant, plunging from the Syrian plain down to the Jordanian wadis, playing memories from an old lakeshore in Wisconsin. I am waiting for the door to open and the women with their tasseled pencils to take notes. I stare down at the cheap leather bag I bought in Damascus to hold my tape recorder. My high heels are dusty, no time to paint my ragged nails. 'You are the most beautiful woman in the room,' the mother in my head insists. And promises and promises, hoping I will believe in her assurance as an entitlement of my own. I look into a Gaza taxi's rearview mirror, and my mother's eyes look back.

By contrast, my father's dreams were as plain as the thousand freckles on his arm, as solid as his fist that threw mock punches, built sandboxes, unhooked fish from the line. 'Monkey pile,' my father would yell, flopping onto his belly in the middle of the living room. The salt on his skin in our mouths, his freckles over our eyes. He was a canopy for us under any hot sun. 'Dr X! Attack, girls! Right hook to Dick the Bruiser! His guard is down, he's taking a nap, playing to the peanut gallery. Left hook to Dr X!' My father organized us into the skins and shirts, taking sides. He loved the glamour of wrestling on TV. For Halloween, he was Gorgeous George, wearing a long blond wig and his red hunting underwear. 'Cry uncle,' I'd holler, tackling him at the knees when he came home from work. 'Porky Pig!' he'd say. 'Donald Duck!' And then my father underwent a transformation.

Hammering nails into the roof of a friend's house, my father, always impulsive, suddenly stood up. Perhaps someone had called to him. Perhaps he had a kink in his spine, or he needed to piss, or his throat was parched for beer and his freckled skin was sweating. He never remembered the reason for the moment that changed time for him. His foot slipped. He went hurtling down the roof, landing on his skull on the sidewalk, frying his cranium. For weeks he lay in a coma, thrashing under foot and wrist restraints with the world a distant sea. Then gradually he swam back to the light with thick, choppy strokes. His eyes opened. He was back on land.

But he never heard another word. My first-grade teacher drew me a diagram. There was an anvil in my father's ear, she said. I knew what that was. And there was a small tympani drum, exactly the kettle-shaped kind my mother played in the Menomenee Legion Band. There was another instrument, the organ of Corti, which was the nerve of hearing. I thought of Corti as an Italian gentleman, dapper and with a mustache, who gave organ lessons in the large empty recital hall at the back of my father's brain. But the organ, the anvil, and the drum which performed all the chords and songs of the sounding world had shattered, and could not be put back together again. He was Humpty-Dumpty. My father had lost all his notes.

When he came home from the hospital, after being gone longer than any time I'd ever remembered, Patrick Lyden was not a canopy of shade against a harsh sun. He did not hoist us girls up to him in a bunch, as he had always done, and call us his Three Stooges. He moved slowly, a Mr Potato Head, a pink bald bulb covered with fuzz. Stitch marks showed on his scalp like a baseball. He sat at the kitchen table and we crawled onto his lap and he pressed his ears, tiny velvet wings, to our mouths. We told stories into his ears, crossed the ocean there. His fingers rested lightly on our throats, and he told us to say our names and sing to him. He shook his head, and then he closed his eyes and told us to walk across the wooden floorboards. He said he could feel the floorboards thumping in his own feet. I recall that his gestures were like a swimmer's. The water came up higher. He was a man in a river.

My father waited for his hearing to come back. You could feel him waiting, as you can feel impatience on the platform when the crowd grits its teeth for the train to arrive. Not long after his return, I saw my father at the big picture window that looked out to the Jimineys', the older neighbors across the lawn. There was a bird feeder beside our house. My father whistled to the birds, but I knew that his hearing had not come back because his whistle, which had always been so wonderful, was a braying, shrill sound, like a chair being pulled away from a table too quickly. The finches and the blue jays darted away. My father stood motionless with his hands in his pockets, stock-still and ultimately defined. His hearing was not going to come back. His mission had been completed and he knew now what he was. He was stone-deaf. He was twenty-nine years old. He laughed.

When he spoke, his speech was as slurred as if he had inhaled one of the spring rivulets running down to Lake Puckawasay. Our conversations spun wheels in the murk of his syllables. If I wanted to talk to my father, I had to get someone else to write down the words I was desperately eager to spell. I loved the alphabet, the very notion of shapes that stuck to the sounds in the air. Now I needed that alphabet so that I could write to my father. 'What does it sound like when you listen, Dad?' I asked him. For my father often stopped and listened, pointing his head at where a thickening reverberation seemed to promise a lost sound. We were sitting on the back steps. My grandmother wrote my question down for my father. My father shook his head, unable to explain. A babble of speech played harshly between his ears. But later, he brought home a conch shell.

'If you had ever been to the ocean,' my father said, 'it would sound like this.' Actually the words came out as they always did now, in a monotonic gurgle. 'If youah hayd evah been to the owshun,' and he passed the conch from child to child and ear to ear. 'It wouyld . . . sahnd . . . lawke . . . this. And inside myah hayd,' said my father, dripping the speech, 'Awe cahan heah the wayves!' And a wavelet boomed out, widening his voice.

So my father had a conch shell for hearing and waves for a

voice, and my mother had a vanity and a mirror that could see the world. The words between them grew fewer and fewer, like broken threads that frayed the bonds of intimacy. My father was like a guest picking his way, uncertain whether to sit back in the most comfortable chair or perch on the corner settee. One Sunday after church, my sisters and my mother and I were having our usual languid afternoon in front of the vanity, stringing odd buttons into necklaces, wearing our Stardust Memory plastic high heels, when my mother turned slowly around, and said, 'Do you girls know what divorce means?' At six, I had never heard the word. 'Divorce is when two people can't live together anymore,' she said, looking straight at me. 'Two people who are married. It means Daddy won't be living with us anymore, though he'll always be your father.' Her voice made the room tilt sideways.

To steady myself, I watched the red rose of her mouth, the slight imbrication of her lower teeth. She might as well have said, 'Divorce means you are going to turn blue today. Your skin will always be blue. You will never return to your normal color, you will just have to get used to being blue.' My mother had bewitched us in her mirror, and I was under her spell. I was sitting in a big yellow grapefruit of a revolving chair she kept by the window. I swirled around and around in the chair, propelling it with my foot. I spun on the circumference of the equator. The walls passed by with a glint and a flash. Japan: the music box on my mother's dresser with the ballerina in jeté on hot pink velvet over black lacquer under painted cherry blossoms. Mexico next: my mother's maracas. Wisconsin: the deer on the deer vase bounding into a thick bramble of orange mountain ash stuck over their heads, antlers of fire. As if a fire had consumed them all and left us three girls behind, stone miracles. I knew of no other children whose parents were divorced, even if they shouted at each other, as many parents did. I had heard the neighbors screaming. 'I'm sorry I ever married a fat cow, fat slob,' a Brobdingnagian monster like you.

Taillights screeched away in the darkness, and high-pitched cries floated over the night crickets on dewy lawns. In the morning, though, the men came home, pale and staggering. Divorce meant that we were different from the families whose fathers returned, took up their old places, and felt their youth leave them.

When two people can't live together anymore, my mother had said, and the words have rolled on with me over the years. She was so much more exotic and younger than all the other mothers. I knew the women on our street, who were slow and deliberate and had veinous legs. My mother wore a size 5A shoe, called a quinn. Even after she had three girls, she had a princess's feet. Other mothers did not trim the fat from the roast with pinking shears, as she did, or turn a cucumber into a rabbit's head for the kindergarten flower show, or decorate the Jell-O ring with real violets. I would not have traded her for five of the slow mothers on the lane, mothers without jewelry or makeup. My ears warmed at the slippery needles in the neighbors' voices as they commented on our household as if I were as deaf as my father. So what if after the divorce some of their children were not allowed to play with us. But that came later.

The bedroom was hot. I thought of our lane on Lake Puckawasay, its surf of loose white pebbles poured on the tar each spring, pinging as the cars rolled past us, tamping the pebbles down into eddies and the shapes of continents. On the lane, my sisters and I sold lemonade and dead wildflowers that we'd picked and stuck in milk cartons. That lane led to the wider world, my mother said, raising her bedroom window, propping her face on cupped hands. All up and down the road were signs. The Krecklows. The Baumgartners. The Mertzes. Signs shaped like fish or miniature shovels, signs like hearts or sailboats or forks and spoons, but as regular as beads on a rosary. I had planned to be famous on that road. I liked to walk up and down it, singing loudly, 'God Bless America,' and hoping everyone would hear.

'We will not be anything without a dad,' I said to my mother. The room and the road outside looked gauzy behind the shimmering heat. The thought of fatherlessness was a free fall from the planet, a dizzy sense of time eternal. There was a mystic father, a father on a gigantic cross, and my own father. A hole inside me worked its way open, like the seam on a glove. I knew it would always be this way, this unraveled love, and I felt myself sliding toward a dark void. 'We will not be anything without a dad,' I repeated. My mother turned to look at me, then looked back at her image in the mirror.

'Well,' said my mother lightly, applying Revlon's Cherries and Ice, her mouth pursed like a fresh cutting of rosebuds, 'let's wait and see what happens.'

Later that summer, my mother cut up the fuchsia satin dress from her sweet sixteen, to make us girls Miss America outfits for the annual Fourth of July costume contest, telling us the story again of her debut party. It had six attendants, she said. Six, and each had made a dress a shade lighter than this one. We felt special that she was cutting up the fuchsia dress just for us, the dress that had premiered at the Knights of Columbus Hall. You might correctly guess, if you drove through our small town, that Technicolor pageantry was called for on the Fourth of July. Patriotism was in demand as a backdrop for national optimism, the current religious rave. It was 1959. Atomic nightmares vanished in the sunniness of our small town's remove from reality. In our kitchen, the dark satin flowed over the table like spilled wine. I touched the fabric to my cheek, feeling the balm of the slipper-soft satin. We were in awe as my mother pinned us into the tiny bandeaux she had cut out to match the tap pants she'd made. Fantasy in her needlework. We preened, and our bare bellies stuck out like marshmallow creams in burgundy wrappings. My mother took glitter and glue and spelled out 'Miss America' on three pink satin cummerbunds, bestowing one on each of us, and we hopped on our bikes, crepe paper streaming, to ride to the assembly point of the parade. Children rode behind the Veterans of Foreign Wars, whose bulges jounced over the lifting and clumping of their boots, lifting and clumping. Next came the boys' corps from the St Columba's Military Academy. They looked lost and abandoned and hot in oversize peaked hats and serge. I felt sympathy for these boys, who had no homes and no visible parents. You'd see them at the drugstore, sucking Popsicles in their uniforms, and now they sweated and lifted stiff legs, marching forward, while my sisters and I rode our bicycles, as cool in our finery as we were rooted in our identity. I stuck out my belly. Miss America, you are so beautiful to me. At the costume contest, my sisters and I shared first prize and received rhinestone tiaras. All the winners were invited to a little stage to sing the national anthem. My father was in the crowd that Fourth of July, his face round and shiny and genial. No matter how hard I sang, he couldn't hear the words, but he clapped as if he could. It made me angry, his embrace of the air.

I couldn't comprehend what his deafness cost him. I feared that my father had given up on the difficult parts of his life, of which we girls were one. A woman speech teacher had come to our house and formed words on his lips, pulling at them like rubber bands, twisting his mouth into E's and A's and U's. Later, when my father and mother wanted to have adult words, they spoke silently, shielding their mouths with their hands lest we children read in their lips the rubber consonants and meandering vowels. I didn't need to hear my mother and father talking out loud to know that they were angry with each other. I could tell by the way my mother held her hand up beside her face and moved her head in nervy twists. We unconsciously started to use our hands to speak to my father in invented signs. Big: stretched hands. Small: a pinch sign. Faster: scroll your hands. More: gesture with your right hand toward your chest. Usually, we merely wanted more.

More time, more ice cream, more of him. His station wagon pulled up mostly just on Sundays now, and Sarah began to call him our Sunday father. 'The Sunday father is coming today,' she would say, 'and we will have to go with him.' The Sunday father is taking us to the park. The Sunday father is taking us to the zoo to see the bears.

'Oh hell,' my father now shouted at my mother. I thought I had heard him yell it perfectly clearly, through the Fourth of July crowd's fervent clamor for patrimony, for country, for themselves. My father felt the crowd's martial thrill, the thrill he had felt as an army paratrooper. It was as if he could speak again, as if his words had finally dried out and stiffened, could stand up straight by themselves. 'Bullshit,' he said clearly to my mother. 'To hell with you.' Then he turned and walked away. We girls now had full citizenship in another country called Yesterday. At home that afternoon or the next, he hugged us good-bye in our living room. My father's boxes of junk and tools and fishing gear, long packed, moved with him to a new place. He tugged them up from the basement, put them in the car trunk, and was gone. There was nothing left of him in the house. I felt the pain ring around my rib cage. I had seen such rings in the sawed stumps of big trees. He himself had shown me how to count the years there, in the sable cinctures of the tree stumps. When I am old and dead, I thought, then they can cut me open and count the cinctures on my ribs. I knew that day would leave such a shadow ring, big enough to see on an X ray. I knew it then, and I know it now.

And then once he moved out, my mother was free, really free. Levitating with freedom. Oh my God, she sang silently to her reflection. I'm free. She piloted her two-tone aqua and white Chevrolet with its miles of chrome trim like a rocket ship, parting the air with a clear sense of where she was going. Our car hummed and radiated with her energy. She was twenty-seven. She drove us to the beaches and small lakes nearby, lakes that glowed in the sunshine like pearls on green baize. We girls kneeled on the back seat, damp sweat on our necks. We rolled down the windows to stick our heads out and let the wind blow through our hair. Kate's red blond hair bounced from her head in curls, Sarah's was a curtain of wheat and fanned straight. Waves of green corn flowed past the windows. The wheels brushed over the highway. We stopped for root beers at the A&W, we stopped so that we could spell out the words in the Burma-Shave sign because I was trying to read: Ben met Anna, Made a Hit, Neglected Beard, Ben-Anna Split. We stopped for sweet corn, eighteen cents a dozen, the same as the price of a gallon of gas in the summer gasoline wars. We stopped for no one, no one in the world. Until we met the Doc. And we stopped for him.

I knew the Doctor slightly. I'd met him again when we went to watch my mother play in the Menomenee Legion Band. He played the first clarinet in a saturnine way, with deep attentiveness, like Buddy De Franco. In fact the Doctor invited various musicians – like De Franco, Clark Terry, Raphael Mendez – to play with the Legion Band, and sometimes, idling on the summer circuit, they came to Menomenee, pleased to be in lake country, they said, after the coast. Coasting where? I wondered. Is it my memory? Did Buddy De Franco really sit in our living room, telling me he had married his first wife when she was fourteen? I know that Clark Terry was the first black person I ever spoke to. He handed me his publicity photograph, on which he'd drawn a little trumpet. 'Stay as sweet as you are,' it said. And I wondered how he could possibly know.

The Legion Band played every Sunday night in our band shell in the city beach park on Lac La Jolie in Menomenee. Our mother was one of the band's chief attractions. As the timpanist, she was its beating heart. Notes swelled like ticking time bombs until she exploded each and every one of them with a crack from her drumsticks in the John Philip Sousa marches. Thunder came from the smears of her drumsticks, lightning from the gold epaulets on her shoulders. She was the crescendo rising to the stars. She wore a cap like a policeman's, they all did, the whole band, midnight blue with gold trim. They were all splendid, but my mother's timpani spoke the whole hidden meaning of the music, which I felt sure was about glorious conquest.

As far as I was concerned, the band was it. Notes ricocheted off the band shell, boats floated up to the shore to watch. Once the weather turned an evil green, staining the canvas of sky, and within minutes a tornado tore over Lac La Jolie. Half the audience ran. The rest of us huddled together in the band shell, a giant Tilt-A-Whirl that might at any moment become airborne. Then the skies calmed, and my mother fiercely resumed the drums that had heralded the extreme weather. On Sundays, you knew the concert was over when the conductor, Mr Laufenberg, who was young and handsome, stabbed his baton up to the heavens and then laid it down and bowed to the crowd. His bow never failed to get thunderous applause. We girls rushed to gather up my mother's sheet music and put away her various cymbals, drumsticks, glockenspiel and other assorted tribal noisemakers. Most fascinating to me were the red maracas, which had an authority of their own.

One night I was suddenly as aware of the Doctor as if he'd swept from the sky like the cyclone that passed a few weeks before over Lac La Jolie. His gaze and voice carried through to us girls in the postconcert clutter of snapping music cases and squawking instruments. I shook the red maracas slowly in his direction, chanting gibberish, but he failed to vanish. During the daytime, I knew, he belonged to the small hospital he operated in Menomenee in an atmosphere suffused with ether and noiseless white shoes and hands that intruded with needles and peering instruments. He was contained in his clinic, where I went sometimes with my grandmother, whose physician he was. He was by that time my mother's doctor too; he'd delivered Sarah a few years before. My grandmother told me he did not live with his family, which made him even more ominous and mysterious. In fact, she said, he had three little girls of his own. Keep them, I thought.

And now here was the Doctor in his brown Cadillac (there was a new one each year) on the highway, dressed like a civilian with a fedora on his head and gesturing in a friendly way to our mother! No band uniform or white smock! Out here in the woods and fields, the thousand byways on which my mother and sisters and I would cruise and drift, picking blueberries and wild asparagus and daisies in a limitless stratosphere, out here where I'd thought we'd always be safe, he'd found us. Out here, in our Chevrolet with our mother, this tall dark doctor was a forbidden stranger and the ancient green man in the woods. I was completely mystified. Perhaps my mother had invented a new way for us to get shots and he would soon take out his stethoscope and hypodermic and come after us. Left behind in the Chevy or hiding in the long grass, we girls spied on their courtship, could hear riffs of intimate laughter rippling from the Cadillac. I tried to think of some plan to get rid of the Doctor: a Comanche raid, a cyclone for one, a stealthy maraca blow to his left temple. My plans often foundered over the fact that he possessed a secret weapon: a genuine Kodak Instamatic camera. It was a bronze contraption of precise, jaw-dropping beauty. It brought me running the second it appeared. In the Kodak's flash, I froze in fascination. You could photograph the violet as it died in your hand. You could photograph a dream and have it. If he brought the Kodak along, I would beg him to let me hold it, feel the power of time locked in a box. I watched our images distill onto white paper; watched the hugely antiseptic Doctor carefully coat our pictures with a bitter clear lipstick to fix our afternoon, sunlit bodies, before they disappeared into oblivion. As if a surgeon, and only a surgeon, had the power to capture our faces and bodies on paper. I still have the instant Kodak pictures he made then. Kate and Sarah and I stand beside the road, garlanded in daisy chains, holding hands, a nosegay of little girls. I wonder if it would have been different had we been holding rubber tomahawks and toy pistols. We three girls look so tame and shy above our wild hearts. So pliable, like children. I think of the lawless world I've known. I think of grenades like lanterns in children's hands and the other lethal things they carry, half knowing. The armed hands of children do not surprise me in the least. Children are fierce, without nuance or hesitation. Children's hands hold grenades that are invisible to all but them.

The Doctor could not see the weapons I carried, but I could feel his hands probing somewhere around my heart, and they were freezing, dipped in mercury. His voice dazed me, caught me in a way that made me think of ants trapped in amber. 'Dummy,' he would chide, jotting in red ink over the stories I wrote in my notebook, red ink spiders that wriggled on my good words. 'Dummy,' he would say, untying and retying Kate's shoes. 'Girlie,' he called to my mother. 'Pretty dolly.' As if my mother too would obey on command as dolls did and girls were supposed to do. Spank it and tip it over. And then I felt stupid, started to stutter, to say my words backward to myself. I who had always loved words found them scattered someplace I couldn't reach. I listened for the oiled timbre in his voice, the distant fugue before a summer cataclysm. The timpanic voice. 'Think you can get it straight, chum? You tie your shoelaces like this, not like a moron ties them. You close the door after you leave the house, not leave it open like an idiot. You button a button like this.' There was no action too small for his scrutiny. 'Is that how we're going to do it, chum? Don't be asinine. Good. I'm glad we agree.' I felt thick, thick and slow.

'Dearie,' he'd say, an instant later, and I panicked at the oozing intimacy. 'You keep your voice down, and we'll be friends. You show me you know how to be polite.' The low notes of my mother's timpani had thrilled me, but the broadsides of the Doctor's voice struck irregularly and without warning. Left my knees buckled and brain hollow. Out on a drive with the Doctor, I didn't know whether he'd buy me a soda or call me stupid, or quite possibly both. Both could happen in the same moment, yanking from polite calm to terror, so that I felt witless, drugged, a million miles away. I felt guilty for making him hate me so much. Just as suddenly I'd go weak with relief that he seemed to like me, pals, smiling while the two of us yakked it up with the gas station attendant with the dogboy face. Buddies, perhaps, the Doc and I.

'Which do you want, Dr Pepper or grape?'

'Grape, please.'

'Grape it is, pardner.'

And then a look that hung you on a meat hook, my cheeks warming like the soda warming in my hand. I'd stare out the window, trying to deny that anything was wrong, to disassociate myself from myself. I had no words for menace, and my mother had no sense of it. She was falling in love. I was excelling in school, though always marked down for talking too much. The teacher said that she thought I would indeed talk the paint off the walls. My mother hummed in the kitchen, and sang for him the songs I had thought she reserved only for us.

'If you don't happen to like it,' she sang, 'pass me by.'

Whatever fantasies of harmony and patriarchal order that the Doctor may have harbored, he stepped into our games and lives as a ringmaster, refashioning the rules, recomposing our voices into a conditional tone. My mother and the Doctor were dating openly by then. One night I couldn't stand it anymore, felt sorry for myself, worked up a keen feeling of neglect and injustice. I marched into my mother's room. 'Don't go out with Doc tonight,' I bullied my mother, imitating his tone of command. She sat at her vanity, combing her hair, and her gilt brush caught me in the mouth, the shock of the soft bristles between my teeth, as soft as a stolen kiss and as stunning. 'What was I to do?' my mother asks today. 'Three little girls. Who knew? Who could have foreseen what would happen? He was the love of my life. Tall, dark, and handsome.' And rich. I nodded as she spoke, but inside I felt the old scales and pulleys, braced for her adjustment, roll down into their final position and lock. I'd colluded in the past. Even as a child, I knew the Doctor was the ticket out of the ring-bologna life that my mother abhorred and which I had begun to sense could take us only so far. Maybe only as far as the edge of our small town. Our father was gone, and not coming back. And I was greedy. I wanted Disneyland, to which my mother and the Doctor had gone just days after Sarah was born, marching in the Rose Bowl parade.

'There's your mother on the box,' said Mabel, Kate and I looking for the little thimble doll that looked like her on the television set. And there she was in Pasadena, 1961, stamping along with the Doctor and the rest of the band in the Tournament of Roses Parade. That was before they were together. The Doctor entered our lives a couple of years later with what he took away, which was our mother and her carelessness. Our moments with our mother before the mirror now had an urgency lacking all enchantment. I did not wish her well as she walked out the door, arm in arm with someone large and glacial. I was seven now. I wrote purposeful short stories in which large men died suddenly, the victims of mysterious accidents. Rocks fell. Motor-boats hit buried sandbars and sank. One of my characters was fatally bitten by a rabid raccoon. Medicine only prolonged his agony. None fell off roofs and then hung around, wordlessly dissolving into the fate of his own impotence and the loss of his senses.

In the brief time between my father's leaving and the Doctor's coming, we were happy enough. Mabel sat in the kitchen when we arrived home from school, buttering Wonder bread, a special treat. Mabel was there because for a year or so after my father left, my mother worked, and loved it. Mabel drove us to meet the Milwaukee Road train each day as it brought Dolores home from her old job as a legal secretary. My mother was dazzlingly happy to see us. The air around her thrummed and sparked as she skipped off the train to run to us. She showed us the packages she'd bought on her lunch hour, told us we would do the same someday when we were grown up. I thought we could stay like this forever, watching her descend from the Milwaukee Road on its way to St Paul, reading the boxcars emblazoned with the words Soo Line and Blue Earth Minnesota. Blue Earth Minnesota. I had never heard of anyplace so beautiful. My mother laughed and my grandmother planted her feet beside the rail-road. The wind from the approaching train blew back the tops of the brown-eyed Susans, wrinkling like sea anemones at the train's shadow passage as it hissed and spat to a flaring stop. The beast disgorged our mother. Gathering up her girls in her arms, she cried, 'It's Punky and her Pals!' citing my favorite television show. 'Punky!'

'What would you have done?' my mother says and sighs quietly decades later. She is sitting on her bed and I can see the gray roots where the henna has not touched her hair. The curve of her back has for two decades borne her waitress trays like hods. A manicure is a luxury now. She is sitting in Mabel's bungalow, looking out at Puckawasay's water lilies. Mabel is long dead. What would you have done, my mother asks, and I can't answer her. For years I used to think I knew what I would have done in my mother's straits, but to my astonishment I have never raised even one child, much less a brood. I know only that I myself have been drawn to men with despotic natures. The way they give orders, the way they justify their majestically cruel behavior, smoke pouring out of their beautiful nostrils like ancient dragons. I once loved a man who held my hand in a flame, another who twisted my flesh with pliers, a third who raped and beat me. A desperado helps one live dangerously, and perhaps that is how we know we are alive. Perhaps that's what my mother needed. Maybe that's what I thought I needed, centuries ago, when love was fueled by hardnesses and the desperate sensation of powerlessness balanced against power, as in war.

Mabel was on the Doctor's side as well. Didn't I want something better for my mother? my grandmother chided. Didn't I? Maracas shifted in the mirror, a dancer danced in Japan, an animal crashed free in a thicket of brambles, bounded into the dusk. Yes, of course. Yes indeed I wanted something better. I wanted to come too, wherever she was going. Even if it meant we were going to live in the Doctor's house, I'd go.

In the summer while my mother worked, Mabel sat on the back stoop, facing the farm and the cows. She liked the farmer; he gave her fresh-killed chickens. Mabel sat with one now, its head hanging over her knee, dangling like a wet nylon stocking. Her hands flew through the scalded feathers, plucking each one until a gray snow pile drifted at her feet and began to swirl in the breeze. Mabel singed the skin with matches, sulphur rising from each filament, an acrid incense. She dragged on a Lucky.

'You dassn't go saying bad things about the Doctor.' My grandmother's cigarette bobbed at me, its orange ember glowing like a hazard light. She had picked up her new husband's idioms, and he spoke English savagely with a Slavic accent. Even then I thought my grandmother's English was as old as she was, which was ancient. She singed another quill follicle. 'He's good to your mother, and I'll betcha he'll be good for you. You girls are jes' wild Injuns. What you need is a big stick with a nail in it. You have a mouth on you that runs overtime. And besides,' she said, knees splayed, the floppy chicken getting the worst of it, 'what other chance does your momma have?'

I laid my head on her shoulder and watched while she shook the chicken like a tassel. My grandmother talked roughly, coarsely, but never touched a hair on our heads unless she was smoothing it down and tying a bow in it. Her fingers were so stiff with arthritis that she couldn't tie bows very nicely, but at chicken-flicking she was better, her fingers working somehow deftly. After plucking the carcass bare, she took it to the kitchen sink to cut off its feet and scoop the unformed eggs from its intestines. Mabel then pulled out the whole aubergine mass and stuck the chicken's feet in a pot, boiled them until they were yellow, and dropped in the liquid eggs with a spoon. She pointed out correctly that they tasted twice the egg of anything we got at the store. Mabel's cooking was like voodoo, primal and full of things that grew in the yard or came back from Louie's traplines. Things that looked odd and were tossed together as Mabel muttered. And that's what our lives were like – disparate contradictory things patched with voodoo spells, stirring and bubbling. You could hardly tell what you had started with because it had all stewed together. I sat in the kitchen and felt sure that the Doctor would make a fatal mistake, that the adults would see him as I did. I had on Superman X-ray glasses, I could see where he had holes.

'Hey, chum,' he'd gloat. 'I gotcha!' They'll see, I thought. They'll know.

We hardly ever called each other by name, the Doctor and I. Sometimes he addressed me as 'little girl,' but because he also used this name for my mother I hated it. In all the years we lived with him I don't recall that he said my first name a dozen times. It was as if by ignoring our given names we could cancel each other out. I felt the earth spinning faster and faster. The Doctor swung me by the ankles, pretending he was going to drop me. Faster, here comes the grass, tickling my head just where it brushes the ground. There's the swing set and the sandbox, smack where the clouds should be. I could feel the Doctor thinking about how small I was. A smile appeared on his mouth, never in his eyes. Yet sometimes when the Doctor visited us, he whistled. It was the only beautiful sound he made, and it was gorgeous, a fluttering three-part whistle, a primordial note. Floating and haunting, a tripartite chord that could have been the sound of rose petals coming off the stem, it was that lovely. I try to remember that he did at least have the ability to make a lovely sound. An ability my father had lost.

Sundays were the days my father came back, everyone knew that. He collected us after church, heading outdoors and pulling us over the fields on a toboggan or, if it was raining, to the bowling alley or the movies. We saw dozens of films – *Prince Valiant* and *Twenty Thousand Leagues under the Sea. Your Cheatin' Heart*, about Hank Williams, starring George Hamilton. That was the best, where they got married by putting washers on their fingers. My father had plenty of things to sort out besides us. Work, fluid locomotion, flash cards, mouth sounds, revved-up rhymes like Peter Piper. He was re-inventing his world; he still had a place in the universe. He had moved back home with his parents. From time to time, his older sister, a seriously unhappy woman, took it upon herself to ask me who I liked better, my mother's boyfriend or my father. 'Both the same,' said Kate and I, lying through our teeth, feeling that any other answer betrayed either our mother or our father. But Sarah, who was four by then, disagreed. 'Our Sunday father is our real father,' said Sarah quietly. 'He just comes on Sundays, but he's the real one.' Even then, Sarah always cut to the chase.

One Sunday evening before Christmas when the dark and ice

seemed both lock and key, my father brought us home and stood beside the Doctor's Cadillac, parked in our driveway. It was an affront, that Cadillac. It had overstayed its allotted hours at my mother's house, hours that until now had ended long before our return. My father looked over the glossy car, taking its measure as he shuffled in the snow. He put his hand on the hood, as if to verify the car's presence. My father had been building us a toy kitchen in the attic as a not-so-secret Christmas present. He was great with his hands. The miniature kitchen was an absolutely wonderful testimonial, but it would never be in league with what the Cadillac represented. That automobile might as well have been a ballroom that my father would never be allowed to enter. My father stood for a moment, and then on impulse led us to the front door and yanked it open. My mother stood there cradled in the Doctor's arms, as if she'd been caught falling down. The Doctor had on his hat and coat. He'd been about to leave. Everyone stopped breathing. Electric Christmas chimes on the mantel bleated repetitively in the stillness like Morse code, their lights clicking on and off the startled faces before us. My mother and the Doctor, a fleshly fact.

Far above me, my father's pink head roared in its own silence, a Roman candle firing in a vast empty night, one thought streaking to its destiny like an asteroid. 'Whaaaaaaaaaaaaaaaaaaaat are youah doing in mah hawse?' my father screamed, knowing the answer. 'Do youah know whoah built this hawse? Awe *built* this hawse, goddamit. Get your handddds offa mah whofe!' The Doctor and my mother recoiled but did not step back. Then we were all inside. The Doctor, a foot taller than my father, put his hands on my father's shoulders, restraining him. We girls bobbled at my father's knees, suspended, unwilling, too dazed to let go of one another. Words were frothing around the room somewhere near the ceiling.

'Fathead,' the Doctor said, a revolting word. 'Idiot. Get out.' I looked up and saw my father's face scrunched, trying to lip-read, his skin as slick and shining as an old burn, and then his fist hammered out and struck the Doctor in the chest. Whatever else he knew, or didn't know, he was being thrown out of the house that he considered his by the interloper himself. He gave the Doctor a big push. 'Stupid jerk,' said the Doctor, flailing backward but not too far. He reeled forward and shoved my father reciprocally, and my father staggered. Everybody had gone crazy; everyone was *flying*. My mother hauled Kate and Sarah up in her arms, and I slipped behind the mesh curtains by the picture window, watching the two men grope through a room that was crowded with things I was beginning to understand.

The Doctor's face hardened but did not fundamentally change. A lock of his waxy brown hair looped over his forehead, his finger skewed into my father's chest. If he punched my father in the head I knew he would kill him. Presumably the Doctor knew it too because he held my father by the collar, like a child, shaking him up and down. There was too much flesh in the room, and too much movement. No one could stand or walk straight. My mother cried, 'Pat, Pat,' but of course he couldn't hear her, and his own voice was crazed, monotonal from syllable to syllable, just like the bing-bang, bing-bang of the Christmas chimes. My father seemed to focus all his energy and rushed at the Doctor, shouting, 'Wah, uh, you, ah!' in an incomprehensible gaggle. He was a goose man. His glasses had fallen off his nose, and he was dumb-reeling blind.

For a few minutes, the Doctor pushed him back rhythmically like a punch toy. Between pushes he removed his camel hair coat and elegant fedora and scribbled little notes on his prescription pad, furiously muttering, 'Fathead,' 'Loser,' 'Pipsqueak.' The Doctor jammed the notes into my father's shirt pocket. My father tried to read a few of them but couldn't see for the sweat and the steam over his eyeglasses. Patrick wadded the papers up and flung them into the Doctor's face. The Doctor pushed my father backward, hard, really hard, and launched him into the Christmas tree.

Airborne, confused, Patrick Lyden flew into the tree, soared through his silent world of color and light. The tree crashed explosively against the window, pulverizing the uniformly blue Christmas balls, upending the spotlight that made them shine like small blue planets. Crushed beneath my father were the antique Christmas peacocks that had been clipped to the branches, and the train set that he had given us the previous year, which ran around the tree's base. He lay with arms and legs tangled like a big Raggedy Andy dropped through the ceiling. The fine white powder flocking floated from the tree and transformed us all into figures in an overturned paperweight. Daddy was a big starfish, hardly human at all. I stayed where I was, behind the curtains, watching. Maybe my father would float away without ever getting up again. And in a way he did.

The brilliantine helmet peered into my cave. The Doctor eyed me. 'Are you OK, little girl?' I yanked back the curtains, my barrier, smelling the chemicals of the dry-cleaning fluid, the stale sunlight and dust motes, the world that had lived and died in the summer in our picture window. A cancer had started in my stomach. The clarity of my hatred for the Doctor, my shame and humiliation for my father, welled up in me as nausea, like the cloud of flocking powder. I closed my eyes and was far, far away, alone over the rainbow in a land of children who engaged in fierce battles with one another and lived in snow forts, amid snow furniture. All the world was snow and falling snow. We were at war in the snow, and we would live there together and I would be their tribal leader.

When I opened my eyes, I felt older and could see that my mother was now bending over my father with a washcloth, but that he was getting up, that he was Patrick again. I became dimly aware that Kate, Sarah, and my mother were all crying, but the girls sounded and looked so very far away, clutching each other somewhere out in the land beyond the hallway. As my father sat up, white flocking mashed to the back of his wet shirt and speckled his rump and stuck to his bald head. The snowman. He looked as if he wanted to say something, but speech was a knack misremembered and he was mute now as well. My mother's arms were pulling at something invisible, like a lever yanking up and down, trying to crank the axis of the world back to a sane angle, and she was saying over and over, 'Let's all have some Christmas cookies. Let's all have some Christmas cookies.' And the Doctor grew there, planted into the room like a sequoia, grim with his hands on his padded hips. Finally he bent and made a gesture as if to examine my father, who pushed him away, much more feebly this time. It didn't matter how long my father sat there. Our home was the Doctor's domain now, and everyone under that roof knew it.

Before he lost his hearing, my father had taken me to see a northern lights show when a new gas station had opened nearby. I knew that these were not the real northern lights, of course, but a spectacular imitation, a force of nature under our control. The lights bolted from tipped barrels, shooting great spouts of illumination that painted the night sky. My father in an eager voice explained that searchlights like these had combed the sky for *him* when he was learning to be a paratrooper, and that he had floated down between the crossed hatches in the darkness as part of the American 'Victory over Japan.' I could see him in my mind's eye, a small figure hurtling through the inky sky, bravely swerving to avoid the searchlights, and then his parachute opening, like a crocus bloom. I imagined him in Japan touching quietly to the ground, listening keenly for the slightest sound of the enemy. I looked at him beside me, standing tall, gazing rapt as the barrels tipped out their light show. My father was looking up, seemingly taking the measure of the bands of light, and gave the sky his full attention.

That Valentine's Day when I came home from school, my mother showed me the diamond solitaire on her hand from the Doctor. She held it up to the light in our picture window, and said, 'I want you to call him Daddy.' But I couldn't call him Daddy. I couldn't without choking, feeling the lie in my throat like a fish bone. 'I already have one daddy,' I said to her. 'And no one I know has two. And anyway, he's not my daddy.' She said I would have to learn to address the Doctor that way eventually, but she was dead wrong.

The Doctor married my mother late the next October, just after I had turned seven, on a night that held a thousand kinds of cold. The stars were cold and so was the moonlight patterned like a ziggurat on the church steps. The camera flashbulbs and the teeth of the adults were all cold stars. We three girls were dressed identically in tiny white stoles of mock fur like rabbit pelts and matching cummerbunds of pale rose. Maybe it looked like we were all getting married, the whole family. The cummerbund felt as tight as a tourniquet cinching my waist. I had learned that cummerbunds were for formal occasions. I also learned some other things. I had new instincts about the absolute fragility of love, of its tendency to be friable and powdery when what is required is a bulwark. My mother had a platinum ring from my father that said forever, but forever turned out to be finite. Betrayals looped through betrayals in the shape of a love knot. I was looped inside that knot. I swallowed the whole idea, the platinum circle without end, the inscription that vainly called on eternity. And Sarah and Kate and I held hands, lacing our fingers together and steeling ourselves as if for an earthquake. We looked toward the altar, at the tableau that seemed as if it couldn't be.

It was only 1960. All the adults must have believed, surely

believed, that things would get better now because the worst was over. I might well have believed it myself, had I been one of them. For her wedding my mother wore a gold brocade sheath, one of two dresses that the Doctor had ordered from Hong Kong's Kowloon Road, and a matching gold bolero. Her hair was teased high but still waved down her back like a flume. She wore gold shoes and her runway smile and she looked like a radiant queen, a golden queen on a parapet. Darkness swam outside the church windows. My mother turned to face the world, convinced that everything could now begin. My fingers still locked into my sisters'. Somewhere in the distance I thought I sensed my father's presence, like a ribbon of spilled milk. My mother beamed and walked down the aisle, parting the waves which rolled back at her feet. We girls were not at her side.

TEOTIHUACÁN, *M*EXICO, 1960

THE POSTCARDS FROM MEXICO said that it was indeed a land as wonderful as we had always dreamed it was, with señoritas who really did wear ruffles of many colors and pile their hair on their heads, and pilgrims who walked on their knees for miles, dust coming from their clothes as if they themselves were steaming or sending their souls to seek God. And my mother wrote that the fruit was so sweet you would have thought it was made of sugar, especially the mangoes and papayas. Postcards, paper flowers, real orchids on the tables of Acapulco. I dreamed in her wake, as I always had. My mother saw what she wanted to see, in people and in places. Her tone in the postcards sent from her honeymoon was bright and gay and infatuated. I am sure I have sounded that way myself in recounting the people and the places where I have fallen in love. She was not ignorant of our unhappiness over her marriage, but she must have prayed for a miraculous change. She willed us to change. Her need for belief was larger than life – life that was either belief fulfilled or as empty as a turned-out pocket, you could take your pick. Her belief was the same kind that built the hanging gardens in Babylon or told girls named Norma Jean they had a future in the movies. Extraordinary people have such belief. Think of the citadels of despots, the vanities that begin wars, the hubris of the conqueror. Such belief predestines that we will make fragile walls bear the weight of our longing until time and gravity and the trumpets of Jericho bring the whole thing down. I was happy then, we say, when I only dreamed of what might be. I wonder if I will be so happy again. I say, be careful what you pray for, for my mother received her heart's desire.

I had proof now that Mexico existed: cards with exotic stamps and postmarks, honeymoon treasures for us girls. There were also gifts of rosewood boxes, round ones like miniature hatboxes with the word *Mexico* carved into the tops. They smelled citrusy inside, not like lemons or limes exactly but bumpy exotic fruit that gleamed lushly when slit open. There was also a cotton señorita doll for me, with black cotton braids and removable clothes, and an assortment of enormous oversize paper poppies in rainbow colors, piñata burros, our own maracas, and best of all, a black lace mantilla and a red taffeta skirt with a black voile overlay for me to dress up in like Dolores Del Rio. What I did believe, clutching the Mexican mementos, is that a wonderland existed somewhere beyond our home and our understanding. And yet now that I had these proofs, these truths, these stamps of the revered face of President López Mateos, I could no longer think of Mexico as a place of escape and my own dominion. The Doctor's honeymoon visit there obliterated that.

'I want you to know that Dockie loves you just as much as one of his own girls,' my mother said upon her return. She was referring to my stepfather's daughters by his previous marriage. Her words were a lie, but I knew she believed them, squeezed from a stylized, cinematic American hope. *Dockie* was her word for him. It was not a word I could say, it was not a word to me. It was a loathsome reflex I felt as he swept my mother into his arms and I gazed out at the fields and the road and the way that the bird feeder had iced over now, birdseed sprinkled on the snow like cinnamon. And anyway, I knew he did not love us because whatever love was it could not be a place where a wrong word was a trapdoor and a false step meant oblivion.

When the Doctor moved into our house, I felt as if the very light had changed in our old familiar territory. His clothes hung in my mother's closet where my father's once had, but I had never before seen so many suits. Though they sometimes smelled of ether or antiseptic, other times they smelled of forests and salt brine. To this day, I associate Old Spice with manliness. I smelled his clothes when no one was looking, sniffing lapels and pockets where they crowded into my mother's dresses and hats and bags. I shined my leather shoes on his electric shoe polisher with black and red scuffs that reminded me of the crowns on the King and Queen of Hearts. His leather doctor's kit bag stood beside our sofa, sometimes spilling out charts of the central nervous system, the skeleton, the intestinal tract. I picked them up if he wasn't around. The pancreas was a muddy pool, the heart a basin of rivers. I looked at pictures of diseased organs and thought of all the things that could go wrong in the body. Our voices, hushed and thinned, lowered to a little staccato of whispers. Unconsciously, we girls had begun to imitate my father when the Doctor was home. We trolled about the house and, if we had been the most beautiful women in the room, perhaps it might have turned out differently.

He eliminated the skins-versus-shirts games because there are no skins without undershirts on, that's why. Because I told you so, that's why. Shut up now. I looked at the Doctor reading in my father's chair. I handed him my book, *Pippi Longstocking.* On a whim I hurled myself into his lap. 'Read to me,' I said. He pushed as hard as if struck. The book flew to the floor and me with it. Tell me I'm pretty, I wanted to say from where I lay on the floor, looking at his shoes. Tell me I'm smart. If you can't do that, then tell me you like the way I stack the dinner plates on the counter. Tell me you like the way I pump the swing to the treetops. Tell me whatever you like, but tell me I exist. His silence was the loudest shout I'd ever heard and it filled my ears with sludge. His silence communicated itself to you, and his eyes found you out and executed you. My mother's smile said she didn't know and didn't want to know. 'At the end of the day,' she would say, slipping out of her pedal pushers and into a dress, 'you should freshen up for your husband and welcome him home. Try and look nice. He's looked at other women all day, you know. Put on a little lipstick.'

'Kitten,' he'd say to her, purring as a tiger purrs. 'Dolly.' 'Lambie.' His hands roamed her body, and I felt suffused with an agony for which I had no name. Rows of little bottles lined up in the bathroom cabinet, with 'Kitten' or 'Dolly Girl' scrawled on their prescription faces. Medicine, my mother said. Little bottles for serenity in a stressful life. My mother said we were a real family now, but a real family would have suffered with much less self-consciousness. There were indeed times we'd drive off with the Doctor in the big Cadillac, and then I would exult, 'We're rich!' I was the betrayer of the betrayed; I was a phony and I knew it, biting into the succulent filet mignon at the fancy restaurants where the Doctor took us for dinner. At home though, when I looked at the Doctor's shaving mug in our cabinet, his stacks of white starched shirts in a drawer, his enormous shoes lined up in my mother's closest, I felt spasms of mourning. Then the silence closed in again, and I lost the old rhythms of life. The natural sounds were all still there of course – the doves cooing at the feeder, the cows' rumbling lows in the morning, the hissing wheels of the road. I was deaf to them because I was roaring with fear. A footstep could land on a crack in the world, a spilled glass could bring an apocalypse. A jagged vocabulary entered our lives – *pig, jerk, chum*, and *fathead*. I took to ordering Sarah around and calling her 'pig' and 'jerk' when no one was looking merely because she was defenseless. I became a bully. I made Sarah suffer, stripped her and whipped her until I raised welts on her tiny pink buttocks. She cried and didn't tell our mother. Our powerlessness mixed somehow with a new fear in the airwaves. The Bay of Pigs meant failure and the force of something atomic that would cause us all to implode. Deadly atoms danced in the dust motes. I had no problem understanding that the nuclei of atoms, of any life-form no matter how elemental, could be split to blow up. Hadn't my sisters and I been split from our old lives? At the height of the Cuban missile crisis, the Doctor took my mother off to a medical convention in Miami. We trembled in our school lockers, preparing for a nuclear attack. President Kennedy was on the loudspeaker. My mother would be atomized. Fear was coming, fear had arrived. The lockers felt like coffins. The whole world as I knew it was threatened with annihilation and extinction as a universe, right down to the molecules, and it was only the third grade.

One night not long after they'd returned from the honeymoon, Sarah, four years old, waking from one of her frequent nightmares, rose and felt her way to my mother's bed and curled up lengthwise at its foot as she had always done. She nudged at the Doctor's toes, which, she remembers more than thirty years later, were chill. In the kick from his feet she was knocked to the floor and, in the subsequent shock of his hands, dragged back to her bedroom. The Doctor leaned against the door like a sledge. Her night-light with its tiny blue stars was confiscated because only babies cried in the dark. Sarah's small fists beat inside the door, bleats like a lamb's coming from her room. Her cries reached Kate and me, where we lay in the upstairs bedroom, our limbs interlocked.

The dark. I think of it like another opponent of my youth. A dog once bit me in the leg while I played at a friend's. It was only a dachshund, a wiener dog we called her – Queenie, not a dog with much of a bite. Queenie was a dowager dog who hated children.

She got me just for standing there, biting the back of my knee. I walked home on our road in the sun, the blood dripping down my leg, and I was not afraid. I thought I was brave and noble, the survivor of Queenie's nip. But then my mother had called the Doctor as I lay fevered on my bed, and he loomed over me in his massive starched white doctor's tunic, bigger than God. He could cure or kill. I had told my mother I would take my chance with tetanus, rabies, anything but a shot. I was silent while the Doctor drew a long needle out of his satchel and then squinted it into my backside while my mother lifted my night-gown. After that, the dark held dogs that lay beneath my bed waiting to sink their teeth into me. They were black dogs about knee-high. I could see and hear them, snuffling monster snorts. And as bright as day, I heard the click of their jaws, snapping and ripping sounds that interposed between the bed and the doorway. My mother's room was continents away. Queenie got closer and closer, and I screamed and Kate screamed. A face in the doorway. A monster shadow in the shaft of light.

'If I hear another sound, the night-light's going with me.' An ax trembling near us, like a fairy tale come alive in which a woodsman's voice chops the past from the present.

So Kate and I whispered in half words at night and often in the daytime, partisans in our own country, talking in code. We were learning a secret language of defense and the cunning of those who inhabit occupied territories. Our minds began to construct labyrinths and whole corridors and interior passageways of escape. The characters from my stories were there, the tribe of snow children and the six-foot Pooka and Pegasus the winged horse. My Sunday father. I put into the chambers of my imagination all the things I would have put into a bomb shelter. My sister and I could live in there, I thought, we had provisions for fifty years. Sometimes I wonder if this is what my mother has done, made her own shelter against annihilation, but she shakes her head. Insanity she can scarcely recall, but the stone-cold timbre of the Doctor's voice, this we all – each one of us – remember like yesterday.

I was stunned by all the new rules. You had to remember to put the toothpaste cap back on tightly, and not squeeze the tube in the middle. If you failed to do that, the air filled with an electric charge. You were warned, you'd been warned. Objects had to stay in their place. My stepfather may have believed like certain Chinese geomancers that things not returned to their proper position released the Furies. Perhaps the toothpaste, blue and alive, would snake out of the capless tube like a cobra. 'I saw that, chum,' my stepfather would say to me with so much venom that I felt the fangs in my skin. I am a chum, chum, and do you know what? It rhymes with dumb.

The bottle cap rule was almost as niggling. Sarah, Kate, and I all liked to run as fast as possible, with filthy feet, from the front yard around to the side door and through the living room, through the kitchen and out the back door to the fields. We would yell at the tops of our lungs, yell even louder because the Doctor was away, chase one another, head for the meadow, disappear. Reappear. Slam. Slam. Slam. We're in the house, we're thirsty now. Drag a chair to the refrigerator, open the refrigerator door, swig from a bottle of soda, leave it on the shelf, out through the back door. Slam. Slam. Slam. We were wild and dirty. My mother and my grandmother agreed that Kate and I were tomboys and monkeys. We ran all day long with the boys on our street, trying to be keen and tough, toppling our bikes off ridges and daring to jump from trees. I scraped my knees and elbows most days of the summer. The pain was nothing to Kate and me if it meant we got to play with the boys, but Sarah hated their loudness and rudeness. So we'd grab her and escape; we ran into the house for soda. Many times we left the soda uncapped in the refrigerator, causing it to go flat, enraging my stepfather, who lived on Pepsi-Cola,

usually going through a whole six-pack at night. I would defy
him. I wanted to change the imprisonment in the air around
us. I wanted to write with cool blue toothpaste on the bathroom
wall, but I knew that at seven, I was too old for something that
infantile. I wanted to fill the sink basin with Pepsi and launch a
hundred bottle caps on the sticky brown sea, like the water lilies
on Lake Puckawasay.

In the kitchen, my mother believed in fairy tales. She was a little
girl too. She was more fragile than we girls, who were not fragile
at all. She sang in the kitchen, humming for him the songs she
liked to sing for us, 'Easter Parade' and 'Red River Valley.' She
invited us girls to join her. I had forgotten the words again. I
had become so absentminded that my mother pinned or sewed
to my jacket anything really important. I lost eyeglasses, books,
dolls, homework, and retainers. I was a sorceress, anything given
to me vanished into thin air. But I shouldn't worry, my mother
said. 'Perhaps you are really a great genius like Albert Einstein and
we don't know it. He knows how the universe works, but there is a
story that he does not always remember where he lives. One night
on his way home, he lost his house. He called his laboratory, and
said, "Do you know where Dr Einstein lives? Do not tell anybody,
but this is Dr Einstein."'

I was beginning to forget, actually, where I lived, in what time
zone, what country, what street. Where I really lived there were
dancing girls and Indians and horses. When *The Rifleman* came
on TV, I thought I would like to live in a desert town of sagebrush
and moral rectitude, doing gritty chores that got me as dirty and
callused as a boy, learning to shoot a rifle and making a cherry
pie like the girl in the song 'Billy Boy.' When *Make Room for
Daddy* was on TV with Danny Thomas, then I wanted to go
home with Uncle Tonoose. Kate and I wanted to cannonball into
Uncle Tonoose's arms, convinced of the protection they afforded.
My mother said my imagination was becoming a problem, and

now, besides talking out of turn I was getting bad marks for failing to pay attention in class, but I had no idea how to change. I then performed cloyingly self-conscious good acts, like writing poems for other children's Mother's Day cards or teaching the Brownie motto to my sisters. I empathized with people on *Queen for a Day*, like the foreign woman who shyly let it be known she wanted a dictionary to improve her English, but got a Kenmore washing machine instead. Kate and Sarah and I acted out all the parts on *Queen for a Day*, wearing our rhinestone tiaras and pretending a jump rope, with its wooden handles, was two microphones.

My secret and magic notebooks were black with red binders. I had several of them in which I wrote stories about unhappy people and unhappy families, like Lulu the ugliest shell on the beach, who no one would ever pick for a friend. She had a curveball of a mouth on her so it was a good thing she was so small, but all that lip was just her way of taking on the world. And the heroic Broken Candy Cane, who had lumps and humps, and who would never be chosen for Santa's bag. All the other candy canes busted him into a million pieces when he tried in desperation to hop into the sleigh. Then Santa took pity on him, plastered him back together with sugar, and took him to some sick children for their holiday. From Santa's sleigh he got to see the whole world and found zillions of lumpy candy canes just like him. I punched holes in the pages of my best stories, collected them in a large black folder with red steel snap binders, and called it 'My Famous Book.'

One day I found the 'Famous Book' lying open in the living room. Red ink corrections in block capitals, the Doctor's hand-writing, crawled over its pages. The Doctor had gone through the stories and corrected the improper grammar. The spelling I had right, but he had changed tenses and pronouns. One story in particular described a little girl trapped beneath a woodpile while her stepfather, a wizard, searched for her so he could cook her in the oven. But she had befriended the birds, who surrounded her stepfather and shooed him toward the spot where she had planted booby traps of sharpened toothbrushes. He fell on one and swiftly died, while she sat above him, drinking Pepsi and throwing the bottle caps over her shoulder. Now he knows, I thought. His fingers have been on my pages, and he knows how passionately I hate him. I felt exposed and naked. I took the 'Famous Book' upstairs and hid it under my pillow. That night I watched him in the living room. He was tall and dark and handsome. He spoke into his Dictaphone, letters to his nurses, secretaries, suppliers, patients, and other doctors. He seemed to be talking to the whole world. He called all his nurses 'dear.' He discounted me because I was only seven and weighed fifty-eight pounds. But I knew I would have my revenge, would reach him even when he would not be reached and make him notice me. Make him never forget me.

It happened at the sink one morning when I was brushing my teeth before school. At the sink I often lapsed into a trance as if on a hypnotist's cue. The sink was so white and gleaming, the silver chrome faucets poised with such priapism over the white basin. The tiny toothpaste cap like a droplet of ivory, all of it an altar. His fist at the back of my head came so fast that my lips hit the sink before I even had the toothpaste out of my mouth. A red tear opened behind my teeth and oozed into the toothpaste, warm and substantially salty. 'Stupid, stupid, stupid moron,' he said. I spit out the stuff in my mouth, replaced the cap, ran the water down the sink. Behind my eyes, the past sank somewhere far out of reach. In this country were fists. Coming at me always from behind, the fists, like snowballs, were random and impossible to predict, hitting the base of my skull where a blow would leave no bruise, unmappable, flung in silence, without words or with just the occasional *stupid*. Or a hand like a vise on my skull, bending my chin toward my chest, thumbs behind my pulsing ears. He was a doctor of osteopathy. He gripped either side of my neck, cracking it with a sharp turn to the right, then the left. The pain was a noose, a tourniquet, a dog bite in the skull. Maybe this morning, maybe tonight, maybe only the threat and that was enough. Try again, I silently told him. Go ahead and do it again. He could not resist me, I was certain of that. We had formed a relationship at last. A blow. The absorption of a blow. A symmetry, he and I together.

One morning, after the Doctor's fist had caught me alone again in the bathroom, I went to my mother's vanity to examine my puffed lip. I pulled up my mother's velvet hassock to the crescent moon of mirror. Oh, I thought, where is my perfume and my jewelry? Where are the señoritas and the cowgirls and the Menomenees in the woods in their quiet villages, and my mother, what can I tell her today about school? I tried on hats, lifted lipsticks, squeezed atomizers. Only recently have I realized that not all men view pain as a part of love, the hardest blows a kind of bond, deeper and more intense than ordinary love. My mother would never know about the Doctor's blows, or she pretended not to know. We cannot acknowledge what cannot be borne. My mother loved him, that much I knew, her eyes as radiant as the sun before its own eclipse. And besides, it seemed almost natural after a while to live in a land of occupation which had invisible locks and keys. But I was determined to learn the foreign language of escape. I have stood on no-man's-land between the soldiers and guns of opposing armies, between the stone throwers and the tanks, the Arabs and the Jews, and watched as legs and arms were gathered into body bags on Dizengoff Street in Tel Aviv. The bomber lies scattered among the bombed. Horror of horrors how familiar it comes to me the way they feed on one another, hater and hated.

At the end of the school year, we would move to the Doctor's house in Menomenee, Wisconsin, a town only eight miles away and much bigger than our crossroads village on Lake Puckawasay. The Doctor's house should have been heaven with its fifteen-foot wall of glass that overlooked Lac La Jolie and white leather chairs and a fountain in the front yard. I could hear the fountain at night from my bedroom, my own room. It was Kate and Sarah who shared a bedroom now. The Doctor's house tempted us and we were not untemptable. I thought how lucky I was to live in a sumptuous house, in spite of everything, watching *The Wizard of Oz* in color on the Doctor's new television. I had been told that Judy Garland wore a blue dress. She didn't, though: it was yellow, and the Munchkins wore blue. Sitting in the Doctor's amazingly huge living room, as big as our entire old house, I knew we were rich. We had made it, or rather, my mother had, and we had gone with her, all the way.

'Don'tcha love to go fast?' my grandmother was saying. It was the summer after my mother's wedding. We were tearing through the woods in Mabel's old Buick coupe between Menomenee and the small town where we had lived with my father. Mabel still lived on our old lane without sidewalks which rimmed Lake Puckawasay. We were taking the S curves outside of Wagner's Hospital, which my grandmother explained was a nuthouse, glazing the curves with our speed between Upper Ipesong and Lower Ipesong Lake. The road doubled on itself in loops between marsh plants and the hidden great houses of the past century. Often a siren came tagging after us, playing catch. At such moments, Mabel hit the gas. Louie taught my grandmother to drive when she was fifty-three, and she had had to wait all that time to discover she was a natural leadfoot.

'Shit,' my grandmother yelled. 'Jesus H. Christ. It's the cops!' Mabel was usually caught by a young policeman named Randy, who was about twenty-one. Now I look at their weekly rendezvous as some kind of date. Sometimes he ticketed her and sometimes he let her go. He wasn't the type to enjoy issuing tickets to old ladies, but he loved catching Mabel. I thought he was a living doll.

'We meet again, Mrs P,' he said. His teeth and shoulders were as even as balance beams. 'You know, Mrs P, there are two kinds of people I arrest in the S's. Teenagers, and you. Have you thought about what kind of example you're setting here for your granddaughter, Mrs P?'

'I know just what you mean, Randy,' she said. 'But today's a special hurry. You reach over there, and feel my granddaughter's forehead. She's burnin' up with fever. She threw up about an hour ago, and I don't know why, but I think maybe she drank some stuff Louie had open in the basement, you know what I mean? I gotta get her over to Northland Hospital's emergency room.'

Randy became all concern.

'I'll escort you, Mrs P.' I wanted to marry Randy at that moment. He could arrest my grandmother as often as he liked.

'You know you are just a dear man, but I think it would scare her, Randy, I honestly do, havin' that siren on, and I don' want her gettin' sick in the car.'

'Then just hold it to fifty miles an hour, OK? Promise me.'

'Cross my heart.'

And we were off. I crossed my heart.

Mabel looked at me out of the side of her eyes, her glasses just catching a ray of sun.

'I drank something?' I said. 'Out of the basement? What on earth, like some paint thinner, you mean? I'm eight years old! Why would I do something that stupid? How could you tell him such big lies?'

'Look,' my grandmother said. 'Sometimes you just gotta bend things a little bit, is what it is, OK? What he dassn't know won't hurt him. You think he was gonna let me go? Shit a brick, a guy like him lives to give people five-dollar tickets when they weren't even hurtin' anyone. It's people like me what gives him somethin' t' do with his time, or he'd be sittin' down there at the station house sittin' on his fanny, nose in a detective comic. Believe me, if there's room for the other guy t' go in the ditch, there's room for me to pass. I hate all them damn road laws. They're for the bohunks, like Louie. You wan' an ice cream, or you wanna go spend my money on a speedin' ticket? 'Cause I could go right down to city hall and empty my purse on the goddamned counter.'

'I want an ice cream at the Scottie,' I said evenly. The Scottie was our drive-in. I wanted chocolate jimmies on my ice cream, and a waffle cone, and I knew I was in no danger of losing it.

'Good,' she said, chortling, pretending she might have withheld it. 'What he dassn't know won't hurt him, and I gotta ration the tickets, or Granpa Louie will bust a gut.' Then she became sober. 'You tell your ma, and I'll skin you alive like a red Indian.'

'Like to see that,' I said, looking out at the tassels of cornfields as we neared Menomenee. The stalks cast shadows on the earth between the rows, and the sun spooled out between the pine breaks. The car window framed the horizon in neat rectangles of country. We could have all we wanted and more would be left over. Real harm was dispelled when I was with Mabel. Even if she'd gone to bed early, gin bottle on her nightstand, washcloth on her face. *Grandma's sick again, don't tell nobody.*

Lies were necessary for us all, for my grandmother, my mother, and for us girls. But we did not think of them as lies. We thought of them as stories, as artful fabrications of real longing, as narrative inventions that made it more possible to live. It cannot be altogether a lie if you believe it, we reasoned, and truth is a bright flag, sometimes long and streaming, sometimes twisting itself around its own pole. My grandmother actually loved to tell outright lies to my mother, and my mother knew it. My grandmother lied to the cops when they gave her speeding tickets, and she lied to the neighbors about things I had accomplished in school. She lied the way other people took pictures to remember things. Events were not my grandmother's until she had embroidered them, and the lies were as real as the psalms on the sides of our home offering box. Those tales were comforts, and I can appreciate now that I am grown the sense of moral certainty beneath our spinning narratives.

Down on Lake Puckawasay, Louie cut off the heads of his biggest fish and nailed them to an immense post that loomed into the air over his battered skinning table. The smell was rank. Ten heads, then twenty, then thirty, then more. Their bones whitened to silver. The sky could be seen through their gaping jaws. Gnats came in clouds, darting in and out of the skulls, giving the top of the post the image of fluttering, mouth upon mouth, bone upon bone. Looking up, I thought, These are our totems, to protect us from evil.

There were two good things about my mother's remarriage. The first was living in the vast apartments over the Doctor's clinic, across the street from Lac La Jolie, in a neighborhood of children our own age. The second was that we traveled. We always headed west, to the Badlands and Rockies, pulling a silver Avion trailer behind a new Cadillac Seville convertible. Pressing a button on the dash brought the canvas top folding down into the car as neatly as a silk evening shirt. The top stowed, we three girls hunkered in the back seat under cowgirl hats, inhaling the new leather while my mother sat up front with the Doctor. Strange animals inhabited the landscape: two-headed calves, fleas in mariachi outfits, horned rabbits called jackalopes. They dominated the roadside gift shops, a signal that other people besides me had weird imaginations. The bizarre menagerie heralded the unreality of our western adventures. We were older, I thought, for having crossed the Continental Divide.

As the Cadillac headed west, the trailer bumbled after us like a circus marquee. My mother sat up front like Rita Hayworth, wearing the black lace mantilla from Mexico over the waves of her hair, streamers flying, a goddess behind sunglasses. We traveled down the slower stretches of Routes 41 and 66, past the diners and bait shops and luncheonettes that are mostly gone now, in an America where there never seemed to be danger at the roadside. Except that somewhere in Nebraska we got the news from the waitress at a tiny café that Marilyn Monroe had died.

The café was behind a Mobil sign, in front of a winged Pegasus flying over antique gas tanks. We pushed through a screen door into the dim little place. 'They found Marilyn Monroe in her bedroom,' the waitress said. 'I heard she choked on her own vomit.'

'Not ever,' my mother said, her face wan under her Copper-tone tan. 'That just doesn't seem possible.'

For my mother, this news was a vortex opening. Marilyn Monroe was a charm, Marilyn Monroe had everything, Marilyn Monroe had come from nothing. She had attained the pinnacle just by being a heartbreaking object of lust (pivot and turn, girls, pivot and turn), just because she was beautiful and knowing. My mother, only a couple of years younger than Monroe, sat on a café stool, her legs hanging down in their pedal pushers, painted toes revealed through her sandals. I was fascinated by the fact that she had hammertoes on each foot. She arranged the wisps of her bouffant hairdo under its halo of net. She was only thirty-two years old, and no woman of her acquaintance and age had ever died by her own hand, certainly not one as enchanting as the goddess Marilyn. I watched my mother's shoulders quiver as she dallied at some blueberry pie. 'I can't believe it,' she said, spooning some pie into Sarah's mouth. The compass inside her spun. 'I can't believe she'd ever kill herself. I think somebody probably killed her. Probably snuck into the living room and put something into her drink because everybody was jealous of her.'

All her life, Mabel had told Dolores that the reason she had few friends was because she was so beautiful. My mother had identified with the isolated quality of the movie star, had no real friends, exposed her vulnerability. She had her own beauty and a child's belief in its salvation. Her beauty was a torch we could all follow through the night no matter how endless. Now she seemed shaken by the intimation that beauty alone was insufficient protection in the world of the flesh.

The waitress leaned over the Formica counter, on which a patron had drawn a road map in pencil. 'That's what all them Hollywood people out there are saying,' she whispered knowingly. 'All them people was jealous of her, and they did her in because she was rich and famous and told them to kiss her fanny.' My mother finished her pie, cleaned the blueberry off Sarah's mouth, then adjusted her hair bonnet and redid her lips. I knew exactly what she was thinking. She was going to beat the odds of crashing, that's what. She had bet on the long journey, set her sights past the edge of our small town. She looked out at the smudgy yellow line of the Nebraska horizon as if it were a string she could pull and follow somewhere. I circled the penciled map on the counter with my finger, a little piece of nowhere, a road the size of the hatch marks on my palm. My road.

When I could put the terror of the Doctor's proximity aside, which came most easily when I was outdoors, then the thing I loved best about those trips west was the sense of exploration. I longed for a prairie schooner and a chart under my arm, the painted topography of a mountain summit, tundra, timberlines, prospectors searching the high sierra for gold, and I loved the idea of a more valiant enemy than my stepfather, like a cougar or a bandit. I thought about heroic acts I might have performed had I been lucky enough to live in the past, like leading search parties for finding water in a dry gulch. I loved the idea of the

Continental Divide, separating water into opposite paths, like
Moses and the parting of the Red Sea as he led the Jews to
safety. I was thrilled by the outlaw Belle Starr, by the mystery of
the Face on the Barroom Floor, the ghosts of Little Big Horn,
the Badlands, and all the other cowboy outposts we stopped at,
for the Doctor had a fascination with the west which I secretly
shared. If only he could have been more like Ben Cartwright – his
most heroic cowboy paterfamilias – rather than his other favorite,
John Wayne. Our home in Menomenee with the Doctor was full
of cowhides and steerhead lamps, wagon wheel chandeliers and
rearing horse bronzes, rope-outlined paintings of Indian wars and
branding roundups painted by Frederic Remington, one or two of
them original. There were also sand paintings from our journeys
west and two old crossed pistols mounted on velvet. And there
were more horses – walking, bucking, shod or driven in teams. I
loved horses. It is a great gift to be given horses to ride as a young
girl, and though it was years before I bought my own horse, I owe
something of that love – the sweat and stink and wild freedom of
motion that comes with equine flesh, the jolting sting of horse
dung in your nostrils – to the Doctor. Yet though he gave us
the means to ride, he was too awkward to enjoy horses as much
as he would have liked. People gave him rough animals to ride
because he was such a big man. But it's hard for an uninitiated
adult to master a bucking horse or refrain from worry about
what will happen to the rattled spine. In the end we girls were
the riders and he was not, though I believe he felt happy out on
those plains. He might buy a gun, he told my mother, in case we
ever had a problem in our trailer with Indians. He might send the
red man to the happy hunting ground. Fortunately, neither event
ever materialized.

At night on those trips my stepfather parked the Avion trailer
in a camp or somewhere on the roadside in a lonely place, and the
farther west we went, the better I liked it. Cacti were bent in agony

beside us as we drove through a landscape so much more hostile than Wisconsin's green blankets, vegetation scrubbed down before an empty bowl of sky. In New Mexico great beetles crawled on the ground outside our trailer, which looked in the night like a glowing zeppelin, or an alien spacecraft poised on the horizon. I could see my family inside their silver cigar like an alien family, my mother cooking and lighting the lanterns, the Doctor at the table drinking his Pepsi. I walked through low sage and cacti, finding a rock to sit on, still warm as the desert around it cooled. From a small promontory, I looked back. I liked looking at my family in their circumscribed ellipse without having to be among them. They looked as distant as angels, except for the Doctor, who even through the trailer windows radiated fatal power only momentarily trapped. A bigness filled the light around him, and I stared on. The basalt beneath me was warm and secure. I had a mission out there. I had been collecting a stone diary. It was my great invention.

The stone diary was my record, one I enhanced every summer on our trips west. There was a piece of rose quartz I found for the day that Marilyn Monroe died, and a piece of fool's gold from the Badlands which reminded me of my wedding rings – that is, those I thought of as mine, my mother's and my grandmother's first marriage rings, which my mother carefully kept in her jewelry box. There was a bit of road tar in my stone diary, a lump of it, from the time the Doctor had been forced to edge the trailer down hairpin turns on Pikes Peak after he'd missed a warning about a low tunnel. I closed my eyes and imagined the Avion's beetled back, the Doctor at the wheel of the Cadillac immobilized, plunging to the valley in the silver cylinder, a human juggernaut. The stone diary also held a piece of malachite that a man at a park had given me, and a tiger's eye, for luck, from the Corn Palace in Mitchell, South Dakota, and also from the Corn Palace a bright red agate that I could wear on a necklace. Leopard jasper from a roadside stand in Wyoming. A small geode from a Buffalo Bill shop fringed with more buckskin than an Indian village. The ribs were my pieces of the molten world, held for all the magical and searching reasons that anyone collects rocks, the bones of the world under our feet exposed. I would keep the rocks for bragging to my friends, of course, especially my two best girlfriends, but they also had a purpose known only to me. One night in the desert in the trailer, sleeping in my canvas bunk that hung like a sailor's sling above the lower bed, I heard the Doctor speaking in the bunk beneath me. Terror seeped like a kerosene fire along my body, racing pinpricks of both cold and heat and coming annihilation.

'Nonmetallic substances,' I heard him whisper. I had no idea what he meant, and I knew exactly what he meant. He meant breasts, thighs, stomach. He meant the soft pink looseness beneath the clothes of the adults. He was crowded into the single bed with my mother, who had for some reason lain down on the mattress bunk beneath me where Sarah usually slept. Perhaps she'd dozed off there.

'That's another nonmetallic substance,' the Doctor said, and his voice struck sideways in the dark, shearing off the breathable oxygen to leave a suffocating miasma. I gasped at his coaxing and supplications, and thought of my rocks and of some dirty turquoise and an opal I had, the first for the dances of the ancient Mesa Verde cliff dwellers with their handholds and kivas secreted high above the canyon floor. The opal was my birthstone. A piece of shale from the Oglala Sioux reservation. I imagined striking feldspar and iron filings together in my hand, trying to spark fire. Then I heard my mother and the Doctor rise and move a couple of feet past my head into the tiny cramped bathroom at the end of the Avion, a space like a shoebox.

The moon that night was a rock. I could see it from my Thermopane trailer window, a Lincoln penny squashed by a passing Cadillac Seville. I watched the moon and listened to the coyotes howl in the hills while the Avion creaked from its rear. The rocks I had were scarcely bigger than marbles, but the next day in a New Mexico rock shop I saw a giant's tooth of petrified bloodstone. The primeval triangle of russet and green-veined stone stood almost eight inches high. It was polished smooth so that all the veins of life that had once flowed there were clear ribbons in its deep core, exposing the visible plasma and the heart as in a medical drawing and very vaguely the same delta of shape.

'I want that rock,' I said to my mother. 'I need it.'

Green rivulets in the dark red sandstone, flecks of gold suspended inside like trapped cavern dust. The paths of trilobites and insect life ran through the rock, and the blood of Mayan Indians, the corn growers and the ritual slayers. The rock was a dagger and a prism that held the ancient world. My mother and I appraised it in its glass case in the shabby store, cooling our slippery, salted flesh in front of a laboring floor fan. The blood pulsed in my head.

'I need that rock,' I said to my mother. 'Please, may I have it, please.'

'Wrap it up,' said the Doctor behind me.

He bought it for me. It was one of the expansive gestures he sometimes made that fell invariably and sadly flat because of its insincerity. For a moment a balance was effected, but for a moment only. He was giving me my weapon, the David stone for Goliath. My first taste of solid irony. Back home, I put the polished rock just above my bed, within reach on a shelf over my pillow. At times I put it under my pillow. It had a heft, a bulgy weight like a flexed muscle. On a summer's night when the Doctor entered my room choked with anger over some minor infraction, I was sure that the rock under my pillow was what sent him away. I pictured the rock in his cranium, and he turned and left. A mythic charm for my mythic terror. I took the rock outside the next afternoon and threw it at a tree, but nothing happened. It was completely ineffectual unless I held it in my hand. Palming it, I felt like a giant killer, both calm and fierce. Today I wonder if that is not the reserve of sociopaths, whose hearts scarcely elevate a beat when they strike their prey, coolly, sincerely, with accurate and greedy ferocity. Then again, I never did see him coming.

My friend Becker, for we girls had adopted the fifth-grade boys' habit of calling each other by our last names, was turning eleven at a birthday party that called for foreign costumes. Becker's mother was the Girl Scout troop leader; parties at her house were always wild and noisy affairs, littered with unfinished craft projects and a yelping mutt or two to add to the uproar. I thought that in my Carmen Miranda outfit I would be the most exotic Scout. I was finally big enough to wear the skirt, the red taffeta, my mother's white lace blouse, and the black lace mantilla. I had screw-on silver Mexican hoop earrings and the red maracas.

On our way out, as my mother went to the car, the Doctor summoned me to the kitchen where he was having lunch before settling down to a Green Bay Packers game on TV. He never missed them. 'Try this caviar,' he proffered. He had the hammer look on his face. He was smiling; he knew I hated fish. Caviar was beyond unthinkable. I stared back at him impassively, mentally transporting myself far, far away, folding my arms wordlessly. I looked at him, and he at me, and he sat chewing without affect, with no expression on his face whatsoever. Then he was on me in a second, one lunge of his enormous bulk. He held my jaws open with one hand and crammed the caviar glued on the Ritz cracker into my mouth, then forced my jaws shut.

'Eat it, dummy,' he said evenly, with a deft orthopedic crack and twist to my neck. 'You have the taste buds of a baby. Morons eat like you do. Farmers eat like you do. Taste it, if you think you're so smart.'

He held his hand over my mouth so that I had to swallow. I felt myself gagging on my vomit, breathing through my nose. He let me go then, and I ran blindly to the bathroom where I could retch into the toilet, barely hearing my mother's voice rising somewhere down the hallway. We never did get the smell out of that skirt. I went to Becker's party in one of Dolores's old maternity muumuus, a white thing that came to my ankles, with purple pansies the size of shovels, and some big plastic leis and my summer thongs.

Not long afterward, I was rubbing my hand across my lips, remembering. Distorting my mouth around whatever sour taste remained. 'Creepo,' I said. I had invented an onomatopoeic name for the Doctor. 'Creepo,' I called him behind his back. It had to do with his hulking movements, his padded bigness. I thought the name was perfect. Put your lips together, make them creep, spit out a po. Creepo. How it must have cut both him and my mother, whispered furtively among my sisters and me. He was a bullying man, and I invented a bully's name for him. Almost a decade later, when they were divorcing, the Doctor told the judge, 'They call me Creepo.' The thought of him sitting there in the court dock pronouncing that word fills me with regret and shame.

'You have the manners of a pig,' the Doctor says to me in front of everyone at dinner. He takes his plate and holds it over mine, as if he might drop it there. My sisters stare. My mother hangs her head. Another meal in which peace is shattered as suddenly as if a sniper fired from outside the window. The Doctor sweeps from the room, removing himself from us and retreating to his office downstairs in the clinic, where, over the plate of food my mother dutifully brings him, he makes clandestine calls to his girlfriend in a distant state. School is about to begin, seventh grade. My mother retires to her room, the master bedroom bower looking out over Lac La Jolie. She curls up in her chair, a girl like me. She sits looking out at the lake while the tears run down her cheeks. She looks over at me. There's an autumn glint in the air.

'I feel like I failed you,' my mother says. I look back at her and play my game of no tears, not giving her the satisfaction. She is very beautiful, somewhere in her mid-thirties. We both know she is right about failing me, and what can you do about it, not a thing. Somewhere a veil is tearing in a faraway temple, and I hear the shouts of the neighborhood children who are chasing one another on the lawn under gas jets of summer fireflies. I hear the red maracas shaking, it all feels so long ago. My mother cries and cries as it grows dark outside while I muse on my petrified bloodstone, holding it in my hands. It is my reproach to her when I think she has been weak, to be as still as a petrified, shining piece of stone. After she has worn herself out from crying and my refusal to cry, she tells my sisters to be good for an hour, and just the two of us go out to the Scottie for an ice cream. We drive along the edges of the little lakes, two girls going nowhere very fast. We sit in the car in the dark at the Scottie, listening to the little explosions of other car radios tuning in to Milwaukee stations, the Beatles singing 'Michelle, ma belle,' eating our cones lick by lick, our knees touching.

We reached Mexico at last that summer. I had been sewing dresses for the trip with my mother's help. To say that I was in love at the age of twelve with foreign soil does not do justice to my feeling of coming alive, of being free. In Puerto Vallarta I watched one evening as my mother spun in an aqua cocktail dress trimmed in matching ostrich plumes, shining in the arms of a Mexican osteopath. We were at a medical convention, free to wander by day while the Doctor attended meetings and surgeries. At night there was entertainment in a low hacienda open on one side to the sea. I watched from the sidelines as my mother danced beautifully. Ava Gardner had just made a luscious movie that everyone in Puerto Vallarta was talking about called *The Night of the Iguana* with Richard Burton. On this very beach in San Ysidro, she'd danced lasciviously with her houseboys in the surf. Everyone talked as though she might be out there still, shaking her hips, soaking wet. At dinner, the Mexican doctor who'd been waltzing with my mother sat beside me and offered me red snapper from the ocean. At the look on my face when I explained my aversion, he touched my hand and promised that our meal would not be fishy. Suddenly I was eating fish. I got it down, dumbstruck. After each bite, I took a drink of Coke, pronouncing it with a Spanish accent. Co-co-co-LAH. The Mexican doctor smiled.

Then the Doctor took us inland to Mexico City in an immense rented Buick, and at last I saw the great cathedral that my mother had described on her honeymoon. It was cavernous and rose like a mountain, and inside it smelled of incense and suffering. I was moved by *los milagros*, the thousands of tiny silver arms and legs pressed into the walls to commemorate the miraculous healing of the sick. They shone dully in the dark, as affecting as the hands that put them there. I wanted to press my own *milagro*, a tiny silver *corazón* perhaps, into the wall. A day or two later, we were walking down one of the city's broad boulevards where poinsettias and birds of paradise grew in quiet frenzy. Dappled walls with broken glass teeth held secret, ecstatic gardens. A day or two later, the Doctor walked with us and stopped with me in a park where I admired a flower seller holding a huge bunch of pink and yellow rosebuds like those in the pattern of my dress. The Doctor gave the man a few pesos, as vivid a gesture as anything he had ever done, and, grunting, handed me the flowers. I had been learning Spanish from a book all that summer, *Español por los Niños*, while I ate blueberries on the back porch. I said, '*Gracias por las rosas,*' and the Doctor seemed pleased. Perhaps it was an act of conscience. Perhaps he had seen the hairline cracks in my mother which we girls had not seen and which would appear in a more obvious way just a couple of months later. We walked together down the boulevard, and I kept my eyes on a giant Orange Crush sign that glittered at the edge of the city – *Naranja Crush* – but it was the roses that I smelled, only a little less pungent in my imagination than the fact that he had bought them for me.

A day or two later I got lost in the Aztec pyramids at Teotihuacán, fifty miles north of Mexico City. It was deliberate and not deliberate. Teotihuacán was the deserted city of the ancients which the Aztecs had made their own long after its abandonment in the seventh century. Now it was swarming with men and women selling piñons and juniper berries to the tourists, cactus fruit and limes split open and speckled with flies. We were with a tour group of doctors' wives. We listened as Miguel, our guide, explained that this ziggurat before us was called the Pyramid of the Moon, and perhaps a kilometer away at the far end of the broad Avenue of the Dead, rose another ziggurat, the Pyramid of the Sun. The dust blew freely, skirling a veil over the pyramids and our faces. The Aztecs, Miguel was explaining, had fascinating gods. There was Tlaloc, the rain god with bulging eyes and fangs that made him look like a panther; and Chalchiuhtlicue, his consort, the deity of lakes and rivers, who wore a jade apron. There were also, according to Miguel, though I could hardly make them out, gods in the stones around us, carved as plumed serpents or hurling lightning bolts that dispensed water in the guise of a shower of jade jewels. Teotihuacán was a paradise of stone. I asked my mother if I could climb the Pyramid of the Moon, and she nodded absently, as I knew full well that Miguel and his lecture were occupying her attention. The Pyramid of the Moon was a gray pyramid, tall enough to pierce lower clouds.

Lizards ran away from me as I climbed, each step of the great terraces fairly steep. I looked back at the lowering plain of this birthplace of the gods, about thirteen miles square, pyramids and crypts and ruins laid out on a map that divined the rotation of the planets. I thought that an ancient girl my age might have climbed these very steps thousands of years before, and I was acutely aware that she would not have descended them again except as a blood sacrifice. The whole of Teotihuacán spread before me when I got to the plateau at the summit, and there was still an immense stone altar above me. I looked down at the shrunken people on the ground, and I knew that my mother would be wild with worry at my disappearance. I sat on the summit of the Pyramid of the Moon for what seemed like a very long time, wondering what it would be like to have a priest dressed as a condor or a panther seize me and try to throw me down on his altar. I imagined the moves I would put on him to reverse the situation. I wondered if the sacrificed girls were terrified or too dazed to be terrified; if they wore cloaks of feathers or anything at all. I thought if I jumped from the Pyramid of the Moon at that moment I would land in a bed of pink and yellow roses, dead but not dead, and pass straight into ancient history, speaking an unknown tongue. I felt that I could go anywhere, and in that I was wrong, because I had yet to learn that I could never follow my mother to the places in her mind, or fly off temple towers and be borne back again on the strength of visions.

When I finally climbed down from the summit and back to the Avenue of the Dead, I was in a stream of men and women murmuring Spanish in syllables that I found soothing. Boys tried to sell me postcards or lime soda, and I knew I should be anxious. For another half hour I wandered in a desultory way, smelling the sweat of the crowd and their cooking, feeling the grit scour me in the Mexican wind. It felt good to be eleven and lost in such a crowd. It felt good to be alive. Finally I saw my mother and

Miguel tearing along the city's broad plaza, Miguel's face smiling and concerned and my mother's an avenging Harpy of fury, not unlike the gods around us. She needed only a lightning bolt on her head. She cuffed me and dragged me by the hand back to the air-conditioned bus, where all the ladies were waiting, late for their lunch, shooting me dirty looks, and who could blame them? So Miguel, who'd met us at Teotihuacán, offered to drive me back in his car, a dirty Nash Rambler, and we lurched over the roads far in advance of the coach. He sang 'La Cucaracha, la Cucaracha,' which I had learned in school, and told me not to worry because he could make his car fly, and the ladies would get their lunch and forgive me, that I shouldn't wander off, but now that I had, how had I liked the Pyramid of the Moon?

I smiled back at him. I wasn't sure how to convey what I had felt. How the world had soared beneath me, as distant as lapping waves. How I had the power to leave it behind in the company of elemental deities who could scatter jade raindrops and spill blood to plant corn. And when I think back now, I think of that as the time I began to dream of my mother at the bottom of a deep green well, while I dove down ever deeper to save her, never reaching her or knowing what she knew, her lips parted with her secret for centuries.

Then came the autumn, and with it her vision.

HUNTING SEASON IN *W*ISCONSIN

WE COLLUDED, my grandmother and I. It had something to do with the way we both loved the smell of gasoline, burning rubber, swamp water, and her cheap romance magazines. Maybe all grandmothers and granddaughters fuel each other in the liberties of self-invention, and more. 'I live through you,' Mabel told me as I turned twelve, and the statement terrified and thrilled me. I decided I would live twice as hard, with twice the energy, or three times more if that was what was required. I have retained her – her swamp green eyeglasses, her brogues, her stained apron and the creased postcard on which she has written her dill pickle recipe in a round hand. These things comprise my *wunderkammer* of Mabel – my miniature chamber of her wonders. I keep them in a wooden box and I have it right here, the last talismans that make her as alive as the curses that brought my mother and later me such embarrassment. 'Louie,' Mabel would say to him after one of his provocations, 'go pee in the wind.' And Louie sometimes did of an evening, off the back porch if he thought we girls weren't looking, a delicate rain arcing into the lilacs. 'Jesus Christ,' he'd bawl at her. 'Go stick your tits in the ringer.' The ringer stood in the basement, under a shaft of light from a window, where its two round white dowels cleaved the darkness, like Louie and

Mabel themselves. Theirs was a rough house, but not a cold one. The amazing heat of their profanity zapped the air like an electric current sizzling flies. My comfort had something to do with the words between them, slipper words flapping about and tattered like the old clothes they wore to streamers on their sun-darkened bodies. No fear of words, no fear that the language would stop.

Sanctuary meant escape. A retreat to Mabel and Louie's house on Lake Puckawasay, to the cognizant rhythms of the seasons instilling themselves in her house, as if seasons too had to dwell in some frame of human experience that made them manifest or be lost. I loved that house so much that in the summer I thought it was the epicenter of the sunrise. At night, the sluicing moon spilled wavy lanes across Puckawasay to the bungalow's back door. Mabel and Louie made fudge and meat juice jelly called silts in winter, he muttering in Czech over pans of cocoa and trays of clear congealed pork fat, leaving both of them on the unheated porch to harden. In the spring, my grandparents shouted and jabbed elbows at each other as they colored eggs with onion skins and beet peels, creating strange dozens of root-dyed eggs in baskets of swamp grass which Louie and the old men had braided. My mother was revolted by Louie and Mabel sucking on panfried squirrel bones in summer. They were forever slaughtering some animal for food, waggling bright knives at us girls, and then skimming them into the evening damp as the meat went into the pot or smokehouse or brine vat. They ate rabbit, squirrel, carp, deer, raccoon, and turtle, most lake birds, except of course the herons and egrets. Anything wild, Louie caught. I waited at Mabel's dinner table, safe except for the uncertainty about the origin of the meat in the soup. 'It's turtle,' she said to me one day. 'You dassn't like turtle? We got mud hen if you want.'

It was understood that I was a confidante in my grandmother's house, that I was not to repeat the blitzkrieg curses I heard there. I could pull out the forbidden *True Romance* magazines stored

underneath the twin beds in Mabel's room. It tantalized me
that my mother hated for my grandmother to read them. To
Dolores, the magazines were tawdry in their cheapness and thin
paper and gaudy stories, featuring tormented women betrayed
by their men and devious blondes. I remember reading a line
in which a house-keeper says, 'Your husband phoned and he
wants you to wear your red dress. Only this time, don't put a
scarf in the neckline.' She must have worn a cowboy bandanna, I
thought, probably the wrong choice for evening cocktails. Mabel
would open *True Romance* with an air of Lana Turner abandon and
prop her sandals on the table, while I looked at the Martian attire
of peekaboo babydolls and tassels on the bullet-shaped breasts
in the Frederick's of Hollywood drawings at the back of each
issue. 'Midnight vixen,' they said. 'Coco-quette. Fringed Fantasy.'
Mabel wept loudly as she read, but by the time Dolores returned,
the magazines were shoved back under the bed, crinkled from
perspiration and the lake's humidity. And I was stated in the
momentary feeling that the world out there was as palpable as a
piece of her sugary red rhubarb pie, a piece I could just about taste
as I watched Mabel wipe the back of her hand on her mouth.

I thought we were honest with each other in that house, but
of course I was wrong about that on many levels, and Mabel
would not have been the head of our matriarchy had it been
otherwise. Mabel had a secret that had its own sacrament in her
notions of sacrifice. And like all sacraments, it brought eternity
closer, perhaps dulling my grandmother into the curious passivity
through which she endured both fate and my mother, yet seldom
challenged either. Mabel's father's name was Red Taylor and
he had come from somewhere Celtic and slate gray and cold.
England had been his last port of call. No one knows where he
started from because he wouldn't say – Northern Ireland or maybe
the north of England. Red existed when he set foot in America,
and not a minute before. Mabel speculated when she was small

that her pa had killed someone over there in the prehistory he referred to as 'that bastard place.' He hated anything English. He bent to unload the railroad cars on the dock beside the track in Pewaukee, where his coworkers called him Red because of his hair, like a glowing brand, and his igneous temper, which kindled at any slight. When I knew him he was so old and incontinent that Mabel spread plastic sheets on the furniture. Still she doted on him. When Mabel knew Red best as a man she was twelve. I think of us as 'sisters' of secrets then, engaged in homely rituals that dispel chaos. Mabel had seven younger brothers and sisters. Her mother was busy with all those children, and she allowed Mabel to quit the fourth grade and start drudging for the family. Red was working one day down at the switchyard and probably drinking and certainly cursing, and he kicked the hitches of two railroad cars he was putting together. I imagine he saw the boxcars coming toward him like rolling caskets, pinning him to the track, slicing off his foot. In his mind, that foot lay there on the tracks always to remind him that he was no longer complete.

After that, Red used a wooden leg or lived on his knees, and Mabel would take the suds pail to the tavern in the morning and return after lunch. She returned again at midafternoon and 'afore supper,' telling the other children to pick themselves up, get on their coats, get on with it. Somehow she had learned piano, and she played, even giving some lessons herself, she said, holding up the hand now so curled with arthritis that it looked like a baby's trying to reach for a rattle. She played when Red was so stone-drunk he could not hear her, played after he'd cursed Jesus and Mary and all the saints. Mabel kept two odors, two essences, in her head. One was the smell of Red's inner exile. She swabbed Red's room daily with bleach, a room saturated with his vomit and urine and worse, the whole house stained with his ignorance. The other smell was the summer perfume that evening brings even to a dilapidated railroad shanty full of what is missing.

In the nighttime, free, Mabel went with the boy next door to lie under the honeysuckle bushes in an overgrown garden, the petals of peonies drifting over the ground, an Edenic grove not twenty yards from her father's bedroom. Amid this garden, she surrendered her rage and transformed it. There was no more stifling stink in her nostrils. I can imagine that the neighbor boy had skin like clean white sheets and hair that nestled into her mouth like taffy, that she felt in the redemptive comfort of the darkness and his flesh a lambent happiness none of us is allowed to keep.

When Mabel's pregnancy became the talk of the neighborhood, she retreated indoors, back into the squalor. Pa Taylor, goaded by the local priest, sobered up and suddenly one morning the two of them boarded the Milwaukee Road for Chicago with a baby in a basket. Mabel never saw the baby again. It was a girl. Mabel was fourteen and had named her Beatrice. I think of that baby as if she had floated down a meandering river, like Moses in his basket of bulrushes, and that Mabel's father, unlike the nurse-maid, had come to steal the baby in the middle of the night.

The baby who disappeared into time belonged for only a moment to a fourteen-year-old girl, who, when she was fifty, looked into the face of the distant locomotives each weekday on that very same railroad track: we picked my mother up only a mile away from where Pa Taylor had boarded the train. If Mabel was looking for the face of another woman as she searched for Dolores among the descending passengers, if that is why she looked and planted her feet until the roaring train engine became her whole life, rushing past, I never knew.

'Sometimes Mabel did say,' my mother told me after Mabel's death, 'that you can get over any hurt. That you can make a mistake and not die. She said that she made a mistake once, and that she thought her life was over.' And sometimes, when she was ill, Dolores would draw pictures of phantom women who

might have been her real mother and curse Mabel and pierce her
with the stigmata of righteousness. Mabel had a baby. Mabel had
some trouble once. When I think of my grandmother now, I think
of how those she loved had the habit of vanishing. Mabel learned
early the finiteness of mortal love, and yet Mabel and Dolores
together proved this much to be true: You can survive your heart
cracking into a thousand pieces, and even if your once-loved
enemy parades the pieces of your heart on sticks, you will not
die. They will wave the sticks in your face and mutter Ha! and
poke at you. You will not die. You will survive even the loss of
your child, though surely this is the worst loss I can possibly
imagine.

The first thing that Mabel and Dolores survived together was the
death of Ray, the lost husband, the vanished father. I never met
Ray, my grandfather. The events of his life, always told with a
dizzying rapidity, a rush of adoration, played out before I was
born. Conjuring Ray, they said how strong he was, how tall, with
his wavy golden brown hair and square shoulders. He could sing,
tell jokes. He had muscles like the hauler and stacker he was.
Mabel, sweat-larded, dough on her hands and squirrel blood on
her apron, glowed like coal light, and said, 'Ray treated me like a
queen.' And indeed, to marry the young woman with an uncertain
past, Ray had told his own family to go to hell. He'd met Mabel
when he commandeered her from another boy in a park by saying,
'I'll be taking her home tonight, Ruben.' For the next forty years,
they were never apart. Ray's views were authoritarian and quashed
all argument. He was a Christian Scientist who believed that only
God healed, that only God affirmed the flesh, and for that his
children suffered. He also believed in silence, and Dolores was
not allowed to speak to him unless he spoke to her first.

'His motto was that children should be seen and not heard,' my
mother would tell us in front of her vanity, and we girls screamed

with disbelieving laughter, trying to imagine anyone gagging *us*, unaware how soon silence would come to claim our lives. Descending to their basement apartment in the alley, Dolores had to be invisible if her father were home. 'He just didn't want to hear my voice, my chattering. He didn't want to hear nonsense. If we had a guest, he'd call on me to perform a little dance or a little song, and then let me sit on his lap. He never hit me, though he threatened to many times.' Yet her brother, Ray Junior, was free to say whatever he liked and sit with the grown-ups.

Living much like an only child then, and one on an enchanted island of silence at that, my mother began to daydream. Wordlessness filled up the house like smoke. Sometimes, when Mabel allowed her to break the gloom in the kitchen at her child's table, Dolores would whisper out her secret plans to Billy and Junior, her best friends, who kept her company when she couldn't talk to anyone else. Billy and Junior were invisible to everyone else, but they had about a zillion outfits that my mother sewed in her head and they looked fabulous every day, even when she dressed them like girls, which she liked to do for a joke. Early one summer evening when Dolores and Junior were seven and Billy was five, they wanted to go back outside and play before it got dark, but they hadn't finished everything on their plates. That meant their fannies could sit there warming their chairs as long as they wanted to be stubborn. Usually, they were pretty good. Usually, they complied. 'But that night,' Dolores recalled, 'my mother served us refried fish and refried oatmeal – the worst. Ray and Mabel ate it themselves. But I couldn't.' So Billy and Junior zipped their little lips in solidarity and crossed their arms and that meant they couldn't leave the table. The sun went down over the kitchen prisoners, and my mother talked on to Junior about a surprise party for Billy, who was much shyer than either of them but an eternally good sport. Before long Billy nodded off at the table like an archbishop. In due time, Junior fell asleep too, and

Dolores wanted to tuck them into bed, but of course she couldn't ask the adults in the next room to release them, unless she ate her refried perch, so she just sat at the table watching the lamps turn on in the alley the way country children might watch a moonrise. It was the longest day of her life. Eventually she dropped off too, and when she woke she saw that Mabel had gone to bed and that her father sat snoring against the paisley nap of his chair in the living room. Dolores tiptoed in and bent down quietly and tied his shoelaces together. Then she painted his fingernails as bright as the twinkling alley lights with her purple nail polish. Her father roared with laughter when he woke up.

She never defied him again that she could recall, abandoning, as he wished, the dreams of higher education, the perfect test scores, instead taking a job in a bakery the day after she graduated from high school, adopting his religious creed, and eventually marrying Patrick Lyden. Because her father wished it. In the mid-1980s when I was at home in Chicago, on a stunning winter day, two large brown envelopes arrived. One was from my mother. By amazing coincidence, the other envelope was from my father. These two people had scarcely spoken to each other for over twenty years. And the envelopes contained exactly the same thing: pages of their life stories, chronicles of personal history, large and small epiphanies about themselves. Why either of them had suddenly chosen to write these stories down and in what sublime synchronicity I received them, I wasn't sure. Memento mori, I thought. Remember you must die. My mother wrote on the occasion of her fifty-eighth birthday. My father's pages dealt deftly with his experiences as a paratrooper in Japan, his hunting seasons in Wisconsin, growing up in La Crosse. My mother's paraphernalia contained a long letter about her mental health, a defense of who she'd been and was. But her childhood biography contained only one page, which began and ended with the single sentence, 'My father always said, children are to be seen and not heard.'

It was on the night of August 2, 1950, shortly before my mother was to be married at the age of twenty, that Ray called to Mabel and gave her the byword that ruled their lives: 'Let's go down to the tavern.' Dolores stayed at home, pleating and ruching her handsewn trousseau, and Ray and Mabel ascended to the street. It was a hot and velvety night in Milwaukee, and I expect the moon was up, pearlizing the city sidewalks as only a moon can. They walked hand in hand, two people solid in their middle age, but Mabel said she felt as young and alive and foolish on that night as she had when she was a girl, walking the same city blocks they had walked as teenagers. I am as in love with him tonight, Mabel thought, as on the day we met.

Ray and Mabel entered the tavern together. The place was called Gaynor's. From the descriptions I've read in the newspapers, I get a sense of a dark but cozy place, with red plaid wallpaper and the Schlitz sign, like another planet, over the bar, a globe imitating the wider world, spinning on a sea of midnight closing times. Underneath the globe is Ray Junior, who is tending bar. As it happens, he is twenty-seven, a fateful age, the age at which my mother told me a woman is at the height of her beauty, which must mean that a man of the same age is at the height of his vulnerability. Ray Junior is even more handsome than his father – it's the red hair again like Pa Taylor's, the deep brown eyes as soft as old sweaters. Only his skin is odd, chalk white, doughy, the pallor of the livid and untreated rheumatic fevers of his youth. God heals, not man. Ray Junior has never been to see a doctor in his life. His pulse is irregular, and often to steady it he takes a good long pull of hair of the dog, his hands trembling, and there are those who unkindly say that Ray Junior is working where he's living. But it's not too bad yet. There's something a little unfinished about Ray Junior, and for that there's hope.

Father admired son, and son admired father at Gaynor's, where the patrons' voices meshed in heavy harness, plying together from bets to drink, from the laugh to the curse, all of it a daily and familiar syncopation. There was the sour, yeasty smell of Milwaukee's breweries, which steamed a dank yellow cloud after the hops were fermented in the afternoons, mingling now with the disinfectant that Ray Junior had splashed about. On the walls hung the usual paraphernalia, the Arlington Park racing forms, a 1949 World Series betting lineup, Yankees versus Dodgers, and a photograph of Ray in a moment of glory, brandishing a royal flush from a poker tournament. One barstool is Ray's and Ray's alone, by unspoken consent.

At Gaynor's, Ray has his boasts and his supporters, men to whom he is fraternity. He nods to his friend Dietrich, a house-painter, and Tetzlaff, a mason. 'My kid brother finishes high school and now he's too good for me, the little mutt. Too good for a man the likes of me. But work for a living like I do, like my own kid here is doing, pulling you guys your brew, and you never forget who you owe your thanks to.' He grins and throws out his arms. 'My own two hands,' he says, slapping one down on Mabel's ass. 'Ray,' she says moodily, but gives him a hard pinch underneath his jacket. It is after all what Ray believes and the patrons here believe too, and the proof is at the end of his arms. Ray's hands are enormous mitts the texture of leather. They have unloaded trucks in the maw of winter, shoveled anthracite into furnaces, shown his lessers who's boss. His mitts double up or unclench quickly according to the tides of emotional weather. They can raise up against wife or daughter in a threat, and the women of her circle respect this as my grandmother tips her glass of draft to him, the man she so plainly adores. So when a stranger enters, one who does not take part in the toast, whose own hands don't look like they could ever perform the herculean tasks by which Ray has kept the blood sausage on the table, no one takes any notice except Mabel.

He's a slender young man whose delicate posture is all wrong for Gaynor's. He's a player, not a worker, you can tell that from his coat and just by the way his arms crook on his hips, like he might draw silk stockings from his pocket. There's something wrong with the cant of his shoulders, which jut forward slightly into his sharkskin jacket. And the other men's voices bounce off him as if he were no more than a child or a woman, an insignificant stranger in their midst. The patrons bubble with the canards of old stories.

'Sure, Wally's a pecker, but Jesus Christ, didn't we know that? I wouldn't trust him with an ace if it was dealt by St Francis. When that loudmouth is not lookin', I'm gonna swipe that deck because I swear on my mother's grave if I find anything funny you're gonna meet Mr One Hung Low.'

'Didja hear Kovack's kid popped his cherry with Bartz's widow?'

'It's more than Bartz could do for her.'

'Hallelujah, rest in peace, Bartz.'

'Get over, this is a stickup,' someone says, almost singing, and it's only then that the men look around to see what Mabel sees. A white fedora hovers over there, and under that a pair of pale eyes. A feline-looking man in two-tone shoes carries a .32 revolver. The Schlitz world glows and turns so imperceptibly that no one realizes that in one revolution they have been overtaken by chance. It is 1950, after all, and these patrons are more accustomed to orders from the boss, the drill sergeant, even their wives, than from a small and insignificant kid, armed or not.

'I said, "Get over, get over,"' screams the trembling gunman, waving the pistol as the others step back against the wall. 'Wallets out one at a time on the bar. Open the till,' he shrieks. He is not from around there. He is from another and unimaginable planet. Irv Dietrich's wife decides to take him for human. She throws a handbag, and then a few wallets plop on the bar like dead carp

tossed in a barrel. Mabel's coin purse bounces off the glowing
mahogany wood and hits the floor, and as Ray Junior makes
to open the till Ray Senior comes to life again, egging on the
gunman.

'Rum at the job, sailor,' Ray baits him. 'You think this is money.
This is just suds change, this is just I-bet-Irv cards money. You
light in the head as well as light in the feet, fella? A cheese-baller,
are yeh, fairy?'

The gunman's head whips round at this sexual gibe, and so
does Ray's. He grabs the gunman by the arm so that he cannot
get to the till, where Ray Junior stands dutifully ready to scoop
out the cash. Ray Senior knocks his son's hands away with one
arm, goes for the gunman with the other. Their fingers grope in
quick mimetic movement, pas de deux, two people caught in a
blast of wind. Ray is so much bigger than the gunman that the
patrons cannot even see the white fedora. He will flatten the
punk in a minute. The crowd is yelling, 'Take him, Ray, take
him,' and 'Get his gun away, palooka,' when there is a roar that
could have come all the way from the war in Korea. It consumes
the room and makes a hole in the world. Ray Senior soars away
from the gunman, shot through the heart. The gunman winks
into the dark, does not collect his hat, vanishes into the altered
atmosphere of those who have killed. The gunman follows a map
of his own making. Mabel runs after him, throwing a chair into
the next world, but it doesn't change time. Ray will be a hero now,
or something very like it. Ray Junior stands stunned, too weak to
move for a moment, looking numbly at his father and mother.
Oh my God, Mabel cries, but God is disposed to do nothing for
Ray, not in this human world, and Ray is staring, a thick black
line around his iris, at the moment of the greatest determination
of his life.

Oh, Ray, what a dodge you took by dying as you did. You who
never aged past fifty, you who never admitted weakness, whose

descendants may or may not have loved you. No one ever took your place. Mabel moved crimson hands through auburn hair. A peony petal fell in her mind. A last taste of him, and gone.

A newspaper photographer takes a picture of them all within an hour or two. I am looking at it now, under banner headlines that read 'Murder in Midtown Bar,' 'Wife and Son Witnesses as Patron Thwarts Robbery. Bandit Flees.' Mabel and Dolores are seated together, arms around each other, and their faces look like someone has pushed them down. Their mouths are wreaths of sorrow. Ray Junior is so white that it looks as if someone has taken an eraser to the print and started to rub. There is a picture of the floor. Ray is missing, and around the bloodstains the police have traced a white corpse. The outline is thick and sinuous, the legs astride, the hand thrown up, reminding me of the Great Lakes as they finger into the middle of the country. The space that was Ray is empty, and over the years my mother and grandmother will color it in with pigment after pigment until underneath Ray is a kind of pentimento. They must agree on at least this one thing, that Ray was good, because theirs must be a coherent construct on which to hang the story of a man who gave the finger to destiny one night. And destiny, as it often does, gave the finger right back. Next to that outline on the floor that is Ray, all other men are found wanting, and there is no man who can take the measure of the husband and the father whom they loved and trusted and in whom they shared such perfect faith.

Not two months later, in September, my mother walked down the aisle with my father, the twenty-foot train of her dress trailing on the floor like a river of dreams soaking into the ground. The invitations had been sent out before the murder, she explained. And Ray Junior's fluttering heart finally froze not long after, quite irretrievably stuck fast where the horror had touched it.

They found the killers and they let them go. I am now staring at a picture of Philip and Virginia Jaeger. Philip is a twenty-five-year-old ex-soldier turned drifter, small and dainty, who has already done time at San Quentin. Virginia is a graduate of the Missouri State Prison for women, armed robbery. She is ten years older than Philip and sexually aggressive, you can see it, I swear, in the bushiness of her hair. She is taller than he by far, 'a good looking woman of about 35' who wears what the *Milwaukee Journal* calls 'an affair of plaid cowboy shirt and bolo tie and boots.' Milwaukee detectives, hounded by the daily headlines, have gone to pick them up in Texas, tracing them through a string of gas station robberies and bar holdups all the way from Wisconsin. And the case against them looks concrete, but four witnesses in Milwaukee cannot identify Philip. The hat taken from the bar does not fit him. No one tries it on Virginia.

Her culpability is my own theory, this Virginia, a woman whose ancient smile at the flashbulbs is somehow familiar. I think of Sheba; I am looking at Virginia. The *Milwaukee Journal* reports that she jokes with the detectives about the food she ate in Texas, about the motorcycle she and the feline Philip have bought, about the countryside she's seen. The detectives politely address her as ma'am. I can feel her charming them. One of them will later become Milwaukee's thirty-year superintendent of police. I look into Virginia's eyes in the news photograph and I hear her talking, hear her saying, Hey, Phil, let's go cruising. Hey, boys, slide on down and make room for me. Ray honey, come down and get me. I have a secret I'd like to tell. Hey, boys, let's get some action here, something going, something nice. In this photograph I conclude that Philip and Virginia are together more than the sum of their sexual parts, parts they molt and change, like some species of fish. They are people who lived in the nether-world long before my mother descended, people who change form and guise and gender as they please because it pleases them to be protean, to rob, to kill.

Slipping through the hands of the Milwaukee detectives is a pair whose indeterminate coupling is like quicksilver; evil not so easily identified. The man and woman are the sexual doubles of each other, and you do not know who you know when you look at them. You do not know who you know when they know each other. Virginia perhaps slips into Philip's hat and jacket and says, Here, I'll do this myself. It is the kind of joke Sheba would play.

When my mother is delusionally ill, she sometimes plays at being dangerous before she actually becomes dangerous. And the odd thing is that, in a way so utterly unlike her ordinary lively, feminine personality, she loses the idea of gender when she's threatening. Like Virginia, the bandit-mother's demeanor is sexually ambiguous and lethal, feline without masculinity or femininity. I do not know if Philip Jaeger and his comrade in titillation, Virginia, actually murdered Ray almost fifty years ago. I do not know it for a fact, but I believe they did. Perhaps it is time to take their newspaper photograph to a psychic. I would put my money on Virginia. If it is she who is haunting my mother, then I would understand this villainess in a way – escaping the force of law and nature, summoning others to execute her whims, wearing a white fedora before which the unsuspecting are slaughtered. And knowing more than any patron at Gaynor's that a sense of order in the world can be jeopardized because we are never quite exactly who we think we are. That is something the insane and the war-weary know and the rest of us struggle to avoid knowing. I want to flee with this knowledge. I flee when I am sick of myself, devious, bored, lethal. I think of the guises we wear in our ordinary lives, and I consider that perhaps when my mother is sick, Virginia and the past have somehow caught her in the snaking outline of a death on the floor of a tavern.

CHILD OF THE TIMES

BY THE TIME I WAS FOURTEEN, religious epiphanies were occurring in our house fairly often, and not only to my mother. I loved Communion because I liked the idea of taking a bite out of Christ Jesus. It in no way diminished his power – it simply felt like payback, teeth on wafer, wine in gullet. I was armed by this tribal ritual, the fallen comrade who has died and given me his vital flesh to live. I also liked the stand-up-and-be-counted part of Communion. I wanted to see who in other households feigned nonchalance until Sunday morning, when they felt the dark waters of oblivion beginning to lap at their heels. In church, we could all go a little crazy. In church, we could all pretend that we were good and would live forever. I especially liked the idea of testifying and evangelism. My teen group was taken into Milwaukee to hear an evangelistic speaker, a Mr David Wilkerson, who blessed us by touching our forehead if we came up on stage, as I did. He talked about all the juvenile delinquents in New York City and how he personally was saving them. He had arrived from Oklahoma to minister to them and parked his station wagon in the Bronx, where the delinquents had stolen his hubcaps. You could read about his exploits in his book, *The Cross and the Switchblade*, available in the lobby. Wow, the New York! Full of juvenile delinquents, Sharks and Jets. I went up on the stage in Milwaukee and testified so that all delinquent New Yorkers might be saved, and that I might be too. Saved for what, who could be sure. Perhaps we were being saved for purity, for order, for the ideal dominion of the next world. I had heard of a Catholic family whose father took them all back to Ireland because of the liberalism of Vatican II, and I applauded this because, after all, they were going somewhere. Meanwhile, Pastor Nordstrom had added guitars to the ten o'clock service, bouncy notes hitting Protestant hearts, played by some hippyish people singing 'Where Have All the Flowers Gone.' Whatever was awry in the world, whatever failed to conform to our notion of value in Menomenee, and however I had lied or plotted that week, I was redeemed at Dr Martin Luther Church, with its clean, sunny Communion. 'Love,' preached Pastor Nordstrom, 'is wonderfully simple, and simply wonderful,' and he never missed a beat. Pastor Nordstrom's life undoubtedly *was* wonderfully simple, and you hated him for it. And yet life was changing. Even just standing still in Menomenee you could feel it and hear it. We caught broken notes, distant edgy elegies, as riots broke out in faraway cities, boys next door grew their hair to their shoulders, and the sounds of faith shredding got louder and louder. The war in Vietnam began taking away young men, even in our town, and brides in Menomenee got married barefoot in dresses made of muslin, a natural fiber. With mortality the shape of a mushroom cloud on the horizon, some of my friends' mothers decided to get hip before they turned forty. They bought Beatles albums like *Rubber Soul*, a record that Leonard Bernstein – *stine* – had recommended, bobbed their heads like dashboard dolls and swayed from side to side, grooving as they listened to the Milwaukee rock-and-roll station while driving the neighborhood car pool, tapping their wedding rings on the steering wheel. In the distance, Chicago's Grant Park came under siege and riot by hippies just a few years older than I, and Mayor Richard J Daley said, 'The policeman is there to

preserve order' and 'Shoot to kill' and the Black Panthers Fred
Hampton and Mark Clark died in an ambush of police bullets.
But my mother, thank God, was unmoved by the outside world.
My mother never pretended to be hip. She was conservative. I
would have died of embarrassment if she had been like the other
mothers who tried to groove to the words of Nancy Sinatra's
'These Boots Are Made for Walkin'.' My mother was against
personal revolutions in her well life, and of course when she was
not well had her own style, which made theirs painfully trivial.
And while I liked the Beatles, I felt real passion for cowboy
ballads harping of shootouts and I loved Marty Robbins and the
West Texas town of El Paso, and a Mexican group named the
Sandpipers who sang 'Guantanamera,' which is about being loved
by a man from the land of the palm trees. *Yo soy unhombre sincero.*
I needed an *hombre sincero*; I didn't see too many in the offing.
Meanwhile I strained to hear what the outside world was saying,
and talk about it came in as hot and as garbled as if I had been
listening to Radio Rebelde from Havana on a shortwave at night.
The Doctor, in the very rare moments that I recall him noticing
the outside world, spoke of his fears of David Rockefeller and
the Trilateral Commission and the international domination of
the Jews. I could not follow his line of thought. The only Jewish
family in town owned a wonderful old kosher summer resort *and*
the local toy store, gave great mahjong parties for children, and
had the best floats in the Menomenee Halloween parade, such
as a huge wooden shoe built over a van. The Handelman children
waved from the shoe, and later we all played in the two-story float
parked in their back yard. That was before the Handelmans gave
up on assimilation and sent their children to a Jewish day school
in Milwaukee, never to be seen by us again.

I was beginning a split-level life, as I would think of it for
the rest of my high school years. On my miniskirted outside, I
wanted the same things the other girls wanted – boys and good

grades, the adoration of my friends, the best part I could get in the school play – and after a fashion a few of those things were to come. Inside, I felt eternally odd and restless and bored. I was terrified of not being accepted and uncomfortable with it when I was. I was passing, thinking one day I would never remain here, never wanting to leave the next. I shook my pompons with the pompon squad, feeling both proud and ridiculous. The world was out there and I just knew it; I could taste it, but we were here in Menomenee, where the fireworks display was so unvarying each year that you could set your watch by it. Spangles were followed by imitative sonic booms, followed by the Niagara Falls cascading off a rope, followed by the American flag branded in sulphur into the sky. I resented all the sameness, but I also took huge comfort from it, while being keenly aware that there was only a three-letter difference between comfort and conformity. The outside world had multiple pages that stretched across the equator like an origami chain, each page connected to the next. I wanted to read them. I learned about masturbation from Mary McCarthy's *The Group*, about illicit sex from Elia Kazan's *The Arrangement*, until my mother found the books and actually confronted the librarian who'd given them to me. As to my mother, she was well, she seemed healthy, even if her marriage was in an emotional deep freeze, and even so that merely put her in the same camp as lots of other people in town. Still, somewhere I knew my mother was more isolated than all the other mothers could ever be if you put them together. They never shared her imagination, and she was never a joiner. Partly, she was too busy at home. But also, in the real world, she was not an easy confider of her problems, even if she could have readily identified them. She was separated from the charity ladies and golfers not only by her youth and beauty, but by a shy strangeness that she sometimes covered with posturing. She did not have sorority stories to tell about UW-Madison. No one ever asked her about her hospital stays, and even if they had, my mother would have smiled and said that everything was fine. More to the point, she would have allowed herself to believe it.

I knew my sisters and I were growing up like bumper cars in an arcade – the brakes applied harshly and erratically here, and no brakes or direction at all there, and all the time spinning around and hitting the edges. I felt Kate and Sarah and I were growing up in Ping-Pong trajectories that no one else could follow, perversely desirable because our experience would protect us in dangerous situations. And I had my books, stacks and stacks of them. I kept them beside my bed, hauled them and myself to the library on my bike, and read there for hours until I felt as if I'd emerged as a distinctly different person from the one who had parked at the front door. You could disappear in there; make sure your old self never came back. The Menomenee Library had casement windows and was situated almost like a millhouse between two lakes. Anywhere you sat you could look up from your reading and stare out at either Lac La Jolie or Belle Lac. The library also had a pirate trove of *National Geographics*, tied in bundles spored with fungus in the basement. Those moldy pages were the world of my curiosity, distant lands under dust and smelling of linen. On the second floor of the building was a museum of molting fauna, in which one-eyed animals gave Cyclopean roars and forgotten baskets held ossified bits of pots and Menomenee, Fox, Blackhawk, Chippewa, and Winnebago arrowheads. The library was a perfect temple, guarded by winged griffins. The griffins, bronzed black with age, had once stood before an old hotel in Menomenee where Abraham Lincoln had allegedly stayed. The hotel was then turned into a convent for beautiful old nuns who wafted through the white columns outside the building in full habit, like parasails out for a stroll. I rode my bike between the columns, thinking they would be there as long as the Parthenon. In the new epoch for religious reform and self-empowerment sweeping America in the sixties, the convent was torn down, beginning an ecstatic appetite for architectural destruction in which Menomenee participated with avidity. The griffins wound up at the old library before it too vanished like the convent. History was its own target. Demolition became the town religion, the vainglorious side of civic virtue. From the destruction of the fields and farms rose something as efficient and bland as white cotton underwear. Each quirky thing – the mullioned and gabled old library, the Gothic fish hatchery, the doddering great hotel, the old lake road, the mansions, the European bridge between La Jolie and Belle Lac, and eventually even the lakes themselves – were as threatened as they were to me beloved. Menomenee turned its back on its charms, tore up all the farms, and a few of the farmers became real estate agents and cornfield developers driving shiny Buicks, not weather-beaten pickups. It was anything for a tax break. Menomenee went after history as if it were giving off a bad odor.

It was in the old library that I came up with the idea of running away. I thought I would shave off my hair, get dark glasses, and take a boy's name. Gus – a name belonging to highways. I thought that if I looked like a boy, I could get pretty far on the Greyhound bus before anyone got wind of the fact that I was a girl. I would go to Red Cloud, Nebraska, where Willa Cather wrote in her journal that 'our necessities are so much stronger than our desires.' The plot for running away was laid out in a library book about a fourteen-year-old girl who does just that. The problem was that the novel gave few clues about how this girl might sustain herself. Her ruse seemed to work chiefly because absolutely no one challenged her disguise, and she seemed to have more savoir faire than I could ever have dreamed of, had I known what that term meant at the time. Running away was Holly Golightly, Huck Finn and Jim, the circus's Toby Tyler. I knew running away was a fantasy, but even so I started saving my baby-sitting and church money. One Sunday, singing with the church choir with whom I occasionally had a very tremulous and earnest solo, the offering plate was left unattended in Pastor Nordstrom's office. I raided the plate for about thirty dollars and waited for a lightning bolt to strike me right down to hell. I felt driven by necessity, convinced that I was more deserving of the collection that day than anyone, including Christ Jesus, who'd understand and want me to have it. I put the cash theatrically in my trainer bra, size 28AA, utterly self-conscious. The powerful attraction of religious fervor is righteous justification in the face of overwhelming evidence of one's shortcomings. I have made a specialty of such fervor in the countries in which I have traveled. I have seen reason vanquished, and I have no illusions about it happening anywhere, anywhere at all.

I told Mabel not to worry if I disappeared someday, that I would be heading to the Badlands, riding horses to check fence posts, that sort of thing, maybe teaching some small children to read and write before settling down among the Navajos, my people. Of course, I never expected my body to change and betray me as it did. While I still fantasized about escape, my plan began to seem like a cliché. What if I were discovered, or worse, broke down and called my grandmother to come get me? I dared not be uncool. Kate was cool. She was a cheerleader and gymnast. I was not cool, could not get the hang of cool, which seems to choose who it will redeem, not the other way around.

Without knowing it, I had become hollowed out when not actually angry; hollowed out with the same static sense of mid-western dread I would feel in similar small towns almost twenty years later, when I was assigned to drive from endless farm to endless farm in subzero weather to learn of ruinous debt, the death of dreams, children who had left crops for the cities and never come back. The few farm families I liked clung to their land like biblical tillers and were washed away in a flood of debt anyway. They were grit families with a grimness that went down with their poor meals like potatoes and lime Jell-O and potted Spam. Their old people lost the farms and became janitors and maids if they could still work, recluses if they couldn't. The lucky ones, that is. In one Iowa town to which I traveled, an indebted farmer had gone crazy and taken a shotgun to his wife, his neighbor, and his banker, killing them all before putting the pump action shotgun to his own chest, pulling the trigger, and then pumping the shotgun and firing again because he was only half dead the first time. Four dead, many others lost. Life as it had been lived was ending.

But in my teenage years, I shared with rural people their burning religious fervor. I read the Bible for the phrases that spoke to my least complex emotion: hatred. I had a fanatic's wish that it would engender strength. In my head I carried around a graven tablet on which I kept track of all of the Doctor's hostile acts. I have not really laid the tablet down. I've entered the records of other moments: where the suicide bomber killed twenty-three in Tel Aviv in 1994, the blackened bunker where the American missile killed the Iraqi children in the Baghdad shelter in 1991 – and the rim of black at the back of my eye still looks. I have seen a dismembered foot, a child's imploded plastic doll. The family of a Protestant landowner near Belfast in 1989 told me how slowly 'our Michael' died, Michael who knew that his arms and legs had been blown off. And when I encounter hatred, the Doctor is always present. I can feel him surging from his living room chair, a ball of fist cutting through the chatter of a Washington dinner party, a gag lurking behind me while I speak in the measured tones of my radio voice. He is there at the checkpoint, in the smarm of some self-righteous believer. Sometimes my heart scarcely quickens thinking of the Doctor, but I can always hear his voice.

Once at a county air show I'd forgotten the prescription lotion for my face, which had been treated for acne the day before with dry ice and ultraviolet rays. The dermatologist had given my

mother and me instructions to keep my skin out of the sun.
But the Doctor wanted to see this show, and my mother was
still hoping against hope that we might be a family. An air show
qualified as a family event. This one was only three hours away
from Menomenee. It was a boiling bright sunny day in early
September. There was no shade in the broad fields where the
planes took off and landed. I had a hat, so the Doctor would not
hear of our driving home. I darted in and out of the sun, sitting
in the car until the heat drove me out, trying to shelter under a
lemonade stand awning. By the time we drove home, the sun was
going down and my eyes had swollen halfway shut like bashed
oranges. My face had oozing, blistering welts. I could think of
nothing but the bottle of lotion in the medicine cabinet.

'Hurry,' my mother implored the Doctor.

But he did not hurry, and by the time we reached Menomenee
I had worked myself into a first-class frenzy, and my mother was
frantic too. I ran into the house and flung open the cabinet door.
My bottle smashed in the sink. I howled for my mother, who was
just a few steps behind me, and we picked out the pieces of gooey
glass and put them in a strainer. After we'd swished them around,
we got exactly enough lotion to dab on one piece of cotton.

'We'll get more from the pharmacy in the morning,' promised
my mother. 'I'll call the dermatologist.' We both knew the Doctor
could write a prescription, probably even had some type of lotion
downstairs in his clinic. I caught the Doctor's eye before I went
to bed that night. I wore his hatred like a badge.

Change comes, wresting the known from the unknown, cracking
the world off at its axis. The farmhouse washes away in the flood.
The farmer pulls the shotgun trigger. The mother screams a
bloody litany, the pickup rolls into the lake, and finally, one
night, the Doctor sought me out. That was an event so rare that
I immediately felt as if we were scouts from opposing armies,

squaring off in a foreign battle zone. He looked directly at me, a challenge. I felt my tongue get thick.

'Where's the paper?' he said. The tone of warden to inmate, but the fact remained that he had talked to me. He had acknowledged me, and I was both triumphant and scared. He would have to talk to me now; he had cracked at last. The paper was in my bedroom, and I ought to have remembered to return it to the living room. It was an unspoken rule that I never broke. I saw my opportunity.

'In my bedroom,' I said, thinking.

'Get it,' he said. His coldest voice. I went and fetched the newspaper, walking with the slowest step possible.

'Fold it,' he commanded. I folded it. Not well.

'Fold it straighter,' he said.

'You mean so it looks like I haven't touched it?' I asked. Suddenly I was giddy, I was laughing, released. The absurdness of our years together seemed to be collecting into words like a geyser, words I never thought I'd have the nerve to say to him. I was sick of being frightened of him.

'Your paper? Should I fold it so that it looks like an airplane, or a hat you can wear? Like Yankee Doodle Dandy! Shall I fold it up this way?' I ripped the paper in two. I spit the words at him, little marbles zipping from their slingshot right into his eyes.

He leaned over and grabbed my throat and cracked my head sideways. His hands were a collar around my neck, and he dragged my head down the hall. I felt the hair lift away from my scalp and my feet were not on the floor. Pink lights flew past, old dreams, snapping dogs and invisible pookas. And then we were in my bedroom, the Doctor and I, my bedspread like a lagoon, my beautiful petrified rock balanced on a promontory above it. I grabbed for the rock and, feeling it in my hand, was in Communion with it. It was a shelf of land below a submerged continent, a piece of earth like a dagger. I swung it in his direction, hitting nothing, dropping it as my breathing got harder and my lungs threatened to burst.

'You big oaf,' I gasped absurdly, and I bit him, getting at least one of his hands off my neck. I couldn't bring myself to call him anything worse. I got a clear look at his eyes and, seeing the dead-on hatred, I kneed him in the groin. But I could not get to his head, which was above me at an unbreachable distance, like the top of a pyramid. I could not implant the petrified rock into his skull and rip through the gray matter like some sort of high priest. He had me by the hair again, was lifting me off the floor. And then the wall came smashing into my face, flattening the left side of my jaw. The pain was like colliding with a truck. I heard Kate screaming, 'Stop, stop, you're going to kill her!'

I thought he would at least try. He threw me down on the bed, his fist knocking everything off the shelf just above my head and from somewhere, I heard my mother imploring him, 'Please, please, please.'

He turned away from me and grunted, and suddenly sauntered out of my room, a room so much more vacant without him. I wanted him to come back, I wanted to finish it. He pushed my mother into the wall as he went. I was very much alive. I ran past my mother, who was crying in Kate's arms.

I stumbled to the bathroom, half dazed, locked the door and peeled off my clothes. I lay in the shower until a lake formed under my head, the water a cooling rain on my face. I thought of the Queen of Sheba and quetzal feathers and why hadn't I seen her in so many years? A long time later, but only minutes really, I realized that the bones in my jaw had been whacked out of joint and I could not fully close my mouth. I reached up and put my finger inside my cheek. On the left side was a sort of hollow spot where the jaw should be, where the Doctor with his deft thumb and forefinger had squeezed tight at the juncture of upper mandible and skull. Looking back, I believe that, as a doctor of osteopathy, he knew how easy it would be to dislocate the lower left jawbone from its socket. For half a moment, I thought of going out and asking the Doctor to push it back. But then I thought I would rather rot in hell. I got out of the shower and took the sagging lower jaw in both hands and shoved it hard, back to the right and up, looking in the mirror. In a second there was a crack. I could open and shut my mouth again.

The truth never goes back together in the same way. I cannot close my jaw without cracking it, without feeling a sideways motion as it slips with a small click back into place. A maxillary surgeon once offered to fix it, saying he would have to break the mandible and rewire it and that if he did not do so an excruciating arthritis would set in when the cartilage was finally gone. Something to remember the Doctor by in my old age. But I do not see why, having failed to vanquish me thus far, I should worry about arthritic pain in the future and, besides, the maxillary surgeon may well have been dead wrong. I feel my jaw click sideways and out of a sea of dreams old memories are rendered clear. In my jaw, I feel my old stone diary, my fossils and the place I was finally made real to him. I put my hand on my jaw and feel the smooth surface of my petrified rock. If he never knew my middle name, if he never knew what I liked to read or dream of, if he never noticed the color of my hair or the sound of my voice, if in fact I never existed for him, which I am sure I did not, then I can open my mouth and remember that I was real. I was there. It is the opposite of love, that click in the bone, but it is where love is supposed to be. For years thereafter, I often found that violence accompanied love. A blow always shocked me, but it reminded me of something, of how much those who deliver one really are, in their hearts, consumed with desire. And that was something I understood because at fourteen my desire for vengeance had nearly consumed me.

My family had already become to family life what a black hole is to a star. We had burned ourselves through at the center, but we were of the same shattered world, exiles who could not escape one another, and so we continued in orbit. After that night, the Doctor looked neither at me nor at Kate, nor at Sarah, nor really at my mother, ever again. He never came near us and we stayed out of his way. Our eyes slid by each other, avoiding connection. This was the calculus of our space. The Doctor had my mother carry his meals downstairs, where he ate alone in his office in the clinic. My mother lived in limbo. She put up seasonal decorations, took them down, put them up and took them down again. The tracks through the house happened centuries ago; no one deviates from the Mesozoic footholds on our rotating piece of planet. Kate swallows pills, dozens and dozens of them, is rushed to the hospital. The Doctor does not look up from the *Milwaukee Journal*. 'My daughter tried to commit suicide,' my mother says in little words that sound like flies in a jar, but the Doctor never listens to her.

Nor does he listen when she speaks more loudly in secret rhythms. Only I hear her, and recognize sounds that are her private mysticisms. The actual crumbling down of her real life gave her a kind of momentary boldness. My mother stalks through the back yard in her nightgown, scattering the pages of a dictionary she's made in her notebook. She finally works up the nerve to ask the Doctor, 'Are you happy?' No, he says, he is not happy. My mother discovers another woman's photograph. The Doctor has a parallel life in a parallel universe and a parallel woman in a distant state. A parallel family. Your children, he tells my mother, are venomous snakes, your love is poison. The drama is over at last. He leaves her, or rather, it is we who must leave the Doctor's residence and return to the cornfields. Divorce, which my mother had hoped would never return, that blue cutting word slicing the world in two, has come again.

My mother puts on waitress shoes and takes jobs to pay the bills. In the Depot restaurant, she wears a mini train conductor's outfit and little engineer's hat. She likes the job, she babies her customers. In the German restaurant where she works at night, she puts on a dirndl and apron. She always has at least two jobs. My mother is just turning forty. I am seventeen and in college. As the months pass into spring and summer and fall again, one of her patrons threatens her with a death X ray, or a crossbow. The patrons turn into bandits who wear white fedoras and who plan to rob my mother of her life. And the telephone hisses and Mabel cries and the words I hear are Can'tcha come up, Jack, can'tcha come up.

I visited the Doctor once, twenty years later. He was broken, and for a man who had made a small fortune, nearly broke. I went to his new condo on Lac La Jolie, which, oddly enough, was built on the site of the convent that had been torn down all those years ago. He occupied their flower garden, one of the very spots where I used to hide. Now it was the Doctor's turn to hide, along with his TV, in the room farthest away from La Jolie and its expansive views of sailboats. His new wife lived with him, the woman from another state. She hated him and bled the rest of his money and he hated her. He used a walker. He'd had a massive heart attack. Don't go, my mother pleaded, protecting a memory after all that time.

The Doctor didn't look at me when I came in. He didn't look at me as I spoke to him. He lay staring at the TV, eating sugar cookies. He acknowledged my presence and went back to the TV and asked me to hand him the bag of cookies. I used a few to coax him and his walker into the living room, lurching him past all those old cowboy paintings now moved to these walls. I made him sit in the environment of the lake, the day, the world. I recited the headlines of my life, my geographic patchwork. He ignored what I had to say as he always had.

'You'd better get married pretty soon,' he said, 'if you want to have a baby.' Then my jaw opened with a click. I smiled, and I said, 'You used to hit me, remember that? For years, usually when I wasn't looking, always at the base of my skull. Finally you tried to kill me. Remember? That night you kept banging my head against the wall, over and over.'

'No, dear, I never did,' he said adamantly. His mind was going. I looked at him, an old man. Remarkable in his late age, his head still dense with shiny brown hair, not a single gray strand on him, and him in his seventies.

'We tried to kill each other once,' I insisted, sharing it. 'You wanted me to die, back in those days.' I'm meeting it out, trading it. After all, I wanted him to die too. There's something coiling in him, his eyes burn into mine. I have nothing to lose, he can do nothing to me now.

'I wanted you to die too,' I say.

'No,' he says. 'I never did. Never hit anyone. You're wrong.' He suddenly shifts direction. 'You know, after my heart trouble, there's an awful lot I don't remember.' And then, 'I was too hard on everyone,' he says, and gives me a sharp look. The old freezing wind. 'You don't think you were responsible for some of the trouble?'

'I don't think children are in a position to take that kind of responsibility,' I say evenly. I know he remembers. I can feel him remembering all of it, stacking his memories around him like bricks.

He snorts. He says he should never have left my mother; that was a mistake. He wonders if I will come to visit him again. His world is his TV room, his car, the places where he can hoist himself with his walker. My mother waits on him when he comes to the restaurant alone for lunch, or for dinner with his new wife, the one he left her for. My mother is pleasant to them, and gets the orders promptly, and when the Doctor is alone she treats him especially well. But you would not guess that long ago they were married.

You would never guess the way she fell for him. You would never guess the hell it was, the way she makes excuses for him.

I say good-bye to the Doctor, leave feeling unfinished and hunched in my skin. I don't get back in the car. I know I will never see him again. I brood beside the waters of Lac La Jolie for a long time, until I am myself again, the girl I was.

My mother's hand was like a bisque cup, all porcelain. And Christ Jesus appeared to her like a tall white vision, there in that town in the darkness. She said I am the Queen of Sheba, and I offer to each of my daughters a country. For you, Jack, Mesopotamia. In my head, I tell her I accept.

HITTING THE *R*OAD

WHEN I WAS ABOUT NINETEEN and my mother was forty-two, we would both have considered ourselves to be in the very middle, the very center of our lives. I would have considered it the middle because I could not have imagined any sort of life after forty. By then I assumed marriage and children would have retired me from the fray. I would plod on, ruckled and hunch-backed toward death. Why I should have thought that when my mother was at that very age and moment, her children nearly grown, her marriages behind her, putting together her new modeling portfolio, I'm not entirely certain. I could give you her snappy portfolio right now. Photos fall out like six kinds of brochures for holiday resorts at Camp Dolores. The woman in the photos looks ten years younger than her age, a bit of family legerdemain, the result of genetic effervescence and the refusal to know what time it is. And then there are her poses – sailoring behind the wheel of a yacht, billed hat atop burnished hair massed into cumulus clouds; her head at twelve o'clock, as the merry-go-round on which she rides sweeps her arms out like the hour hand. In this photograph, she is an errant milkmaid, swinging on a swing, inexplicably flouncing a red apron over a black dirndl – that is my mother at forty-two. She is still young. The grin on her face says,

'Isn't life a bowl of plums?' She's determined to swing, bounce, scamper into the future as if the past never existed, wipe out time in institutions – the institution of marriage, number one, and second, the institution of the county mental hospital. And if the means to do this is to edit history, then who better than one who can create and re-create herself? Woman Invents Own Life Story. The night before I left for college, my mother called me aside. 'There's no money for college,' she said. 'I lent him your college fund to buy a boat and he won't give it back.' I vowed I would leave. And yet what kind of gypsy looks for excuses to run home, her mother's gold earring in her ear?

So I went to Valparaiso University, Valparaiso, Indiana, without any money. In my junior year, I spent a term studying in Cambridge, England. I lived at Number 26 Huntingdon Road, a nook-and-cranny house, full of sags and angles and stairs that led three steps up to surprise landings or a single room. Each day at about six A.M., the milkman, his face as red as a dried cherry, pushed four bottles of milk against the door with a salutary clink. Lights winked on up and down the street. From the perimeter of the city, edging toward town, lorries gurgled as they shifted gears crossing the bridges to the market center. I would open the door and find the letters, the post, as we called it, and be reassured about the way another day had begun, with its morning accoutrements of post and newspaper and milk bottles, the milk fat bursting up in the necks and rounding the tinfoil heads like something lascivious could be expected to pour forth. Number 26 smelled of menthol sachets and wrinkled laundry, cigarettes smoked by the American students who lived there and who, for the most part, would return to America virtually unchanged by their time abroad. Number 26 made me think of Mabel. I suggested to her in a letter that she could imagine Cambridge by thinking of the gothic Waushara Fish Hatchery. She wrote back that she could not imagine me so far away, fish hatchery or not. In Cambridge at Number 26 Huntingdon Road, the mail slid through the slot two or three times a day, like poker chips from her life spilling into mine. And I thought that if my mother tore a strip of paper in two, one half would stay in her hand and the rest would somehow find its way to me.

What I studied in Cambridge – the Romantic poets and the writers between the wars, Woolf and Lawrence and Forster, as well as England's writers of the 1950s – was less important to me than the fact that I was there. I tried to get away each day from the American world of the other students by riding around town at four o'clock on a bicycle, passing the college backs, or back gardens, where crocuses flooded in deep purple pools on the riverbanks in spring. I stopped at evensong at St John's, listening to boy sopranos levitate oval notes up to the clerestory. I flirted with English boys whose fathers paid their pub accounts at the college drinking establishment.

Baxter, our art professor from the Polytechnic, had a shock of prematurely white hair, like Andy Warhol's, and Baxter's face also had the surprised wonder of the eternal boy. He arrived with art books spilling from under his arms and placed them under a projector. As we sat in the dark, Cézannes and Manets and Picassos leapt up on the walls. Baxter's lilting voice slipped around like silver trout in a stream. His voice swam beside the apples and bathers and gardens of the paintings on the wall. When he stopped talking and turned on the light, a few of us sat dazzled. The rest of the American students snoozed peacefully on the worn Persian carpet, where peacocks spread their tails, peacocks so brilliant that you could almost hear them strutting. Here, I thought, safety lies.

I bought a Victorian fainting outfit with a corset and full sleeves at the Cambridge market for five pounds. Then, for extravagant money and intending to return it, I bought a creamy Victorian silk hat with peach organza roses and orange blossoms dripping off the brim. This way, I thought, I will keep my love from slipping away. We were engaged, he was back at school in Indiana. I wore the outfit beside the river Cam at dawn, having asked one of the harmless English boys to take my picture. I arched my back and leaned over the water. I thought I looked like a dryad, or a naiad perhaps, hovering between dry land and mist, fusing the mortal and immortal worlds. I was exactly like Dolores, trying to fix in illusion what I could not hold on to in life. It turned out that my fiancé, a law student, was secretly having an affair, a fact revealed to me in a letter from his roommate. The letter caught up with me on my first day of travel in France, and I carried it with me as I crossed the English Channel in tears. And something else: when I looked down at my hand as our train left from Calais for Paris, I noticed the naked socket that once held the fiery opal of my engagement ring. The opal had been a gift to my fiancé and me from Dolores. The ring with its empty socket was, I thought, one of nature's perfect moments.

At the end of the college term, I went to work as a waitress in a nearby hotel called the Old Bridge in Huntingdon, Huntingdonshire. In those days, British hotels, like hotels everywhere, would hire American, Chilean, or Dutch students – anyone young and willing and reasonably pleasant – to haul trays of cream desserts and haunches of beef and high teas on silver plates to customers who tied up their pleasure barges on the river Ouse. I loved the Old Bridge. Sometimes at night we pushed back the furniture and danced to American songs, or went out to the great houses in uniform. All the non-English help were encouraged to speak as little as possible. The tiny maître d', Jad, was from Beirut, the Paris of the Middle East, he assured me, and his wife, Vicky, who wore platform shoes to attain five feet, was from Spain. One night I turned on the light in my dormitory room, only to find my American ex-fiancé. It was a shock, and the tumult that followed afterward was even more of a shock, the supplications and the violence and his disappearance before morning arrived. And not so long thereafter, I stood looking at the Ouse, thinking of Ophelia and a weedy death. I saw honey-combs in the light, double vision in the gardens. I craved sleep. I remember sitting with the village doctor as he announced loudly, Preggers!, then took a phone call to answer his wife's questions about what he wanted for his dinner. I watched his hand, as big as a boxing glove, holding the heavy black receiver, while I felt the ground give way beneath me. I had befriended a girl a few years older, Mary Jane Snook, aged twenty-three. She had raven black hair and a hooked nose. She was the bartender at the Old Bridge and a rapid polisher of glasses. She had a worldliness and sense of security that astonished me in the middle of her nursery rhyme name. And she had a mother, who was a social worker at the Cambridge maternity hospital, who arranged everything because I told her the truth – that I would kill myself before delivering the man in question's child. I intended to drown myself, my last act as a river nymph.

Suddenly one night I was living in Cambridge for the last time, and Mary Jane and I were cutting flowers in the garden and giving them to each other and intending to be friends for life. As the plane took off, I thought that I could not stand going back to America, that I wanted to stay in Cambridge where the streets felt like my veins, the river a balm, the cadence of speech my melody. The pilot announced that Gerald Ford had just become president of the United States. I had largely missed Watergate. I leaned back against the cushions and thought of the rivers Cam and Ouse flowing somewhere beneath me, and how their bends crawled through the fenlands. I thought of those who were pursued, who Baxter had told us about on one of his rambles – the outlaws and outcasts who hid from the Crown in the marshes. The Fens, he said, for centuries protected the secrets of those who hid themselves there, and I felt that I had added a secret of my own.

ON THE RODEO TRAIL

FROM A RENTED ROOM AT POLYXENY

KOULIOPOLOUS'S HOUSE

FALL RIVER, MASSACHUSETTS

JUNE 1975

Dear Mother

I'm thinking of you on the rodeo trail. Who would have thought it would be like this – cheap motels and rented rooms. No, I expected that – what I wasn't prepared for was the ugliness of cheap, the tackiness of fiberboard, the ashtrays dumped in hummocky chairs, the acrid smell of vomit in sinks. I've made an escape from my escape and found myself a boardinghouse to live in. My landlady is a Greek woman named Polyxeny Kouliopolous. She is in her seventies, an avatar of Mabel. We pick rose petals from her bushes which she makes into jam, burning her hands, and she heats a paste of beauty. On Sunday afternoons she shimmies on the porch in her slip to Greek love songs in which lovers wander off never to return. Her slip, with its yellowed lace, and the coiled rosettes of her iron hair make me think of a very old and unattended wedding cake aging in a shop window. I would go mad without her.

Perhaps I should not have run away and joined the rodeo so soon after graduation, but then again, why not? They were there and so was I and I thought: subject, photograph, pursue. A photo-essay on these carnies, picturing a rodeo and all the lives it touches. Maybe sell the pictures to *Life*

'in the names of poor children who would otherwise be unable to attend this dramatic re-creation of an actual Wild West rodeo in your town.' It was like pouring cream on bananas, a pitch we purred into the telephone. Who bought our pitch? Rubes, generally. Good-hearted rubes we conned and plucked, from Massachusetts to West Virginia. I was Fagin. Elderly women answered our lies with money and little notes that went, 'Although I am seventy-eight years old and have a plastic hip and sometimes fear I will have to eat cat food, I want to give you this four dollars so that a crippled child can go to the rodeo in my name. Matilda Tutweiler.'

I shuddered, should have quit, didn't. Too proud to go home where everyone had said the rodeo was all blast anyway, too accustomed to the enchantment of chaos, too angry. I could avoid my employers by taking rooms in houses with old ladies like Polyxeny Kouliopolous, while Mary and Gordon lived in seedy motels at the edge of town. On the Fourth of July, Mary poured herself into a dinky motel swimming pool with a winner's cup of gin. Her face hit the water first. She looked like a sheet being floated over a bed. Her glass drifted to the bottom of the pool, much more slowly than Mary herself. Gordon dived in after her. 'Barmy, aide kin go bilde arrude 'er,' which was, 'I'd go wild without her.' Once, to escape them, I traveled with the rodeo itself, not an advance person, and became briefly a cupcake rider, the girl who carried the gizmos to the guys – flags, torches, lariats, guns – as the horses performed familiar antics they could have done in their sleep. They were fake wild horses, nudged on by tin cowboys. But it was Sheba-perfect, a distant never-never land. The Diamond S was on the lam from the law, God, wives, taxes, permanent retirement plans, and every other form of human responsibility. The rodeo was bad at many, many things, but when it came to human irresponsibility it was outlandishly good. You never had to apologize. You never had to live with your mistakes in

the same town for more than one day. You made children happy,
women dream, senior citizens with plastic hips feel as though they
were helping humanity. I took pictures when I was not absolutely
mortified at what I was doing, dreamed of submitting them to a
photo magazine. But after a while, I stopped. I knew I would be
living with the evidence of my daily betrayals, and the only record
I wanted was whatever my memory could make. I had seen my
mother do that, and it seemed the nub of art. She dreamed
imagined beginnings and exotic outcomes. I'd squint harder and
find out I was in places like Nitro, West Virginia. Nitro was the
end of the rodeo trail for me. It was my Living Allegory town. It
was a good place for innocence, if any remained, to be used like
iron filings to detonate sulphur. Everything else could perish, and
a girl like me could make her escape.

JULY 5, 1975
WASHINGTON, D.C.
EN ROUTE TO NITRO,
WEST VIRGINIA

Dear Mother:
  This letter is a lie:
  What a nice time I'm having! I'm making pots of money,
and all the rodeo people are just one big happy family –
so reminiscent of last year in England. Everybody helps
everybody else – to steal from whatever town we're in.
Just kidding! Have you ever actually seen anyone pick a
lock? Not a safecracker – I mean with a screwdriver and
crowbar. But things are getting better. Polyxeny took me
to a kalamatiano dance, and I met a Greek student from
Amherst College who is brilliant, I think. Why didn't I go
there? *I assure you I have more balls and brains than he, but
it's amazing how people underestimate 100-pound 21-year-old*

girls from Wisconsin. Look at Georgia O'Keeffe. What else – what are you doing for the Fourth of July? I was supposed to go to the Mall in the nation's capital to watch the fireworks, watch a city of spun sugar melt under colored icing, but my new employer got drunk and fell into a motel pool. Oh, and I bought a car – a British Ford East Anglia with lefthand drive which I named Nelleybelle. It cost 800 dollars. It's my boon companion. *So, mother, I'm trying to figure out – why that student is where he is and not me. He took me to a party but left with a much older woman poet named Erica Jong. She thought she was pretty hot stuff.*

Love,
Jacki

JULY 11, 1975
GOD, IS IT HOT HERE!
MENOMENEE, WISCONSIN

Dear Jacki:

For the Fourth of July – what else? I marched in a parade! Felt great, wrists like steel putters, hitting notes through a barrel. The crowd bellowing like it won a prize. I'm going to play timpani with the Legion Band again in Mukwonago. There was a Demolition Derby Days going on before the fireworks with all the funny old clunker cars. Also, I placed bets on a frog jumping contest and watched a dog being spayed. I am a little worried about your sister – changed her name to Ka and has a sun tattoo like a shrunken head on her stomach. She runs around nude in the woods on this commune in Oregon and she told me she made a belt for herself out of leaves. Doesn't that sound awful? Your sister Sarah says she wants to go to law school after college. I say go for it! I am trying to find another job. The waitressing at the hotel has me so tired afterwards I feel like melted butter. I want to ask my doctor if he thinks I can stop the Thorazine. Do you?

        Love,

        Your mother who is kickin' and rarin' to go

AUGUST 11, 1975

        ELLA'S BOARDING HOUSE, NO. 7

        NITRO, WEST VIRGINIA

Dear Mabel:

Well, I did a little stint as a cupcake rider. At least it got me out of the snake pit for a few days. I would rather handle the dime cowboys and nickel Injuns than the characters in any of these towns. They ride when there's no money to be had, but at least they know they're out there on the lunatic fringe, on horseback or off. Not like the mayor of one town in New England, who gave me a tenner and told me to come get comfortable in my bikini while he ate ice cream in his lawn chair. I tore the ten-spot to piecemeal in front of him. Whereas the wastrels I'm with, legs splayed by their horses, mouths puckered from Jim Beam, are too 'wore out' for other kinds of horseplay, I believe. Got dressed up in a cowgirl spangly outfit with a fringed bolero and matching skirt. All I had to do was canter around the ring, a cupcake with a flag – I'll tell you, that horse could have done it without me. Not like those 1940s posters of women standing on the backs of horses leaping over Cadillacs in arabesques and fandangos. Later I came out walking – I mean my horse was walking – and presented a lariat to Mr Buddy, who does the cattle roping. I fanned on horse-back around Elmo, the Brahmin bull rider from Oklahoma, crazier than a loon. He has exposed gums like dead night crawlers; he's about twenty-five. None of these guys are exactly bring-home-to-Mom material, but one or two try to speak nicely. I don't know, Mabel. Think I ought to come home?

Love,
Jacki

P.S. I know the answer to that one. You're always thinking 'come home,' aren't you? But I can't. Yet.

The Fraternal Order of Police sponsored the rodeo in Nitro, a town of a few thousand souls. One of them became my friend. Tiller was the younger brother of our police liaison, Earl Mulles. Mulles watched too many southern lawman movies. He had a gut like Rod Steiger in *In the Heat of the Night*, but that was all they had in common. Still, he was not stupid. One night I sat in my Nitro apartment reading an article in *Harper's* magazine about the superficiality of my generation's emotions, 'the loss of love among young people who expect very little from love and often get less than they expect.' I thought about this. I expected almost nothing from love. I also wondered if anyone else within a fifty-mile radius of Nitro was reading *Harper's*. I looked down to the neighborhood bar beneath me, the Rebel Yell, glowing in pink neon. Right in the middle of the sidewalk was Earl Mulles, peering up at my apartment.

Earl Mulles was probably only in his thirties, but he seemed older to me, a stocky man with a rubescent face made more florid by the sun and Nitro's bars. He mimicked Tiller by stuttering his body sideways like a sand crab, then lisping like radio hiss. Or Mulles would stop and scratch his head, feign exaggerated bafflement over simple tasks, oiling a big grin under the frying sun. At all this, Tiller roiled in anger to his hairline. Why should there be harm from the people who are closest to us? Tiller's dreamy paralysis was something I'd seen and wanted to protect. And the feeling of wanting protection deepened as Mulles watched me from his squad car, cruising by the apartment, or stopped by the phone room, or hung out at the café where I ate gravy sandwiches with Tiller. Shadows felt as thick as sludge in Nitro, like the residue of a sulphurous coal process, which they probably were.

KA, A NAME OF JOY!
BITTERROOT FARMS
NEAR HOOD RIVER, OREGON

Dear Sis:

You sound stressed. I think you need some Divine Light. It's the source of all Inspiration and Understanding. You can get closer to God naked, but if that's not a good idea down there, just go naked around the house. Reveal the truth! Confront your demons! I gotta go to a meeting, I'm captain of the Spiritual Group.

Love,
Ka

Earl Mulles had strongly suggested to me that I hire a grotesquely fat woman named Cordelia Judge to work the phones. Cordelia described Mulles as a tough-minded man, with 'a tighter hand on the wheel than other men round these parts.' More determined to have his way, a man like him. I felt a hot wind blowing up my skirt, a hot and determined wind. I fancied Mulles putting dimes into a slot machine, myself expelling a jackpot. Perhaps Cordelia was in some way beholden to Mulles, a favor needing payback. Maybe everyone I'd hired in the phone room had debts to Mulles, and were somehow beholden to the police department of Nitro. They were watching me. Don't think, I said to myself. I couldn't afford to go crazy in Nitro.

Mulles's squad car looped around and around my building at all hours until I began to wonder, If he were wrapping the house in rope, would it be completely covered by now? Me in a string ball. I made Tiller my constant companion, and I do mean constant. I made him dinners, did his laundry, even let him hang an old punching bag by the back entrance where he could practice his woeful karate kicks. Tiller began to sleep in his van outside my apartment at night, and in the morning I had him come in for coffee. I let him clean up in the bathroom. I pitted brother against brother, and if there was a buzz about us around town in the soft caramel month of August it scarcely mattered. Whether Tiller sensed my fear in the direction of his brother, or merely wanted my presence as a puppy wants warmth, wasn't terribly clear. I was glad to my bones he was there.

AUGUST 20, 1975
LAKE PUCKAWASAY, WISCONSIN
BULLFROG SEASON, BIG ENOUGH TO FRY!

Dearest Jack:

Who are some of these people you're down there with? Jesus, they make my hair stand on end like a spider crawled up my neck. Between you and your mother, it's a wonder I'm not dead yet. I made headcheese today. Does it ever stink! Viola next door complained she was gonna upchuck from the smell. Her ass! She cooks them TV dinners. Your mom and I are holding a rummage sale next weekend. I am putting out my wig she bought me. I've had enough of that bullshit and it makes me sweat bullets. I look like I should be playing piano on Lawrence Welk. Wish I could be. Your mom is always looking for dates to do stuff with. She was dating this lawyer, Roger, from Milwaukee, but he was pretty dumb. I offer to go places with her. She says, 'Mabel, you're not my type!' It's so hot here today I'm sitting almost in the altogether. Now I got the fan on and the doors shut to the outside. Pugh! The smell is going away, anyways. I see Viola next door is down on her hands and knees looking for weeds with an itty-bitty teaspoon. You know how she goes over that lawn like it was needlepoint. I feel like going over and planting my foot on her big round rump roast. Here's five dollars. Buy yourself something nice. My damn neck is killing me again.

Love always,
Mabel

After a couple weeks of cat and mouse with Mulles, he sprang. I found him parked on the speckled old sofa in my Nitro apartment, twilight tessellating the floor around him as it came in through the venetian blinds. He was dragging on a beer from the fridge. I knew he had me now. He could afford to take his time.

'I got rid of your little lapdog,' he said, referring to Tiller. 'Jesus, talk about your dog and pony show. You got him on a bit, don't you? I got him over to St Andrews on a tire dump fire. He gets to set up in the truck and help the firemen. Might take two, three days. You and me, we got a chance to spend some quiet time together.'

I said nothing. If he made a move, I planned to scream and claw. But he'd anticipated that.

'Want a date?' His mouth was like a piece of liver, working saliva into the corners.

'No,' I said.

'You will real soon,' he said calmly. He got up, smoothed the crenellations that his nightstick had made in the sofa coverlet.

'I ain't going to beg,' he said. 'It's like this. You can meet me halfway. Or take the consequences. Your choice. Rodeo brat like you, hanging out with all kinds of scabby people, hands in other people's pockets, you're bound to mess up. Could be I have to get me a warrant says I found some dope in your apartment. Have to take you in, book you. Hell of a mess, expensive. After all, you're guests of the Fraternal Order of Police here. We gotta be cautious, right?'

He fished a small bag of white powder (coke, baby powder, salt?) from his pocket, held it up between thumb and forefinger as if it were a dead mouse. And looked pleased. He put it back. I had never taken so much as a hit of marijuana. I was terrified of drugs. Losing your mind looked like anything but fun to me.

'Mebbe you'd beat the rap. I don't think so. Know all the judges 'round here. Could make bail expensive. I think you will want a date.'

A step toward me, face like a red onion, and he slipped out his nightstick, tapped it on the wall next to my head. He tapped a point beside my ear, over my crown, the other ear. His smile like something oozing from a wound. He leaned down and gave me a look in the eyes. I felt rigor mortis setting in.

'I'm enjoying my date already,' he said. Then he backed out of the apartment like a beetle scuttling to its hole. 'See you tumurrah night.'

'Why don't you get the fuck out of here,' I said, but I am sure it sounded as small as I felt. Real trouble this time. Again.

If I look at us now, at the Queen of Sheba, at that Daughter of the Rodeo, I see the harm that mother and daughter skirted in a manner both oblivious and flirtatious, like coquettes performing before troops in the field. We beckoned harm, a singsong in chorus, kicking high. Our failure to protect ourselves was a measure of our capacity for self-injury. It was also a measure of our greenness and faith. Sheba fought her battles with an invisible scimitar, twisting it as if she were a snake handler before a dazzled crowd. I have been more prosaic and road-bound. I was road-weary when Earl Mulles drove away, and I had a bad case of the jitters as well. Yet as bad as Nitro's crooked cop thought himself to be, I felt I could outwit him. I was not only the more desperate. I had witnessed more escapes than even a lawman could dream about. Mulles dreamed of conquest, I was sure, dreamed from his crotch, but my dreams were beaky coppered hawks, hovering on unexpected thermals of air.

An unforgettable night. I was a skeleton against the wall in a chair, feeling my breath frost against my ribs. Could not move, never had moved. Listening for my heart to stop, waiting for phantoms to line up and take speaking parts. Did you think, Sheba calls in my brain, that you were somehow immune? That you would triumph where I have suffered? I waited for a miracle, and there it was, Tiller's lumbering step on the stairs at dawn. He bounded into the room as if he would do laps in it, smelling like a burned oven mitt.

'I'm back,' he said. 'They don't need me no more. Cain't put that fire out for a month of Sundays. They thanked me for my help. I remembered: ain't the rodeo coming tomorrow? I wanted to see it every night!'

'Tiller,' I croaked, 'coffee?' I was sweating now after a night of paralysis. Mulles was a crooked cop who wanted me to deliver the goods, namely myself. If I tried to file a formal complaint, whom would I report him to? I had no faith in the local powers. Who would vouch for me? And if I left Nitro immediately, I imagined more trouble from the Diamond S, not to mention the squawking unpaid phone hustlers who'd want their last wages. The cowboys were already in town setting up for that night's rodeo. Gordon and Mary were due in that afternoon. I had to stay on at least another week. Live in a netherworld of cupcake riders, and, oh! nether things can happen to you! Make up your mind now, tonight! Sheba, her quirky spears darting at the world from behind her shield. Sheba would take on anybody, say anything, wield monkey wrenches. Hadn't Sheba been arrested by sheriffs, spat back at them, faced them off in courtroom and squad car and told them their faces looked like old socks? And she was right. If you threw some pea meal into an old nylon stocking, squished it around, and added black buttons for eyes, you would have Mulles's jowls and general mien.

Later that morning I handed Mulles a rendezvous letter, wishing I had written it in arsenic. He hung over his squad car like a sandbag on a levee. King Leer. I went to my flat and packed my bags as carefully as if I were storing nitroglycerin. Mary and Gordon arrived, in town as Über-collection agents for that night's cash proceeds. I hung around the rodeo camp during the day, sitting on the newly erected corral. I hooked my feet in its rope slats, listened to the cadences of the shellacked bravado and road swill from the young and middle-aged cowboys. The horses were unloaded, so forlorn they looked as if they were about to become a French delicacy rather than a Wild West legacy in Nitro. I will never see you again, I thought, looking at the men's card faces. I'd named them to myself that way. He's the jack of hearts. He's the king of spades. A man named Buford came over, saying there was something he had to talk to me about. I thought he wanted me to buy him a drink.

'I just want to say something,' he said, hulking and spitting. His cheeks were as pitted as a piece of cantaloupe rind, and he puffed them up and let out air. 'You have the purtiest voice,' he said. 'I never heard one so purty. Are you English?'

Night descended, and the moon was a miner's lamp that someone had hung over Nitro as if we might want to use it to locate exits. Families, grannies, grandpappies, children of all ages came to the rodeo, bestirring themselves from television and arguing, Nitro's two favorite pastimes. I wandered through the crowd to see the exhortational looks from the kids at the home for the mentally retarded (two dozen kids, couple hundred seats sold), cheering on their charity John Waynes. Other children were from the black lung fund, a few dyslexic kids from the reading program, some very little black children who were part of the hot lunch assistance program at a county daycare center. There was a woman I always saw in Nitro who had velvety tumors growing on her neck and body like a pumpkin patch. Cordelia Judge screeched by, embossed in Pepto-Bismol pink stretch pants. She looked like a small dirigible. 'Miss Bossy,' she clattered, 'you all gonna pay us in the morning, right?' You know it, Cordelia. I had written out the checks for somebody to find the next morning in the phone room.

The rodeo began. Buford, Merlin, a hardcase-looking woman I didn't recognize – the night's cupcake rider – paraded around in the ring on the horses, Yankee Doodle, Pop Star, and Spunky, names bestowed by children who'd loved them for a while before abandoning them to the glue factory. The Diamond S got them cheap. As the horses circled the ring, oompah music lent the effect of a carousel spinning round, damned to do so for all eternity.

One member of the audience waited to grab the brass ring. 'Meet me at ten,' I'd told the cop, and I could see him across the rodeo ring, snuffling through the dust. 'There's a yellow rose in Texas,' the loudspeaker blared, 'that I'm going to see.' The music twanged. Got that right. In the ring, the Brahmin bull was all but trampling Elmo. The rodeo fans had gotten exactly what they came for. Mary and Gordon were expecting me in the morning to put the books together. My pulse sped in the dust, as I stared at cotton candy tubes on the grass. I walked to the parking lot and drove to the apartment, entered it from the back staircase without turning on the lights. It was almost ten o'clock. As still as a rock. Thick nails of dust in my snout. Heat under my armpits. I slipped a brick I'd taken from the street into a sock, waiting for Mulles. I could see the Rebel Yell below, lit up like a cinema. Precisely at ten, I heard a crash, and a stool made a tingly trajectory through the storefront window of the bar, a solid launch that pulverized the glass. Inside, Tiller stood swinging a pool cue wildly over his head. He paused and looked up once toward my darkened window. Had I called his name? Then he sliced the cue across the mirror behind the bar, fracturing the glass.

'I'm going to bust up this bar,' cried Tiller, and other men were shouting either 'No you hain't' or 'Lemme at 'im,' and they closed in on Tiller, and on one another, for good measure. Fists bounced off the walls, pogoed off belt buckles and jawlines. Under a frieze of neon, the men danced in a brawny embrace, a beer barrel polka at a shotgun wedding, woozy partners stepping on each other's boots. Off cue and out of sync, sirens bleated down the street. One, two, three squad cars, all that Nitro had in its tiny force, drawing simultaneously to the bar like magnets. Earl Mulles huffed out of his car, glanced spookily up at my place. Smart guy, Mulles. Maybe he even guessed what I'd done, but what could he do? Walk away? Tiller was supposed to get a chunk of insurance money from Joe the bartender to whom I'd given three hundred dollars with the stipulation that he give fifty of it to Tiller. And Tiller wouldn't be able to tell them where I was going because I'd never told him the truth about where I came from in the first place.

No time to think about the old life. *Young people of this generation expect very little from love and get even less than they expect.* A girl with her breath skittering, her knees like petal jelly, throws two suitcases down a stairway, plashes into a pitch-dark back yard, hides herself in Nelleybelle, and, with her lights out and engine in neutral, rolls down the hill and out of sight forever. Drives farther south because she thinks someone might look for her on roads going north. Dawn comes like someone cracked an egg into a glass of beer – too yellow, too putrid. I felt my wits return with the sunlight, pulled the car over to watch a girl my age hang wet clothes on the line. So placid. Behind her was a barn so entirely stuffed with tobacco sheaves that it resembled a cardboard packet of matches. The girl hung up a quilt that probably had a named pattern – Log Cabin, Wedding Ring, Rose of Sharon, something like that – and she hung up a bandanna, and a clownish turquoise shirt. I knew eyes that color blue, like the color of squirting dish soap. What did Tiller's face look like now? I tried not to imagine a dirty egg, a beaten baseball, milk scum in the refrigerator. I saw a purply mottled rag over his head, teeth crowded down his throat like seeds.

I got back in the car. An hour later there was a ripping sound and a nasty hiss of air as the rear tire blew out, a cheap retread sold to me by yet another misbegotten son of Nitro. A hundred miles later, the same thing happened to the second rear tire, another retread. Each time I sat for long, flat hours while I waited for help to come, trying to read Virginia Woolf's *The Voyage Out*. Soon I had less than fifty dollars left – gas money, folded in my bra, the better to ration it. I threw water on my face at the auto shop. My hair felt like a straw hat, my forehead prematurely wizened with dirt and motor oil. Nelleybelle had no air conditioner, and the sun beat down with the strength of a branding iron. I was heading back to middle-class life. Back to my twenty-second birthday, back to my mother, back to my chance to be an overnight journalistic sensation. I intended to stop at the home of a friend who lived somewhere outside Chicago, an insouciant girl, Valerie, who'd been with me in Cambridge. We would shake off everything that had come before us all summer long, like dogs shaking off water. We would quaff beer, throw the bottles over our shoulders, talk about men, and remind ourselves that we would be forever young and good-looking. But Chicago was an unknown metropolis to me, one suburban name more meaningless than the next. I got lost when I got off the Interstate and into the spaghetti of bypasses around the city. I hadn't slept in forty-eight hours. I passed a patrol car. I wouldn't ask a cop for the directions to hell. I pulled off the road to ask the way to a girlfriend's house in the suburbs.

'Keep your eyes on the green light,' said a bored black gas station attendant at two in the morning. He bit off a piece of sausage jerky. In no mood to talk, but his face said, White Girl, Seriously Lost. I was in Maywood, Illinois. But where was May-wood, Illinois? I did keep my eyes on the green light, and on the rodeo, and on Tiller's face, now faded to a bilious shade in my mind, and I never saw the stop sign or the driver who had the right of way. I felt a giant metallic cannon shot hit Nelleybelle broadside, and the car spun like the inside of a kaleidoscope. A telephone pole came into view through the windshield, dead on. I put my head down toward my chest and the steering wheel. The boom of the contact with the pole was seismic. The lights dripped away, and everything was wet. I could see absolutely nothing and hear everything.

Jesus God, I'm blind.

Hands, which somehow belonged to me, rushed at my eyes and, no, I wasn't blind, but blood sluiced into my eyes as if from an upended gut bucket. The bucket was my head, a deep and nasty gash starting at the forehead and parting my hair. My scalp had been gored by an exposed spoke on the steering wheel, the windshield was gone, the back seat zippered metal. A Christian burial for Nelleybelle on the highway. The other driver was unhurt. I tilted my head back while I waited for the ambulance I could already hear, ears so acute that I could name grace notes in Beethoven's Ninth Symphony from the upper balcony. *Justice and punishment, for all the wicked things you've done this summer.*

A couple of days later, when I arrived home in Menomenee, Sheba had preceded me. Mabel had warned me when I called from the emergency room in Illinois. 'She's not so bad,' Mabel had said. 'Just buying swampland in Florida and putting good jewelry in the church rummage sale. People call, tell me to come, she's shoplifted a scarf or a birdhouse. She's writing another will, and she cut me out, I can tell you.'

It was fall. For years, the fall brought exactly this lunar reflectivity, disturbance in Sagittarius, Dolores's swift plunge from reality as Sheba rode in triumphantly with her entire retinue of tricks. Nearly every September, from senior year in college until some years thereafter, Sheba was back from her summer of taking prisoners on her travels, and ready for action. I left the hospital and my girlfriend's house with a bandaged head and a blood-soaked jacket, my hair scraped off jaggedly as if with a scallop shell, twenty stitches in my scalp and features that resembled a topographical map. Mabel screamed when she saw me at the bus station. 'Jesus H. Christ! Did you get banged up or runned over?' And in a way I felt I had been run over by my choices in life.

Welcome home. Mabel put me to bed in Dolores's house, brought me simmering chicken soup, and I drifted off to sleep. Hours later, Dolores came in from her date, breathy but not delusional, though she seemed to be saying that she wanted to make her date crêpe suzettes while she did a cancan, that she'd make syrup out of roses after she rode a trapeze around the room. She'd shot a game of pool. I fully woke up. It was after one in the morning. I heard my mother come up the stairs. She opened the door, and the light behind her announced a debutante's entrance.

'See my bandages,' I said, pointing to my head.

'Gross-out,' she said. 'Do you want to meet Dean? My date?'

'No,' I said, turning over, wanting to start again in the morning. *But I wish I could tell you about this kid, Tiller. Brains like stuffing probably all over his shirt by now. Want to wrap him with my bandanna, sing him a lullaby, ice his forehead. But of course I'll never see him again.* I healed. My mother, for the time being, did not.

A few weeks later, I took Dolores riding in the state forest near our home. I knew I was playing with fire because she was sick again. She had walked into the middle of a parade in a nearby town and tried to march with the drum section. Because of many other pranks and the general state of her mental health, I had filed for a commitment hearing. It was ridiculous to take her into the woods, she hardly knew where she was in her own home. But I didn't care. I was sick of her being sick. I wanted my mother back. I wanted to go for a ride because it was October, because it was the way we had always celebrated my October birthday, because it was fall. It was fall, and everything in the woods was dying as if in operatic *mise-en-scène*: light like a reflection off old brass, sumac a frilly plumage, lavender wild asters crumbling to a color I remembered from sixth-grade science, called 'tincture of regulus of Venus.' My mother and I put on orange fluorescent vests as protection against the bowhunters who were after small game, and we saddled and bridled our horses. I had convinced myself that this would be good for her. There would be fresh air, motion, equine sweat and wild turkeys in the underbrush, and other healing portents of nature. I cleaned the dirt from the horses' hooves, one at a time, smoothed the burrs out of their manes with baby oil and a wide-tooth comb, got impatient and used my fingers to wipe down their dirty backs and ran my dirt-caked palms over the muscles in their haunches. Then I cinched the straps tighter and brushed their forelocks and dusted them with fly spray, and the Queen of Sheba and I moved out into the forest.

She talked about a racehorse she intended to buy, a solid investment. As she has unlimited wealth from her new company, or is expecting a certain group of unnamed investors to come through, it would be easily affordable. Think of the purses, she said, the parties, the winners' circle!

'Yes, Mom,' I say. 'But you don't have money for a racehorse. You don't have money for a hobbyhorse.'

My mother stared at the horizon, ignoring my stupid joke, and rode in a dignified manner befitting her sense of fortune

and power. Sheba in the desert. There was nothing but the
sound of the wind through the jack pines, whipping a whistle
at us. These were the Wisconsin trails and fields I knew best
– a territorial stagecoach route, overgrown now with blackberry
bramble. The pioneer who had abandoned the spent apple tree, I
thought, probably had descendants working at the local car wash,
or writing insurance policies. The limestone fences, cobbled from
the boulders of the kettle moraine, poked through the fields like
knobby tibia and fibula. In the distance I thought I saw a brilliance
like wings flashing, a pheasant in flight or the sheen of a woman's
veil floating in the wind. Sheba drags her veil past Dolores's cheek,
and Dolores spurs her horse forward with a blood certainty that she
can capture the future. Sheba is off and running, and I'm inside
the sound of drumming hooves.

My mother is forty-four at the time of that ride. She lashes
her horse like a woman in battle, Aisha against the followers
of Ali. Chestnut hair streams a nimbus from her head. I wish
for my mother a breastplate and chain mail, even as I stare at
her, horrified. She rides as if she were escaping from a band of
Visigoths, hunched over her horse as if she had an arrow in
her back. 'Go,' she screams at poor old Houston, her quarter
horse, 'go!' And Houston, sensing he has the possessed on his
back, does go, an old cow pony remembering the roundups of
his youth. My Polish Arab, Shadow, is so skittish that he bolts
straight up on all fours at the cackle of rustling wind. Now he's
planted himself stolidly as if bronzed. He no more wants to chase
down a madwoman on horseback than be skinned alive. I whip
him with the reins, but we lope forward only a few paces. We
trail a marauding Minerva who flirts with death, spiking hearts
on her standard. Shadow wants no part of it.

Galloping across the fields is a wrangler from a nearby ranch.
I know him. A monosyllabic farm boy, rawboned and dressed in
a tattered undershirt. Thick tobacco cud moused in his cheek,

which he takes out and holds in his hand when he drinks soda water. As he tears past, he can only be thinking, These broads are stupider than shit. He catches up to Dolores, grabs her reins in a wink. Efficient fucking cowboy. Shadow bucks and dances his hooves at the tree branches and I am on my ass. Look up. The wrangler is staring at Dolores's horse and empty saddle. She is on her feet, screaming, 'You spoiled my trophy! I was going to win twenty thousand dollars, asshole! I'm suing you for everything you've got.' She stomps along the trail, disappears into the woods.

The wrangler looks over at me, mystified by weird-people behavior. He can talk to animals, understands their direct needs for comfort and release from pain. Hay, grain, alfalfa, horseshoeing, that's his vocabulary. Tobacco juice pours from his mouth like a punctured rotten tomato. 'Is she crazy or what?' he asks.

I say, 'She's bonkers. That's my mother.'

I let my mother go because the Queen of Sheba is my quarry. There are bowhunters out there in the black pines, looking for grouse and quail. Maybe one of them will nail her. I hope he gets her right between the eyes, so that I can do the dance of Salome. I'll put *her* head on *my* platter. I start after her, feeling sheepish, calling, 'Mother, remember the bowhunters, hunters! The hunters are out!' Silence answers me. Let her stomp through the woods and get lost. I'll get the sheriff and have her back in the clink by nightfall. An hour or so later, when I get back to the car I find it missing and she with it. I notice a note on the tack house for the wrangler who rescued us.

'I have your dog, asshole,' her note reads in handwriting puffed like birthday balloons, 'your Australian blue heeler. Answers to the name of Lucy. If you want to see her again, you better come up with ten thousand dollars. And a kite.'

I sigh. Imagine the day spent ferrying Lucy back to the ranch, a sweet old dog whose tail is probably wagging right now in gleeful anticipation of a doggy biscuit fed from Dolores's hand. She loves animals.

That same fall a close friend mentioned that she thought her mother had heard of the perfect job for me, traveling and writing and taking pictures. In spite of everything, I hadn't fallen out of love with the road. I thought that, yes, this probably *was* the job for me. It was based in Chicago, a job for a travel trade magazine, and to my astonishment when I phoned the office, the manager said the magazine was looking for an editorial assistant, and she would be happy to see me if I would like to come down. I was ecstatic. On the day I was to drive to Chicago, however, Dolores, totally lunatic, took the car on a secret mission so I had to postpone. When she got back, Kate and I managed to hustle her into a hospital, and though she was only voluntary that time I hoped she might stay there long enough to let me go out and look for a job.

I have wondered, and think it is probably true, that loneliness can be fatal. That winter, my first in Chicago, Dolores had a daytime dream she couldn't wake from. That winter my former stepfather remarried. Dolores went out and got two blood tests. She bought a dress and flowers. She booked the church. She described her fiancé to Pastor Nordstrom as tall and dark, but when he asked her details, like name and profession and where he lived, she couldn't answer. She broke down, left a valentine with a real arrow through it on Sarah's pillow at home. But by then, I was living in the big city, Chicago.

TravelGo was a trade journal for travel agents, and my part-time job was not, it was explained to me, actually traveling and writing and taking pictures, as we'd discussed it might become when I was hired. The job instead consisted of repetitive calculations I was horrible at: logging ads, measuring typeface percentages, giving out prices on the telephone for quarter pages, all things that made me weep with tedium. But it paid eighty dollars a week, enough to move to the city and get a roommate or two. Finally, after several months of horrendous boredom, I was allowed an assignment, the launch of a Greek cruise ship called the *Stella Solaris* out of Galveston, Texas. And it had an especially exciting aspect: it would require a grown-up evening gown, my first. As usual, I had no money for anything, but Sarah, a talented seamstress, helped me by making a John Kloss lingerie-look dress out of a Vogue pattern catalogue, beige crepe, with a fashionable seventies keyhole neckline over the breasts. As I look back I think the designer might have been influenced by Frederick's of Hollywood. The dress looked good with liquid liner and blue eye shadow. It had a rhinestone strap around the back of the neck that worked architecturally like a sling to hold up the gown. I felt like Loretta Young, on the old *Loretta Young Show*, swirling down the stairs to arrive at the Mecca of Glamour. I had silver platform shoes that cost ten dollars in a budget shop, an airline ticket, and a spot at the guest table below the captain's dais on the *Stella Solaris*. A limousine picked me up at the airport. Yes! I was part of the professional travel-writing group; someone else was from the *Houston Chronicle*, someone from the Associated Press, writers from the travel trades. And I thought: I'm *passing*. They probably think I'm older, like twenty-seven. Now cruise ships seem like overstuffed hobbles to me, but then I was thrilled to be on one, having A Paid Assignment. At dinner the first night the captain was charming, the travel writers funny and forthcoming, the wine free, the linen and silver real. I was enjoying myself. The writers impressed me with their knowledge of where to buy the best cigar in Quito and how to get a charter to Yucatán, and I didn't even mind that most of them visited perfectly safe destinations most of the time. And then the rhinestone necklace went ping, and the beige crepe dress fell into my lap like a strip act. I was naked. There was no escape from it: I pulled the dress up and sat there, holding it over my bare breasts, and prayed to God to strike me dead. Think of something to say, Jack! I informed the table, 'This happens all the time!'

A man, I think it was the writer for the Houston newspaper, said, 'Oh my God,' leapt up to give me his jacket, spilling a bottle of red wine onto everybody else. They must have been saying all sorts of things, but I heard only babble, and the room went black. I decided that God had heard my prayers, delivering me to darkness as forty waiters marched out of the *Stella Solaris*'s huge kitchen in double, martial rows with flaming trays of baked Alaska perched upon their shoulders like epaulets. I grabbed the newspaperman's jacket and my dress, now hanging off my hips, and prepared to make my escape on the silver shoes, darting in and out of the column of waiters. It was like trying to make a touchdown in a cloak. I had very nearly gained the door when the lights went on. A distinct snicker of laughter went up from the table beside me. I locked myself in my cabin and sobbed, certain my future was in smithereens. And then I thought, Dolores always got up, didn't she, got up when her psyche was buff naked in front of a room full of people who might not even like her. I changed into the paisley lime green pants outfit I had made myself for my high school's junior prom and went upstairs to face the music. The women writers were sympathetic; one came over to talk. I thought she might make me feel better.

'That was pretty bad,' she said. 'If I were you I'd be commiting suicide right now.'

TravelGo fired me a few months later. By then, though, I hardly cared about the dress incident. I'd lost several thousand dollars by failing to enter ads into forthcoming issues. When the editor fired me, she was wearing a Peter Pan costume and we were handing out magazines at a trade show. You have no future in this business, she said.

Radio wasn't about ad pages, at least not public radio. It was about taking a speaking part, the come-here-and-let-me-tell-you-a-story part. I didn't get to it for a long time, until I was twenty-five. In one of my gazillion part-time jobs before that, I taught journalism fundamentals in Chicago, and a student wanted me to recommend her for a job in radio. I was twenty-four. The job involved getting up in the morning at three A.M. to report the highway traffic patterns for morning rush hour at a big news radio station. 'You won't get up that early,' I told the student, who was older than I. I don't know if she would have or not, but I did. I called WIND radio in Chicago. The station manager said he was looking for someone who'd driven a taxi to gather traffic information for the air. 'I've driven a taxi,' I promptly lied. The guy who hired me said later that he knew I was lying, but that I sounded cute and he wanted to meet me. I wrote traffic copy that said, 'It's heavy on the Dan Ryan from 79th to 103rd.' Once I wrote that there was a snafu in traffic, and I described a car crash like a roller rink, and the editor put big red lines through it and suggested I might be happier as a newswriter. We wrote copy during the long nights and early morning hours, listening to the police scanner, the exhumation of the bodies of John Wayne Gacy's victims as they were reported one by one; we watched the snow pile up and spell the death of Jane Byrne's mayoralty; we got trapped by more blizzards; got drunk; fanned the facts like hard-pitched baseballs.

The first day I was ever live on the air on my own show, at another station some six months later, was the day my mother was seriously missing, just before Christmas 1980. I realized that radio had always been there, like the voices in my head. I believed I could speak all those voices, just as Sheba did. I could take the dreamer's part, or the part of the damned. I could take the voice of the woman my mother wanted to be, the assertive one, the confident voice. If my mother had been Sheba or Marie Antoinette or Dolores Gimbels, president and

CEO of Creative Renaissance, then I could be Zelda Thorne, my alter ego.

Zelda Thorne. I invented her name that first night on the air, just for myself, and for years she did the hard parts for me. As the girl I was, I could do nothing. My dress would fall off, I was too shy, too stupid, I heard the voice of my stepfather in my head. You're dumb, chum. You're a moron. But Zelda Thorne could do and say anything. Zelda had, after all, been the name of F. Scott Fitzgerald's wife, and she was manic-depressive, she was crazy. Crazy people have no boundaries. They can come up to you and ask you your secrets. Asking questions others want to answer is about giving yourself permission to enter their world, however insane they may be or you feel yourself to be. Wouldn't you want to talk to Zelda Thorne? She was so brave, so witty. Radio entered me, like a wave. I thought of Sheba. I thought of talking into the night and traveling into the heart of darkness and looking for shards of truth amid deceit and about how deceptions in time become their own facts and how we invent ourselves with our speech. Speaking on the radio, I was invisible, hidden behind the harem's scrim, speaking to you in your head. On the radio, like Sheba, I became the voices of the people I spoke of – the lost farmer, the dying war casualty, the brilliant lover of life. Imagination and voice, that is all there is. One day when I was twenty-six, I opened the door to National Public Radio, and the world opened to me. After that, all the voices that would not leave me alone had a home in the air. Sheba was speaking to me, saying, 'Go anywhere. Go.' Being alive on the airwaves was like traveling back to the source.

Mabel's currency consisted of fried perch fillets and pork juice jelly, five-dollar bills from her pension check squeezed into envelopes licked for wandering grandchildren, and ice-cold bottles of Blatz. The sweaty things, the sugary sticky things you could hold, were what Mabel gave. Her pennies were the buttons of her button box, her jewels the chicken wishbones drying on the windowsill in case of urgent need. 'Make a wish, Jacki, any time. I got lots of wishbones.' Mabel stuck bits of African violet in old milk cartons, watered them into a moldy muck that never sprouted, hid cigarette butts under stacked towels, her gin bottles among the boat cushions beneath the stump of wasps' nest down under the porch. Restless, she would tie on her rain bonnet and get into her 'good' cloth coat, the one that twenty years earlier had looked striking on Dolores, zebra stripes of orange and black. On grizzled Mabel, it was a carnival awning. Then out to her Chevrolet over the slick roads. If Dolores were unwell, Mabel could be seen stalking her down the streets of Menomenee, a muttering old tiger on the prowl, hem bedraggled and tilting forward on her brogues as if there were always a wind against her. Which in a way there was. Mabel braced herself by cursing under her breath. Life, she believed, was not something you stood and thought about. It was something you threw yourself into, like a vat.

I used my grandmother's home as mine, dragging summer crowds of gangly friends up from the city, bivouacking on the porch floor, crashing in the country to run about in halter tops and short shorts, to make love amid earthworms and mosquitoes, ride horses in the woods of the kettle moraine. We put the boat out on the lake, swatted fly balls with baseball bats under night swallows. One summer at dawn I looked up, startled, from an act of seduction, riding a billowing blanket on the porch, only to see Mabel's face pasted on the window, reminded of the lust in her own past.

'If I were twenty years younger, I could go for you,' she told a baldheaded friend of mine from New York, giving him the eye.

'If you were twenty years younger, you'd still be twenty years older than he is,' I roared.

Momentum, tilt ahead. It's a bond we all shared, grandmother,

mother, and daughter. In her own way, Mabel tried to get to the bottom of Dolores's breakdowns, find out who had come and stolen her beautiful offspring, left her this raving changeling bawling for its ogre parents. In the end, Mabel could not keep up, forgot and poured too much gin in her cup, fell off her chair, decided I would make a better detective and she a better reporter of events as she saw them. Because she was wildly prone to exaggeration, she compounded folly with falsity. What was real and what was not blurred by day's end when Mabel told it. Other times, reality simply didn't matter, got scraped with the plates into the sink. Mabel broke her hip, but who knew, Dolores shushing her, telling her to quit hollering, she'd arrange to bring her supper in front of the Ted Mack *Amateur Hour*. Shut up with you, Ma. It was true that Mabel had broken her hip, but none of us believed her.

Dolores once told her, 'You are not my real mother,' and produced a whole notebook of her imaginary family led by her 'real mother,' her Aunt Martha, from a branch of the family as dull as church hymnals with pilgrim virtues. 'My real mother was a godly person named Martha, like Jesus' aunt,' my mother would tell her own mother. 'Nothing like you.'

Physical, shrill, incantatory, cursing, Mabel railed at life out of a sense of her fleshiness in it, sensed life was to be used like something tactile, like soap made out of animal fat or shoes made from wading boots, which she wore. Strip the rubber, sew it. Make do, use the wax paper to cover the windows if you don't have plastic, use the plastic twice if you rinse it off, store the bacon fat in tin cans, not those ones, they're for worms, give me that chicken fatty tail on your plate cuz you'll just waste the best damn part. Smack and suck, Mabel tickling the pope's nose with her tongue. 'The reason I don't have any wrinkles,' she said to me once, confiding – she had almost none – is because I have used Noxema and water since

I was sixteen.' I couldn't imagine a product having been around that long.

'Jesus Christ, if you dassn't gonna close the refrigerator door, I'm gonna take a goddamn shovel and hit you with it. I'm so hot one minute and cold the next. Burnin' up and then flippin' freezing. It's for the birds, bein' old. Don't get old, it stinks to high heaven. Jesus Christ, my neck feels like your damn horse kicked it. Jesus Christ, I'm going to pee right here in my pants if you dassn't come out of that bathroom.' Other times, running into the house, 'Open the can! I gotta go!'

'Ma, your mouth is a sewer,' Dolores would say, her lips curled in one of her great lady acts.

My mother said to me, 'She didn't used to talk like that when my father was alive.'

'Better a sewer than thinking I should only wipe my ass with silk handkerchiefs,' my grandmother spit back. Mabel could thrust, Dolores parried mightily. Oh, those better mothers! Mary Baker Eddy, the Christian Scientist Church founder, or Martha, Jesus' aunt, or family trees in which powerful Mafioso fathers took care of little Dolores and gave her ponies and presents and spoiled her rotten. Sometimes, unwell, Dolores would rant and blame Mabel for lost opportunities, crushed hopes, attacked her general deportment, her bone sucking, her oily beads of perspiration, the rags tied around her head. But most of the time, whatever else, there was a loyalty between them that braided them together as tightly as a cable.

'She hates me,' Mabel said.

'She hates me,' Dolores said.

'A handful.'

'A drinker.'

'A liar.'

'All the same, she's got pluck.'

'A feisty one,' Dolores recalled. 'Gotta say that.'

Mabel died alone in the middle of the night, in the middle of a thought, in the middle of a dream. A dream in which she escaped from the house and followed Sheba on the bright path across the lake, hardly minding as the lily pads crunched and toggled beneath her feet. Her voice as thick and resonant as the croak of a bullfrog, as regular. Vanished in a second, never tarried, swept out of life with the same burst of energy with which she'd entered it. 'I know how to die,' she'd be saying to herself. 'Ain't nothin' to it!' Burst the invisible band of energy that holds us to earth. Halted the tympanic beat of the heart. Mabel makes communion with eternity, wishes she could use her body twice, smooth out the old skin and start over with somethin' good, but if not, be scattered as fertilizer for the neighbor's tomatoes. She didn't want to leave the children a bunch of old bones and carcass good for nothing and expensive to bury.

Kate and my mother called me in Chicago. Kate in her chopped staccato, that way she has of feeding her words back into herself through her teeth: 'Mabel called me and Dolores last night and said she'd had the paramedics over cuz that she couldn't breathe, y'know? I offered to go over, cuz I made her some dope brownies and I wanted to give her a copper bracelet for the arthritis, but she said no, she was tired. Had the runs. Well, she wasn't tired exactly. More like dying.'

'That's right,' Dolores chimed in on the line. 'I called her three times last night and she never answered, so I knew she was dead.'

'So Dolores went over in the morning.'

'I figured if she was dead, what could we do about it? Revive her? She was eighty-four!'

'And Dolores found her just inside the door with her coat on, like maybe she wanted to go out for a drive in the car.' But she'd lost her license six months before, doing sixty-five in a school zone, cops no longer amused. Mabel grounded and brokenhearted about it, waiting up by her mailbox on the road, waiting for us to come pick her up, not wanting to waste the time it would take to get out of the house and into the car and out again, ready, stamping the ground under her rain bonnet, a goer.

Mabel always said, 'When I die, Sarah gets the bookcases, the lamps, and this box of junk. Kate gets this box of recipes. Jack can have the old books. Want to take them now?'

'Shall I take the sofa you're sitting on, Gram, d'you need it right now? Maybe you'd like to sit on the floor?'

'When I die, don't spend no money you ain't got on some fancy funeral. Who's going to come anyway? Don't stand around yammering. I dassn't want any priests or religious types. Just read a prayer or somethin'.'

'Don't worry,' we'd say. 'You'll be put out with the newspapers up by the road. We'll lash you to a treetop in a red blanket like the Menomenee used to do, down by Puckawasay. You'll be a chrysalis, then a moth with scarlet eyes on its wings. You'll live forever, Gram. You'll live longer than me. You're too stubborn to die, Mabel.'

'So I called the funeral home and the guy came over and right away he wants to talk money,' my mother fumed. 'Was that guy a jerk or what, Kate! Wants to put her in a casket and charge me two thousand smackers! Has the nerve to say, "My kids need shoes!" I said, "Well, my mother's not gonna pay for your damn kids' shoes!" I stood arguing with him by the front door where I found her. Really, Mabel's just lying there. Kind of indecent. I pulled her dress down, I propped her up a little at the foot of the stairs, and I covered her with a quilt. Nice enough.'

Mabel looking out at the lake. I am in the boat, Gram, waving to you. Sheba is just a hint of porcelain on the water.

'So we called the county coroner and found out all the doofus had to do was take her to the funeral home and sign the death warrant,' my mother said triumphantly. 'And do you know what that costs? Fifty dollars! Even, no tax. That's all I had to pay! "You cheat," I said to him. "You give me her body back this instant! My mother would rather ride with me than with you anyway.'"

'We wrapped her back up in a blanket and carried her into the station wagon. The funeral home people came after us then, gave us a cardboard box to put her in,' Kate said. 'Mom says, "I bet Mabel's having the ride of her life!"'

'Stepped on it, you know, just to please her, the old lead foot. I didn't drive like some old crappy funeral procession. Cut in on a few people, gave her a few last thrills. I know she was happy. I know she'd be proud of me. She kept saying, "Don't spend money you don't have, Dolores, don't make yourself broke any more than you already have." If I pay twenty bucks a month for the next two years, I can afford this cremation.'

'When we drove up to the gate at Wisconsin Memorial,' Kate said, 'all them people had quite a turn when they saw we had Mabel in the cardboard box. I guess they don't get too many ladies driving their own granny in like that. But you know, we kind of had fun. At least we were with Mabel all the way to the end of the line, weren't we, Dolores? Kind of like accompanying her on her spiritual journey.'

'I put her ashes in the wall out there,' my mother said. She hadn't buried Mabel next to her beloved Ray. 'Too expensive, and it's done with,' my mother said.

I wanted her to scatter Mabel's ashes over Lake Puckawasay on a gust of wind.

For how many years – five, ten? – I've reached out to the telephone, but Mabel has stopped answering. I want to tell my grandmother, 'Oh God, you won't believe it, what she did today. She took that little cross from Louie's room and nailed it to the old totem pole. She tried to write a check for five thousand dollars to charity. You oughta see the negligee she bought! I tried it on and took it back. She stole another puppy. I fell out of love again. Kate threw the tarot and your card came up the sun card. That's the best! We deal your tarot cards all the time, Gram, we're trying to keep track. Kate saved some marijuana for your arthritis and a new potion she's making out of Chinese herbs. Look, here is your Woolworth's foot powder. I have it here in this box with all your stuff. Your painted lady figurine, your picture of Ray on your twenty-fifth wedding anniversary, just before he was gunned down, next to Sarah's baby bracelet – can you believe she's a lawyer? – and Dolores's high school report cards, those glowing scores. What are these squirrel steaks doing in your freezer? Throw them out, for the love of God, they look like roadkill. Call me at seven A.M., Keokuk, Iowa, the Holiday Inn, next week Thursday. My assignment is another farm story, endless pain between the furrows. Did you ever think about your red-haired baby girl, the one your father took away on the train? Did you think about those dead and lost when you were dying, Mabel? Or did you think of those living? Did you think about us?'

Instead I close my eyes. Your memory, a cotton rag around a cut.

MESOPOTAMIA, *C*ARTHAGE, AND THEBES

DELUSION IS A PRETTY THING. It keeps molecules afloat, pulling lives forward to a shining distant point. To the thorny gates of heaven, perhaps, if the delusion is great enough. Or to the mere quiet that pools at the end of the day, if the delusion is smaller. I am rustling through my boxes, breathless, dizzy, spilling out letters and records, charts, diaries, legal briefs, all of it color-coded and cross-referenced from the year 1988, the year my mother began to revise her history. The year she decided it should all make sense. No, not ill, not ever. Here is the letter from January 27, the one that she wrote on her birthday, a testament to her life's ardor. Woman Edits Own Life, Creates New History.

'I want the right to be a little crazy at times, like everybody else – without doubts! My problems were drug-related. I alone sensed it. Only me. You children with your questions regarding my behavior at times are the worst insult of all! You all feared it might happen again!'

I fear it every day and every hour, a metronome clicking on a back shelf. True, it has been eight years since the sheriff's deputy and the stout matron fetched my mother and took her to the sanitarium. And how willingly I have consigned my mother's lunacy to a bizarre pastiche of memories: The Christmas tree bobs in the plaster of paris, and from its mizzenmast branch droops a pair of panties. My mother cocks her head under a darling little hat that says 'Thorazine' as she answers the murmuring voices offstage. My rude memory, so totally in disarray, envelops the dreams with the facts. Over the years, other people's stories weave into the spaces, from the roads traversed mile by endless mile for the radio. In the interval of years, I have become an intimate of those in confinement. Incarceration of any kind lures me. The young inmate at Marion who sits sweltering all day, naked, filing a hacksaw key from a toothbrush that fits like a comma into his rectum or cheek or nostril. He will escape, he will. He thinks about it day and night. He will stab the guard, climb over the wall through the razor wire, grab, he says, at all the pink colors he is losing out there. His arms are chained behind his back, he wipes his sweating head on his knees. He will leave and take me with him, and after I leave him I go home and dream that my cat, Tealillie, is as large as my horse, Shadow, and that she is running through the fields outside the prison to me in a waiting car and she leaps to the window and shatters against the glass. Or the sixteen-year-old in the Kalispell, Montana, jail who believes he is the next Messiah. Escape, he says, I must escape, and in his mind he walks under the scrubby trees, hails a passing car, and is gone. In reality, he hits his head against the wall until he is dead. I lean closer to the tellers of these tales, position my microphone. I breathe the air they breathe. I feel what they are imagining for their lives, something bigger and greater and as free as high-flying kites. Imagination is their benediction, delusion their Host, but faith crumbles and betrays its followers. No pink colors left to grab. In every story behind walls is a fantasy of freedom. And why not? I have my own delusions of escape, of freedom.

Delusion is the total revision of history, my mother's ultimate escape. By 1988, she has encoded a new past for her present and it does not include twenty years of speaking in tongues to angels and archangels. She is passionate and willful and as determined as Job. She rips up the commitment bills that the county mental hospital spits out and eventually takes her to court to collect. 'What will I pay, Mr Administrator,' she writes, 'for being manacled behind my back, forced to defecate on the floor, to eat food shoved through a slot in my door like a common criminal? Thorazine forced down my throat, tranquilizers shot into my hip? I will ask *you* to pay *me* to remove the shame, the fear, the torture from my records! I will offer not to sue you for further damages. In the way of cash, I OFFER NOTHING!' Though indeed she has paid thousands, hiring a lawyer to help her 'fight back and exonerate my good name.' The hospital counters that she is creating 'a smoke screen of allegations which will only reinforce your erroneous thought process and forestall any further treatment.'

We'll see who blinks, says my mother. She is having another birthday, she is marching into the future like a Christian soldier. She is fifty-eight. She collects the fragments of what she deems is her real story, her true life, thinking she will write her life, beginning and ending with that single line, 'Children should be seen and not heard.' Her legal bills cost her dozens of double shifts at the restaurant, cantilevering the heaviest trays to her shoulder. Her bunion grows, her feet swell, and she develops a nasty chest cough she cannot shake. At the end of each day she is exhausted, falls asleep on the living room floor with her clothes on. She spends hundreds of hours and all the money she earns on her cause of the New Self. '*THIS CASE IS NOT ABOUT MONEY!*' my mother insists to me in slanted capitals in her birthday letter. 'If I die before the trial – I want the case to go on! I will continue to fight for the disaccreditation of this institution!' My mother's pages, sent to me, pulse with her vitality. I imagine her nailing this tract to an oak door, like Martin Luther at the Reformation. I imagine her making a great split in what was and what will be.

And I am thirty-four, the age at which my mother first became ill. Her face bends down next to mine. I search the mirror on rising to claim my lips and eyes as my own, fixed on straight while I wait and listen. Am I going to go mad? The voices that come to me are only the old lisps of memory. Mabel cursing in her kitchen. 'Jaysus, dassn't tell. Dassn't say nothing!' Dolores singing in hers. 'I love you a bushel and a peck.' The wind moans, and I hear the lake whispering the heavy-footed dialogue of our former selves. The one voice that speaks clearly is my mother's. You wronged me, she says. You betrayed me. And astonishing even myself, I decide that she is right.

She was never crazy. She was stressed and overloaded, neglected, abused. Her doctor-husband gave her the wrong drugs for the rheumatic fever, for being his little doll, a doll with insufficient stuffing in the 1960s, twenty years before. My mother writes, 'He brought me Ritalin for narcolepsy and I didn't know what it was. I looked it up in the dictionary. It said '*narcolepsy:* an uncontrollable need to sleep.' With the Ritalin I was flying! Hands and feet so swollen I had to crawl from room to room to put the children to bed. He said I had rheumatic fever! He gave me Indocin to relax my muscles! And then the Cogentin, Haldol, Prolixin.' ('Indocin,' writes an esteemed doctor whom my mother persuades to send a letter of testimony on her behalf, 'causes delusions, feelings of unreality, hallucinations.') 'And what of my ex-husband who began this whole process of unwarranted incarceration? He kicked my children across the room. He lifted them by their hair and threw them against a wall. He tromped on their dog. He exerted extreme mental pressure on all of us.' Spinning, swinging from his arms over a sea of grass.

My mother goes on in her open letter to her children: 'I have decided to ask you girls for something you may not be able to give me. Eight years ago today I was released from Menomenee County Hospital. I want your understanding. I gave you fragmentary information, hoping you would understand, but you didn't. I am not, and I never was, crazy.'

Never crazy. It never happened to you. Ant Trap Zap! It never happened to me. We'll throw out those old pages and get some new ones at the K Mart. There is a life I'd like you to try, size six. We can always take it back if it doesn't fit. You will be a housewife heroine, pushed into adversity by a demanding doctor-husband and prescription drugs, and I will be free forever from the taint of your insanity. Prescription drugs, I tell my friends confidently. Misdiagnosis. Miss Diagnosis. Clodhopper attendants, Nurse Ratched on the case. Dolores naked and chained in a pit. Lions and tigers and bears. In my heart, Sheba is no bigger than a baby's tooth that I might wear around my neck, a reliquary of delusion. She never came, I never saw her, my mother was never, ever ill. For months, I tell myself that this is what I truly believe, and my mother visits her lawyer as if he were her savior, filing motion after motion. He entwines his hand in hers when they have tea. The lawyer says that he will exalt her for all posterity and be with her through all the ages. And I wait, we all wait, while Sheba smiles.

July 1988 unfurls around us like bolts of bright cloth sailing into the air, exuberant and tactile. My boyfriend and I and our friends flee the sweltering city. We are to pick up my mother on a Saturday evening for Heritage Days, the carnival held over the Fourth of July holiday in our small town, a new name for the same fair where Kate and Sarah and I became Miss Americas. It's the kind of night in which you can feel the sounds of summer and its peeping reverberations kissing your ear. Now that Mabel is dead, my mother has moved into Mabel's bungalow. She has carted away decades' worth of hunting and fishing and summer detritus, consigned Mabel and Louie to the spirits of Lake Puckawasay, had the outhouse hauled away, thrown the frozen midget squirrel steaks into the garbage. Zap! Old Mabel's refuse heap! Dolores works her real-life magic – makes the bungalow air-tight and converts the attic into her airy upstairs boudoir, layers the porch floor with Mediterranean tiles, adds dormers and a bathroom and a skylight and bay windows that face Lake Puckawasay and its lilies. 'Come on up,' I say to my friends. 'Waterskiing! Horseback riding! Utter relaxation! Meet my mom!' Bivouac here from the thrum of our busy urban lives.

But when we arrive, the house is dark, opaque in every window but the one where I think I see a candle glow. 'Perfectly ordinary,' I lie chirpily as I turn on the lights and invite my friends to sit and have a nice cold beer, Mabel's old housewarming. I spot a dictionary that my mother has opened and see random words brushed with pink Hi-Liter. Stupidly, I close it, sacrificing clues. 'Thirsty?' I smile, handing round Pabst Blue Ribbons, imitating ordinariness.

'Mom?' I call upstairs, my intestines coiling like a garden hose. No answer. 'Be right back,' I say, giving my friends another grand smile. Phony wattage strains my face. 'She's primping, probably.' I snap on the stairway light and climb to my mother's attic bower, wet my lips. 'Mom?' I can feel her waiting for me at the top with a garden trowel in her hand. How will I explain it to my friends if she pops me one? I round the top banister.

'Hey, Mom, what's going on up here? Holding a seance?' How I hope not.

My mother sits resplendently before her mirror next to a small candelabra, drawing a mole on her face, moistening the thick air with a perfume atomizer.

'Hi, shrimp,' my mother says without looking at me. 'Smell this! It's called Enchantment! What do you think?'

What I think is that she is the regal queen of her destiny, her face brilliantly made up beneath a Marie Antoinette wig, or rather, as she pirouettes, candelabra in hand, I see that it is *her* hair, impossibly waved with gel into so many tight pin curls that she appears to be wearing bicycle gears. It must have taken hours. A side curl is pinned over her ear. She makes it dance on her shoulder, like a long piece of ermine tail. 'Like it?' she says. 'Pretty foxy.' Then, ahead of me, she floats down the stairs.

Here she is. My mom, the One and Only!

Inside the mask of my mother's delusions, she smiles. My guests stand agog, rapt, bewitched by a woman who appears to have abandoned her bridegroom on the wedding cake. She is made of hairdo and lace rosettes, her décolletage is a scimitar, suspended for battle. My mother has stuffed her curves into a black bustier with garters, which dangle over a transparent lilac half-slip. Underneath, some sort of pantyhose hide any real nudity. Yet the suggestion remains, and I look around uncomfortably for a raincoat. On her cheek is the fake mole the size of a shamrock. Coquette on Mars.

'Welcome,' says my mother to my guests, in a throaty and expansive voice. 'Who's ready for Heritage Days?'

'Mom's a little overboard in the costume department,' I say to my friends.

'Who's ready for Heritage Days?' my mother asks. The young woman who is my friend Alex's date lattices her fingers over her eyes, chirruping and peeping. 'Ahahahaha,' she burps nervously, like a little frog.

'Cover up,' I yell at my mother. 'Now!'

She gives me a coconspirator's wink. 'Welcome to my party,' Dolores says to my friends. 'Would anyone like to have a snack? Don't mind Jacki, she's a prude. Alex' – she's known him for years – 'will you be my date until Mr Alfred of Milwaukee brewing fame arrives? You're such a gentleman.' Alex is an old flame of mine, was my date at Sarah's wedding. A boon road companion and fellow fisherman, he's known me long enough to know something of my mother's prior proclivities. But the emphasis has always been on the word *prior*. Still, Alex, a true gallant whose own inner resources are vast, realizes how much has suddenly gone wrong.

'My pleasure, Dolores,' he says courteously, slightly bowing. A saint. The bald spot on his head flushes a little pink halo.

I run around the house peeking into closets, trying to find a bathrobe, a large towel. Should I pull down the chenille bedspread and roll my mother in it as if I were trying to put out a person on fire? I yell at my friends to sit down, have a Coke. But who am I kidding? We are all gob-smacked, giddy, laughing hysterically. I could drink a pitcher of Jim Beam with a very small twist.

'Who are you?' I hiss at my mother in the kitchen, twirling past my boyfriend, who has finally recovered enough to offer her his jacket. He's an older guy who I've been seeing for a while, and he and my mother plainly adore each other. He's in it for the ride. He edits a major men's magazine well versed in the lingerie look. Perhaps he's partly responsible for the Victoria's Secret display before me. 'Psssst. Who are you?' I hiss again at my mother. 'Kitty on *Gunsmoke?*'

'Let them eat cake,' whispers my mother, fluttering false eyelashes and talking to no one. 'I want to go to Heritage Days. Benjamin,' she wheedles my boyfriend, flaunting her bosom beneath his nose, 'how do I look?'

'In my opinion, Dolores, you are somewhat underdressed,' he responds in his nasally Harvard accent. (And to think I fell in love with him for lines like that.)

'Would you cover up?' I snap. 'Get something decent on! Or you're not going to Heritage Days! You look like some kind of a floozy!'

'No,' says my mother, 'I don't think I will. Just because you're an old fuddy-duddy. You're not the Queen of Heritage Days, I am.' She parades slowly around the kitchen, past the plaque that says 'Lord Bless This House' and the ceramic swan holding paper napkins and the antique tackle box displayed on a shelf. The ordinary things of the past. Now she pretends to braid her Marie Antoinette forelock.

'I've been preparing all day,' my mother says, patting down a quaint little yawn that plays, one can only say, merrily about her lips. 'And I don't even have a maid or a charwoman to help me up there in the garret. So you best take me to the party, shrimp, or you'll disappear. I'll have to put you in the dungeon or the vault or the iron maiden thing and cut your head off. To Heritage Days! I've got a date with Alfred there, and we're going to rumble to the rumba. We're going to knock 'em into kingdom come.'

I am buttoning her into a long blouse, right over her bustier and see-through slip, buttoning her up as you would a child going out to play in the snow. The blouse is some kind of paisley sixties tunic. Now you hardly notice the garter straps on her thighs. And I am laughing. Because I would rather go with her in her bustier and tunic than leave her at home with the candles, because I believe that the normal society of our small town – the butcher and baker and candlestic maker – just might jolt the delusions storming the Bastille in her mind. Because I'm relieved. An obsessive part of me wants to see the Queen of Heritage Days in action. All during the drive up from Chicago, I had been repeating the phrase to myself, 'She was never sick in her life, never sick in her life.' For five months I had joined the revisionist campaign of her history, banished every scene of her insane past as inadmissible evidence, mistakes, false memory, hysterical and collective neuroses. Scrubbed the pantheon in my memory free of goddesses and mothers with tiaras on their curls. How much I had needed her to play the role of sane mother, wronged mother, constant mother, good mother.

Now I put this crazy little apparition in the car with the rest of us, wondering if Marie Antoinette will pass with the night, an accidental phantom who detoured here, scrounging a bit of cake, perhaps. Or will she hang around for months until we lock her up and throw away the key? I am already composing the letter in my head. 'Dear Menomenee County Mental Hospital, my mother has been countersuing you under the misapprehension that she was never mentally ill. Unfortunately, recent events suggest otherwise. Please come and haul her away in one of your oxcarts!' But off we go, to the carnival where I posed as Miss America at the age of five and my mother now reigns as Queen of Heritage Days. How secure I felt as we ventured out, what comfortable old ground we were on, the parade ground of poses. My mother and myself and this tilting at windmills. Doña Quixote and Señorita Sancha Panza off through the Estremadura. When I had tried to convince myself that she'd always been sane, it was like letting go of a religious faith, as if I'd become a heretic. The past went blank, and I'd lost my entire concept of Oz, or the Sargasso Sea, or Byzantium. It was boring and sterile and promised a future of more of the same. Now Sheba had returned to my family as our little maid, our Alice and her White Rabbit on Lake Puckawasay, Miss Bo Peep, our Madonna dressed in fetish paint, spinning on her jewelry box, our whirling mother.

At Heritage Days, we sat at tables under tents, planting ourselves around my mother, barring further contact with the crowd. Oddly enough, she didn't stand out all that much in the dark. It was rather like sitting down with a medium who is in filmy contact with another world. My mother did a running commentary on the antics of unseen players. 'Unreal,' she'd say. 'See that woman with the big red nose?' But there would be no woman with a big red nose. She ordered us to bring her lemonade and roast corn on the cob and bratwurst cooked in beer. She insisted on dancing with Alex, and in a gesture for which I shall be forever grateful, he gave her his arm and two-stepped with her smoothly to a cowboy waltz; he was a great dancer. I saw a few heads turning, though not as many as I had expected, and the look on Alex's face said only slightly, 'Help, I've been cast in a Fellini film.' Alex's high forehead declined toward Dolores's marcelled curls. I could see her lips move as she chatted away to him, something about the meaning of various colors. 'Pink is very important,' I heard her say. 'My babies were pink. They still are.' She closed her eyes often when she spoke, reaching for focus. 'Of course, pink is also a blood derivative, and if you spill some pink on the floor, or, say, for example, the kind of negligee you would wear on your honeymoon, it's very hard to get out.' My mother had had such a bridal nightgown and kept it for years in her cedar chest.

She wanted to wait for Alfred and dance with him when the cowboy band started up again. As many times as Alfred had broken her heart and never arrived, she always waited anyway. Sometimes I waited for him too. I thought he might pull up in a pumpkin shell coach-and-four, wearing a waistcoat and cocked hat, only that very morning turned from pond frog to prince. Lake Puckawasay had plenty of pond frogs.

'I won't leave,' my mother said, digging in her tiny princess heels as if to spike herself to the bedrock, her size quinn feet hooked around her chair. 'I won't, absolutely. I'm having fun, and you always want to spoil everything whenever I have a good time.'

'Fine,' I said, staring like I barely know her. 'Walk home, see if I care.' I imagined her bumbling the mile of rural route back to the bijou bungalow, silver sandal heels like diamond drills in the pebbles. Garters snapping beneath her tunic while dark cars pass that look to her like spaceships cruising the back roads for human specimens; she looks to them like Tinkerbell.

We left without her and went to the outdoor drive-in, the Scottie. While I ordered chocolate jimmies on my cone, while I watched the 1988 crop of cheerleaders serve us our root beer floats and Scottie Twosome hamburgers, I thought of how she must appear on the highway, a runaway from the court of Louis XVI. I thought of how my mother and father brought us to this drive-in so many years before, how Kate and Sarah and I crawled on the roof of my father's car and ate there with ketchup and soda dripping down the windows and nobody minded at all. But that was at the very beginning, before everything became the way it was now. She could burn the house down for all I cared, her little garters jingling against her skin. I could feel them as she trudged home, slapping her thighs, slapping and jingling as if they were the coins of her realm.

It is a week later, and we are at a private mental hospital in Milwaukee. Kate locks hands with me, and I lock hands with Sarah. We form a small ring, and inside that ring is our mother. We are catching a mermaid in a net. I begin to walk, and then my sisters crab sideways. Slowly we move like dancers around the mother in our midst. Ring around the rosy. 'I'm concerned about you,' Kate says loudly and solemnly. Pocket full of posies. 'I'm concerned about you, too,' Sarah says, and I say, 'And me. I'm concerned about you as well!' Yes, I'm concerned about you, all right. My concern is that I would like to tie your garter belts around your neck and leave you like Mrs Rochester in the attic. Later, we could do a family reenactment of *Jane Eyre* and perch you on the roof while we set the house on fire. We chant 'concern' like 'Row, row, row your boat,' like Mabel yelling, 'I scream, you scream, we all scream for ice cream,' Louie singing, 'I like bananas because they have no bones.' Me singing back, 'I hate peaches because they've hearts like stones.' My mother is a monument, face to the sky. Ignoring us. Never seen us before. Pretends to file her nails and holds up her hand to see if she's made a half-moon shape or a teardrop.

All afternoon, my mother has been talking to a psychiatrist, for we have tricked her. She thought we were taking her for lunch, and we ambushed her and brought her instead to a private psychiatric hospital, our captive. Take that. When she realized what we'd done, she stuck her tongue out at us and made her when-she-was-horrid face. She was dressed all in white – white sarong, with the straps twisted over her shoulders like a jungle vine, a large fake gardenia in her hair, white stockings and sandals. A missionary from God. She carried Mary Baker Eddy's prayer book, *Science and Health*. A crucifix swung from one hip, a Jerusalem cross from the other. She could have been a Lyndon LaRouche airport proselytizer. In fact, for a day or two we lost her when she camped out at Billy Mitchell Field in Milwaukee, somehow – we never found out how – procuring enough money without a credit card or bank withdrawal to fly to Denver to attend Sarah's back yard barbecue.

'Hi,' she said to Sarah and her astonished guests. Doing the wigging out. 'I'm Dolores, Sarah's party-girl mom! Do you know that Mrs Mary Baker Eddy tells you to go away evil, come back love? Science is the blessing. I am teaching a course about the meaning of colors and moods. If you are in a downcast mood, think pink.' Sarah and her husband had her for three days. So that my mother couldn't escape at night, Sarah's husband slept in front of the door.

Ah! but now we have her where we want her. Sarah bribed her back to Wisconsin from Denver, and we frog-marched her to a shrink. 'Of course this all seems a little odd to my girls,' my mother explains at her appointment. Eyes to heaven. Clouds enter her mind. There are things she can't quite see tossing inside them. The shrink scribbles notes. 'There are so many things I've never told the girls about my past. I'm a marked woman. They're not familiar with counterterrorism like I am. I've found electronic bugs in bars of soap. You know, I used to be the victim of secret medical experiments conducted by my former husband. But now I'm a devout Christian Scientist. Go away evil, come back love. Even if you ordered me to take medication, I would have to tell the court that it's against my religious principles.' She opens her

Mary Baker Eddy *Health and Science* book. Cast out the evildoer, heal thyself!

Crazy like a fox.

Just before the door closes in our faces, the psychiatrist, who'll need five thousand dollars in cash just to sign my mother in, watches my mother's labile face crumple and smooth like people do when you see them walking down the street crazy, the Joker spinning inside them. 'Manic depression,' says the doctor, a tough Austrian, by God. 'Only she'd seem to be dominantly in the thrall of the manic side of the cycle. Very rare. Bipolar, but just the briefest depressive period. No compensatory deflation. Until she crashes, of course.' I study my mother in the hallway, as she smirks and makes notes in *Science and Health*. Bipolar. It's the first time in more than twenty years of mental illness that I've heard that word applied to Dolores. Two poles, north and south. Two maypoles twirling in the wind. I have heard other words applied to Dolores: paranoid, schizophrenic, delusional, neurasthenic, suicidal most certainly. Nervous breakdown, says a 1966 record. Hysterical neurosis, reads one 1979 chart. 'Patient improved through physician consultation.' Really, doc, just through chatting, must've been a miracle worker. But bipolar is a new one on me.

The maypole flaps in my mind. There was a real maypole. I was seven in our small town, Queen of the May, with a tinfoil crown. The other children laughed and teased me and called me queenie and wrapped me in the streaming, colored ribbons. But I cannot think about this. My musty memory springs confusion. I must think about money and the closed psychiatrist's door behind us. I must think about the fact that my mother has no insurance. Can I charge her bills on my Visa? In escalating bursts of frenzy, my mother has shrewdly canceled her health insurance, and life insurance, and liquidated all her other convertible assets, like stocks and a mutual fund. As if she were performing a party trick, she'd hold up a check. 'Five thousand dollars for the Mary

Baker Eddy Health and Science Mother Church in Boston' (I tore that one up). She gave away a car, said, 'I just can't keep up with all my charity donations!' Her divorce settlement has been spent to smithereens. The house could be next. She owns Mabel's house, but has spent a small fortune on its improvements, and the bank that holds the home loan is threatening to take her to court. Then she'll be homeless. Then she'll wind up with *me!* I am desperate, desperate, desperate for that five thousand. As if she'd even sign in if I had it. Who do I know who has money?

I call the Doctor. I call him without forethought, heat-rushed and mad. They have been divorced for sixteen years, and I haven't spoken to him for twenty. It is a code of silence. Now his voice on the line is like hot water pouring through ice, through vertebrae. I feel a sharp crack in my joints. As I talk, I can see my mother playing with a Xerox machine, photocopying something from *Science and Health*. In a sentence I explain the situation and beg the Doctor for the money. Treacly syrup, his voice in my ear, seaming up escape routes. Our voices together for these few minutes. Beads of sweat roll down my face like bowling balls. 'Gee, dear,' he says, 'I haven't got it.' I was mad to have asked him, to have spoken to him. I was mad to have shown him our vulnerability, and when I put the phone down my palms are soaked and there's a thorn in my tongue and I feel dirty all over.

Something skitters down the hall like a child streaking for recess – Dolores, making a break for it. She spies a lunch tray, lifts a banana, and beans it at my head. Bingo! she yells, missing me by a mile. She pounds on, half skips, little crucifixes swinging from hips and rear, a rock-and-roll escapee. My mother yells, 'I hate this place. God, is it ugly. The people in here are so ugly, they must've won the National Ugliest Contest. That psychiatrist! Why did you take me to see that Nazi?'

She prances, and I follow in slo-mo. Where are all the beefy attendants fluent in the half nelson? My mother snatches a brochure from a bulletin board, waves it at my nose. 'Help Coping with Mental Illness,' it reads. Mindlessly, I put it back. Dolores sprints off through the empty cafeteria, out the side exit and into the parking lot, where Kate and Sarah luckily round a corner from the front entrance like girl commandos. We trap her flat against the car, our bug! And that's where we join hands to make the ring so she can't run away. 'I care about you,' Kate goads the rest of us, who have not like her spent most of our adult lives in a twelve-step group for the afflicted. Kate glares at us accusingly.

'We care about you,' Sarah the lawyer says dutifully, her voice small. In ten minutes she'll be so disgusted that she'll try to hitchhike home, a thirty-one-year-old and mother herself whom I'll have to flag down a half mile from the parking lot.

'I care about you too, Mom,' I say. 'Why don't you sing "Over by the Window and We'll All Help You Out"?' An old joke of my mother's like, 'Want to lose ten ugly pounds? Cut off your head!'

'Ring around the rosy,' Dolores apes, slapping at our hands. 'Last one down is a big fat clown. Hey, squirt, you stay at the damn hospital if you think it's so great. Yeah, good idea. Let's put Jacki in the hospital and have her head examined! See if there's anything besides old newspapers in there! An old rat's nest! Hey, do you know she had a secret back-alley abortion! How do we know she hasn't had more than one? Like one, two, buckle my shoe. Three, four, maybe more!' Particle matter moves downriver inside me. Trees slide heavily by as if on a rolling slab of stage scenery. 'Last one to tag the car is *it!*' Dolores cries, nipping Sarah on the hand.

'Shit. Damn it, Mom, knock it off.' Sarah starts to walk. 'Goddamn you. I mean, I care about you!' Sarah wanders toward the edge of the parking lot.

We let my mother go. Sheba has won this round. Dolores

shakes her car keys out of her purse with dignity and adjusts her white sunglasses. There are white gems sparkling on the corners. We're capsized in the lenses. Sarah has walked away down the street and won't get in the car. Hey, Sarah, I call, come back and get in the damn car! My mother has the keys, and that's dangerous, but I manage to make her stop and pick up Sarah. My mother drives home quietly, peering out the window as oddly as if she had been asked to spot gazelles on safari and we were some Water Bearers she'd hired for the journey. I think, I scream, you scream, we all scream for ice cream.

When we get home a half hour later, my mother dashes into the house ahead of us and locks the door in our faces. We stand there. Christ Almighty. Jesus, Mary, and Joseph. It's not that we don't have a key, it's that we've lost heart. My sisters and I trudge down to the pier, feeling like a troupe of very old, fat, and tired elves. Rent-An-Elf, you could call us. We perform at children's parties and loony bin lockups. The sun bounces off our house like radar, and the weather vane glows as if signaling Mars. 'Make it a very large Manhattan,' I tell the bartender in my mind. 'A double. Whiskey, a finger of sweet vermouth – a dash of bitters.' A great blue heron floats down to the pier, gilded icon bird with a sun-silvered fish wriggling down its throat. The heron often visits my mother along with a pair of 'magical otters.' The heron is real, the otters are not. After a while, as we girls sit in the late sun, besotted with thought, my mother opens the door, tapes a piece of paper to it, and bangs the door shut hard as if we're still after her. Fat chance. I run up from the pier over the parched lawn to retrieve what she's written. It says:

'Hi!'_____

'This is'_____

Inviting you to a casual outdoor 'supper' on my deck! I'm

ever so sorry – I won't be able to reschedule at the present
time as I'm busy starting my NEW BUSINESS!!!!!!!!
                                    Signed,
                                    A former friend?
                                    Creative Renaissance, 4:30 P.M.

And so we supped with Sheba, peeling her grapes and eating her
pork chops on beds of rhubarb leaves, with glitter, twine, and
bits of crepe paper tied round the handles of our coffee cups.
Our voices trailed far into the night. Above our lamentations,
my mother's voice could occasionally be heard climbing a ladder
of giggles and swooping off, with a cry of 'Unreal! Oh, girls,
this is just unreal!' Her voice swooped farther and farther until I
imagined they could hear her on the other side of Puckawasay.

If in her well life, my mother was a struggling waitress, why
then, in her mentally ill life, she wasn't. No sirree bob. She was
a slick businesswoman, a jet-setter, a princess with a growing
empire. Never mind that her assets were vanishing. She would
replace them and make more money with her Design from the
Master Planner, namely God. She conceived of two businesses,
both of which had roots in her well life. The first she called
Creative Renaissance by Design, which would redecorate your
house. The other was the Déjà Vu Gourmet Foods Division of
Creative Renaissance, which I learned about when I called home
one day and a strange, secretarial-type voice answered, 'To which
division of Déjà Vu Foods may I direct your call?' Déjà Vu. I
had seen it all before, including her utter reliance on the Master
Designer Namely God. He'd be paying all the bills, incidentally.
If she needed something, she got it. A car, a cell phone, a secretary
to sit in the kitchen and pretend there was more than one phone
line? Done. Déjà Vu Foods would be a family business, my mother
wrote in her notebooks. On her brief trip to Colorado to visit

Sarah, she'd booked a conference room in Breckenridge for our annual Déjà Vu board meeting. We found this out later, when the bill came. Mainly we were supposed to be making Dolores's cookies and gourmet butters. My mother mailed us each her brochure. She had drawn a picture of a Golden Guernsey cow on the cover which looked like a hyperactive wildebeest with awning-fringe eyelashes. Déjà Vu's mascot was a saucy milkmaid (is there any other kind?) in a tam-o'-shanter with a balloon popping from her mouth that said, 'I'm a Déjà Vu mam'selle.' You could say that again. My mother walked into the real Golden Guernsey Dairy offices in Wausau, Wisconsin, and presented her business plan on pink construction paper to an executive. 'You give me milk, I give you gourmet butters,' said the top executive and CEO of Creative Renaissance by Design, Déjà Vu Gourmet Foods Division. She crossed her legs assertively in her peppermint pink suit. 'Done,' said Mr Golden Guernsey. Did he really? I don't know. I do know that at her home, Dolores worked round the clock. The secretary she'd hired was a slow thing named Evelyn, who sat for two weeks typing invoices to potential and imaginary customers. As board members, we girls got copies of Déjà Vu recipes and pieces of literature almost every day in the mail. She hand-painted hundreds of business cards, as well as little crocks, packaging materials, calendars, and mail-order how-to forms. I thought my mother's recipes were sort of fabulous.

> COCONUT BUTTER
> I stick (¼lb.) Wisconsin AA butter,
>   Golden Guernsey of course!
> ½ cup of Clover Bear honey
> I oz. coconut flavor
> freshly grated coconut
> Mix together and be a little coco-nut!
>
> For your dining pleasure!

*   *   *

And there was Sweet Lemon Butter and Raspberry Blossom ('spread on MY banana bread, MY mixed fruit,' my mother wrote on the handmade menu). Country Herb and Apricot Butter, Almond Butter and Black Peppercorn Butter – which was delicious. And then of course, the concoctions named after us: Peanut Sarah's Creamy Butter Cups, Farmer Kate's Buttermilks, and Jacki Promises (customers had to request this one sight unseen; they could get a sample of anything else). Also Black Walnut Logs, Snappy Gingers, Raspberry Hearts, Date Diamonds, and Mabel's Sulze (meat juice jelly, not a big seller if you weren't born before 1915 in Bohemia). But my absolute favorite recipe was Thorny's Revenge, named for her cat, Thorndike-Barnhart, who was rechristened that summer as my mother had been paging through the dictionary while working on her 'new language.' She phoned one of my friends at NPR to tell him about it. 'You wouldn't believe the new language I'm inventing,' she'd said. 'You could broadcast it!' Anyway, Thorny's Revenge was a butter full of secret Cajun spices. On one little crock, my mother attached a tag that said, 'Eat Until You Explode!'

And Creative Renaissance – Déjà Vu Foods got results! My mother waltzed into the Toyota dealership in Menomenee, as crazy as a loon, and piff-pop-zip, handed them her Creative Renaissance business card, 'Creating custom surroundings to fit your lifestyle.' She left with a twenty-six-thousand-dollar fire engine red Toyota Supra with whitewall tires and spoiler and a turbocharged engine. She was flying! 'Evelyn!' she commanded her secretary. 'Here's another letter from Judge MacGill who wants me to pay Menomenee County Mental Hospital only about a billion dollars.' 'Judge Meant Daze!' she wrote on a slip of paper to enclose with his bill. 'Send him an invoice for two thousand dollars' worth of product and one designer sweatshirt. Here's a bill from my lawyer. He's a schnook, always wants money! Give him an invoice for five hundred bucks' worth of Thorny's Revenge and Jacki Promises! And how about a nice crock of Lemon Butter?' And on it went. They sent her a bill, and she sent them an invoice – the mortgage banker, the savings bank, the lawyer and the sleazy brokers, the doctors, the billing office at Menomenee Hospital and then the collection agency with the threatening letters, the car dealership, the department stores and local merchants, even her dentist. Evelyn, as slow as she was, wised up after a couple of weeks, quit, and hopefully billed my mother for her time. My mother billed her back, sent her an IOU for Snappy Gingers, a coupon redeemable for other hand-made goodies. She couldn't waste time with bills, she had a thousand things to do. The butters would come in hand-thrown crocks, the cookies in decorated containers, Ant Trap Zap! She would do it, she could do it, build an empire, build a business, line the stores with special mouthwatering treats she'd concocted herself, the kind of self-invented entrepreneur that you read about in the pages of *Money* magazine, and it would be a family corporation. We would be wearing matching outfits to the ribbon-cutting, Mary Baker Eddy would head the board, Alfred would finally come forth and escort her to the Inaugural Ball for Déjà Vu at the Pfister Hotel.

Kate and Sarah and I watched like village girls under a spell as Dolores spent her money as wildly as King Croesus. Bankruptcy loomed, but credit creaked on. One Saturday I stopped in and found my mother in her kitchen, surrounded by pyramids of carefully stacked purple coffee cups. She smiled at me. On each cup, she'd had her motto tastefully inscribed. 'Think About Me,' said the little cups. 'Think About Me, Think About Me, Think About Me.' Five hundred times over. 'Think About Me.'

Oh, Mother, as if we could ever think about anything else.

In the summer drought of 1988, the Mississippi River below

Cairo, Illinois, shrank like a worm in the sun. The dryness and heat bleached out every green thing in Wisconsin like a faded daguerreotype. Farmers pursed their lips and filed for crop insurance and slaughtered their beef herds. Lawns looked like pipe tobacco. The great blue heron delicately mud-hopped on Lake Puckawasay. On their reservation up north, the Menomenee chiefs did a rain dance, a wasase, slipping their bodies into the dank snakeskins and turtle shells cast off by dying animals. The eastern half of the nation was parched for water and farmers cursed for it. I flew to Mississippi to do a story about tugboats trapped by drought on the southern end of the river, clogged for miles and miles outside Greenville like a child's bathtub traffic jam. Flawn, my sound engineer, and I met a Cajun tugboat captain, Tom, who navigated the *Smokey Joe*. Tom, the socialite of the river, ferried us up and down muddy troughs of water while blaring 'Proud Mary' by Ike and Tina Turner. Tendrils of the Mississippi beat over our bow with trumpets, spoons, and cockscombs of spray. We were rolling, rolling down the river, microphones on, listening for the sounds of river life, water life, worlds we create. Then we transferred to another boat, the *Dread Jadwin*, the Coast Guard's big dredger, which looked like an antebellum steamboat. Flawn and I ate ham family-style in the old-fashioned atrium, and I tried to decipher the Louisiana bayou accent of the *Dread Jadwin*'s captain, which was even thicker than Tom's: 'This heah bigaloo than ya'll kinsee. Hae mose red bees and rise!' Something about the food.

The heat and the thick hours of time clung to our bodies like wet wool suits. The *Dread Jadwin*, shuddering, shived a deeper channel into the river bottom. By midnight, the trapped tugs and barges slipped away one by one, beads falling off a string, and they floated their names out to the Coast Guard's radio as they passed. *Echo Prince. Smokey Joe. Arabella.* I sat on the Mississippi banks and waved good-bye to our friends and thought of Think About

Me coffee cups and my mother. As I have done from so many, many places that she has never seen. Yet Sheba is as close as a breath. When I watch the Hamas gunmen, Izzedine al Qassam, shoot into the air at a blazing rally in Gaza; when I stare at an empty courtyard, palm befronded, gold and blue mosaic where the American hostages glumly sit around a swimming pool in Baghdad; when I climb, half shrouded, away from Tehran on hiking trails past the spring poppies in the Elburz Mountains, *I think about her.* She could do anything, go anywhere, become anyone. She does not even have to leave home to do it. And I wonder who is the greater chameleon, my mother or me.

Her delusions choked around her mind that summer like the loosestrife attacking the cattail patch on Puckawasay. Hours got lost in her mania, days rose and sank there. There was the clown incident. The painting was one of those embarrassingly cloying ones that belongs on black velvet. The clown had tangerine hair, deflated teal inner tubes for lips, oval white eggs painted around his eyes, and little shamrocks meant to remind me of Ireland. Someone had sent the clown painting to me as a present, a someone who lived in what was deemed to be the toughest prison in the United States, if you believe the federal Bureau of Prisons. (A lot of state prisons would vie for the honor.) I'd done a story on the United States Penitentiary at Marion, Illinois, back in 1986, then the Bureau of Prisons' successor to Alcatraz. Marion had had systematically tighter and tighter lockdowns under highly questionable circumstances until riots ensued and the inmates in the worst ward went crazy and murdered two guards. Then the guards went crazy in retaliation, raping prisoners with riot batons, smashing false teeth, beating people already chained in leg irons. The press had been kept out for over a month while bruises and broken bones healed, and Amnesty International would eventually condemn the prison, the only such distinction it made in the United States. Afterward, nearly all the prisoners spent twenty-three hours a day in cells in which they could take one step in one direction and three in another. The warden told me with a straight face that the director of the BOP in Washington had said that Marion was where they 'had to keep all the predators, all the cancer cells, and if you don't contain 'em, they spread.'

'And do you call them cancer cells?' I asked.

'Well, not to their face,' he spluttered.

After the story aired, many of the 'cells' wrote to me for years, and one of them, a bank robber and reputed prison leader of the Aryan Brotherhood, sent the clown painting. I was going through my neglected mail and happened to unwrap it on my mother's porch a day or so after we'd taken her to see the psychiatrist. My mother, scribbling nearby on one of her sketchpads, looked closely at the clown picture and picked it up. She gave it a long, cockeyed scrutiny.

'This clown,' my mother said, 'is speaking to me!'

'Really,' I said. 'What's he saying?' Ears on alert.

'He tells me I have a message from God,' she said, eyes sumptuous with light. But God had so many messages for Dolores that summer that the switchboard jammed. She vanished in the night. It was a couple of days before we knew she'd gone to Marion, USP. How my mother managed to drive her Toyota Supra nearly five hundred miles to Illinois when she could not hold a thought in her head steadier than a dust mote, I do not know. Marion is in a lonely spot, a federally protected swamp not far from the Kentucky border. Even if you know where to look, it is still down the moseying roads where we lock the dark secrets of our human failures. Yet somehow, Dolores, who had had her own experience with incarceration, managed to make out the tiny signs that form a Hansel-and-Gretel path to the prison. The forest there is so overgrown and spangled with moss that it should be renamed the Big Bad Woods. My mother, avenger of the wronged, pressed the intercom button at the gate, announced herself as the daughter of a certain mafia chieftain known as 'Big Tuna,' and was denied entrance. She would have been alone in that swamp, she told me later, but for the helicopter that she claimed followed her for ten miles out beyond the dogwood trees and marshes. And it would not surprise me if it had.

Not long afterward, I found that the reputed head of the Aryan Brotherhood who'd sent the clown portrait wrote my mother tender letters of his great love. My mother responded with letters about magical otters, blue herons, and thunderstorms that frightened her cat, Thorny. He probably thought it was code. This man, in prison since the age of eighteen, had convinced himself that I had posed as someone else to tell him of my romantic love for him. And that in order to do that, I was now writing him under an assumed name – my mother's. I gasped at his longing, for his greatest passion was his fierce yearning for freedom, a convict's impossible dream of space and hills.

'So sorry, but you are not writing to me,' I answered immediately when I put it all together. 'You are writing to my mother, my actual real-life mother. She's not well. She thought she could spring you from prison. I know it's odd, but things on the outside are crazy too.' He apologized profusely and immediately sent my mother four old-rose trees, a Rosa Mundi, an Empress Josephine, a Gloire de Dijon, and Noisettes. Each a different hue. 'Now, pink,' my mother had written that summer, 'that's the color of renewal, and white . . . that's a pure strong statement without fear.' She planted the rose trees beside her front walk, and they bloomed luxuriantly, a color riot, until they were slashed down by a Wisconsin ice storm that came the following spring. We never heard from the Marion prisoner again, and for all I know he is still there, in that other world, in a cell half-buried in darkness.

That was the summer my mother bought the racehorse (a quarter-interest, actually) and the summer that she changed her name legally to Gimbels, for Gimbels Schuster, and for the name of the distant aunt who she had decided was her real mother. It was the summer she wrapped herself in a sheet and did a rain dance for her former boyfriend, and it began to rain. It was the summer she was teaching the special course about Divine Love, and the meaning of Colors. 'This course will be taught by me or I will not be the teacher,' my mother wrote. 'Now we all know that Creative Renaissance by Design is a special gift from the Master Planner to promote healing. This will be a family corporation. I have already instructed my daughter Kate. BLACK, for example, will indicate a lack of fear. That's a strong statement. WHITE will denote a pure, unadulterated color.' It was the summer she spent a night in a county lockup when she became delusional and agitated at a library. 'You don't know who I am,' she cried. 'I am Mary Baker Eddy's daughter. I need to get to the Christian Science Mother Church in Boston!' It was the summer I walked into work in Chicago, and the NPR national editor was on the line, saying, 'Jacki, someone has just called and told us that if you don't cover the big Pabst Brewery summer parade, Gimbels Schuster is going to pull out all of its funding from NPR. Do we get money from Gimbels? Should we do it?' (An editor long gone, I might add.) It was the summer the county's social worker who I called pleading on an almost daily basis reminded me that I could not commit her until she constituted a clear fatal threat to herself or others, and so we lived with her, frightened and giddy, waiting for her to do us bodily harm.

LIVING IN THE LAND OF *B*ABYLON

MY MOTHER TRAVELS in her imagination as I have traveled in my life. There was a time when two weeks in one city seemed onerous to me, when the rhythms of it got overly familiar and strangling and tired. Often I have kept my passport in my purse, as if by looking at it and its strange visas I might confirm that this real world, the North American one in which I temporarily find myself, is not the real world at all but a kind of large airport holding room for tomorrow. Tomorrow is a country of its own, but I always think I belong *there*, taking up residence until it no longer pleases me. In that sense, I wonder if I am like my mother. 'Go out,' I remember her saying in our small town. 'Go away from here, leave, do anything!' I have done anything. I have walked on the bar and crushed a cowboy's glass in the middle of a great prairie of nowheres. Been mugged by car hijackers in Dublin, interviewed the head of Sinn Fein, Gerry Adams, in Belfast wearing one black shoe, one brown – all I had left after the Dublin mugging the day before. Jumped into pools in my underwear at dawn in Amman, and had the PLO pick me up in the middle of the night in Tunis to drive me around in a limousine with the windows blacked out before a meeting with Yassir Arafat. I've pulled on the now-fraying Armani suit bought with Gulf War profit in Rome and forgotten about amoebic dysentery precisely long enough to interview King Hussein of Jordan in his palace. Excellent eminence. I have driven five hundred miles through the desert to Iraq, retching under a scarf by the roadside, spitting out Mr Johnnie Walker while confirming virtually every stereotype of the wanton Western female correspondent for my Arab driver. Arriving in Baghdad, I am wracked with sweat and chills. Cover up, the driver says, for I am so hot I've shed my jacket. Cover up! 'Here to cover the war, or crew for Oxford?' the *Independent* correspondent jokes at the Al Rashid Hotel. I smile. I don't care. I have been here before. It seems like a millennium ago. Thugs in shades stand around in the lobby, extortionists, spies, and torturers. We know we can touch bottom in Iraq. We know this is the date palm swamp. Here is my translator, a good man, a Christian whose family was sent to prison and the front with Iran to force him home from studies in London. Then he was imprisoned and given a choice of rape by a Tikriti goon or a bottle. We meet in secret near the San Raphael Hospital. 'I want to get to America,' Paulus says, deliberately giving an interview critical of Saddam to an Italian TV station. I tell him there is no chance. In Amman, I mention his name to our embassy in Jordan, which doesn't want to know, and to the Brits, who put him on a list. A month later he will make his escape from Iraq, get to Jordan, and there's a call for me from the International High Commission on Refugees in London. Yes, they say, we will help him get to America, and he calls me one day from Michigan Avenue in Chicago, where I am living, and says, We're here, the wife and children too. One chance in hell to redeem the saved.

If only I could save my mother, make some intercession with the International High Court on Reason Against Insanity. When I travel in far places I am not certain who I'm remembering. The mother from my childhood who sang Carmen Miranda songs and baked banana bread in the middle of the night to soothe nightmares? Or the mother who speaks in tongues and dresses up in the bedsheets and thinks she's a queen or a bride or the daughter of Mary Baker Eddy? How can I be sure who she is when I'm on the other side of the world listening to language about human shields and burning up half the earth and drinking the blood of the fallen infidels? You'd think it was the Crusades all over again. What I want to do is vanish, wander into one of these fantastic marketplaces, these *souqs*, and shroud myself in one of these black chador things and lean against the wall where they've painted slogans in ocher denouncing the infidel in a script I'll never understand though I try – *kaf, alif, noon*, letters that sound like music, *wah, ein, rah* – and I don't know who I am anymore or whom I'm thinking about and half the world's gone crazy anyway, and that's one very big hangover I have. Who is she really? The question makes me feel at home here seven thousand miles away under the date palms in Iraq, where boundaries have dissolved overnight and everyone longs to be someone else.

'Paul Marshall Lyden,' read the obituary in the *Menomenee Eagle*. 'Born 1899, died Oct. 29th, 1988. Family from Clifden, County Galway. An Irish wake is planned for Saturday evening. Bring canned memorials to the Menomenee Food Pantry! He leaves four granddaughters, Sarah and Kate and Jacki Lyden, and Dolores Gimbels of Menomenee.'

It was a small thing, I told myself, and it didn't matter. My mother had placed an obit in our local newspaper for my paternal grandfather, making us her sisters. Clues like this baffled me. It was true that my grandfather had died, hanging on until shortly after I'd come home from covering the Olympics in Seoul. I'd taken him to Ireland and his ancestral town three years before, just the two of us. (We're on our honeymoon, he'd say to one and all, isn't that something? Or, You know what Pat said to Mike when he came to America and saw grapefruits for the first time?

Gee, they're so big, wouldn't take very many of them to make a dozen!) But he was my paternal grandfather, not my mother's father, and Paul Lyden and I had grown close only in his very last years. Nor was my mother, I pointed out to an editor at the *Eagle*, our sister. Didn't anyone check these things?

'You never know anything with her,' Kate said. 'You only know that you never know.'

My mother is a worm in our brains that makes us crazy, Kate and Sarah and I. The person she was is vanishing, and I think I am vanishing too. I get a letter from her telling me that she recently heard me on the radio, and did not know until then that I had learned to speak Italian. I get letters all the time, circulars for Déjà Vu Foods, recipes for love potions, tips for looking more beautiful, dresses she's cut from magazines and mailed to me as things I might like to have, or that she will promise to sew for me. She calls my sisters and me laughing in the middle of the night, talking about people we don't know.

'I feel helpless,' Sarah told me on the phone from Denver. 'I'm angry at God or whoever. I can't clean up after her anymore. I feel like her problems are my problems, just like when I was in law school. I wake up, I'm with her. I go to bed, I'm with her. I've got my own family now. I'm supposed to be independent.'

'Well, all I can tell you,' said Kate, another day on the phone, crunching a Farmer Kate's Buttermilk from my mother, 'is that yesterday I bought her old car, kinda t' give her some money, and then she called the police and told them I'd stolen it. That was tootin'! Except, y'know, the police, they don't even believe her no more. Then she comes over in a black leather miniskirt and this hot pink blouse open to there and she looks so coy and so cute I wanna slug her. Y'know how that feels? She wants to help me look for a kitten she let loose in my back yard the day before. And worst of all, she never, ever, ever says I'm sorry. Y'know?'

That was the fall we tried tough love on my mother. We'd make her ask us for our help getting treatment. We would isolate her, make her beg for it, her and her damn magical otters and great blue heron, her Creative Renaissance and endless parcels for Alfred – tennis balls, swizzle sticks, cuff links. The sheriff would call Kate to 'come look at this here room a junk I got for that man.' No more of her one-sided dialogue with the courts and businesses and oddballs who yammer into my ear day and night through her. Our mother, the small-town pariah. Let her loose, as Lear was abandoned by Regan, Goneril, and Cordelia, until she is by law a danger to herself or others. Lethal, the Queen of Sheba. The tough part we were good at, but I must say the love suffered.

NOVEMBER 5, 1988
CHICAGO, ILLINOIS

Dear Dolores:

Kate says you wonder why you don't hear from me anymore. I'm terribly sorry to say I've had it. I'm exhausted by your stubborn, stupid, childish refusal to get help for your obvious mental problems, problems even you admit having. Pride, I think, is a big factor. You relish denying treatment. You love having me jump through hoops. When you decide to get help or let us get help, I'll be there. We all will be. Until then, you're my nightmare. You're not the mother I remember nor a person I'm proud of.

Love,
Jacki

P.S. I won't be coming home for Christmas.

Immediately she sent back all the cards she'd kept that all of us had ever sent her in the previous thirty years. An overflowing box. Three decades' worth of Christmas cards and Halloween and St

Patrick's Day remembrances. Even the plaster casts you make with your hands and spray-paint gold in kindergarten. Corny, but then we were corny. Early stick-figure drawings with blue faces; poems composed in doggerel. My mother included a poem she said she'd written for me on my birthday that year while she was sick, styled in the kind of rhyme that leaves the listener bug-eyed: 'Lord, give me a heart that is heavy no more, and wisdom to know that on wings I can soar. Love opens the door to sweep shadows away, where music and laughter brighten each day . . .' A good thing she doesn't know her own mind, I say.

My baptismal announcement then arrived at my door, a 1950s puffy white satin card with a pink baby lying in a blue forget-me-not cloud. Above the baby, in red ink, on the envelope: 'Jacki must keep first name given her by her parents, may choose middle name and last name. Learn more, read more, about God! For GOD's SAKE.' Inside, she wrote 'Church of God' in red ink over my baptismal name. She changed our family name to that of a well-known Milwaukee Mafia mastermind. Here was the Mother's Day card I'd sent her the year before. 'To the Best Mother in the world,' my card read, 'who is one of a kind.' Undeniable.

Her accompanying note said, 'You can have all these BACK! I can't feel the messages in them anymore!' The handwriting served as a clue, for when my mother is sick her penmanship eclipses with her brain. Scary block capitals scrabbled down the page like cockroaches after a bit of meat, her plump child's cursive tossed on the page like boudoir pillows, and there is the nightmare zone of an upended Gothic alphabet with wavery spider legs. Inverted word sequences distort like a hall of mirrors: W.O.W. = M.O.M.!

NOVEMBER 15, 1988
CHICAGO, ILLINOIS

Dear Mom:

I got your package. I'm sorry you can't feel the 'messages' from those cards anymore. I'm sure there are feelings underneath the present tension we both still have. We love you but perhaps you don't realize that your behavior is totally out of line and stressful in the extreme. We will miss you this Christmas, always our special time, and I hope you will use the solitude to reflect on what harm you are doing to yourself. You need to be in treatment. We want you back, the real you. Let me know what I can do to help.

Love,
Jacki

DOLORES TAYLOR GIMBELS
LAKE PUCKAWASAY, WIS-WE-CAN-WIN!
DECEMBER 5, 1988

Jacki:

This is not a hate letter, this is a hurt letter. You have hurt me to the point where I must say I do not want you to come here for Christmas. I never asked you to be my keeper – and I still do not. I have repeatedly told you how I feel and you ignore it! You are not welcome here for a while! You owe me money for Déjà Vu cookies – none for a dress I am not making you. Perhaps it's my fault you are so callous and self-centered. In fact, I'm sure it is, but as the oldest you think you can boss everyone around and I don't want anymore of your bullshit and 'concern.' So screw you! I'm not your mother and I'm not fifty-eight!

Dolores

I am raving, quarreling with the lost. I send my mother a pamphlet, a brochure about lithium. I have gotten it from a telephone help line, something I have seen on the bus from the office to home. I am clutching at straws. I would buy leeches if I thought they'd cure her. 'Try this, you'll like this,' I write to my mother, enclosing the pamphlet, as if I were offering her a Big Pineapple Hawaiian Vacation! Miracle Cure Included! I write, 'Lithium is a natural salt that works on your biochemistry the way insulin works on a diabetic. As you can see, tens of thousands of people suffer from your same illness. The good news is you're not alone!' Hallelujah, Mom, you can rejoice. Insanity. Blasting the familiar turf like fire or flood, a hot lava flow concealing everything, removing the tree from the path, the path from the mountainside, the mountain itself. Waiting for the future to be invented from entirely new ground.

'LITHIUM WORKS LIKE SALTPETER ON THE "HEAD,"' my mother writes back on an envelope. Inside, she has made her own version of the pamphlet I've sent her:

Manic-Depressive: A mental disorder, extremes of joy or rage, uncontrolled and often violent activity having or characterized by alternating attacks of mania and depression . . . as in manic-depressive psychosis – an unusual fondness or craze, as for BIG MEN, soft lights, dancing, music, laughter, good times, good health.

And on the flip side she has written:

To: Jacki 'Ballistreri' Lyden

Merry Christmas, Asshole!
    Your father was a *little man*. But he could carry a heavy burden. My father was Frank Ballistreri, the Milwaukee Godfather. A *big man*. If I DIE on Christmas Day, it's not my problem!

Jacki, you're an asshole! Your father was a *nice boy*.
love mom.

When our mother is ill, any script of our lives can become an interior monologue for her: a birth, a death, a passage of any kind. Here is a picture from the overflowing box, Kate and Sarah and I at Kate's wedding. The year is 1980, my mother is sick that year and often missing and Kate wants to get married. We argue. Wait until she is better, I say. Kate will not hear of waiting, Kate being Kate. November is her destiny. And who knows when my mother's touring caravan will cross the border to Well? Kate borrows a cape from Sarah and a peasant dress from someone else and stands beside her bridegroom. Standing, in fact, in the same spot and before the same altar in the Church of Cold Stars, where my mother was married – no regard for bad luck. At the last moment, just before the tiny wedding begins, my mother streaks in, cheeks painted with two high clown spots of rouge, a scare-crow in a satin brocade dress made on the Kowloon Road. And I'm looking at that dress right here.

My mother's cheeks are rubescent, her cuckoo's laugh forms a crescent in the air. 'Unreal,' she says, laughing at the 'death do us part,' laughing at the 'dearly beloved,' cackling contrapuntally to herself in the pews. There's a comedy in the cloud in her mind. She points at Kate's exchange of vows with her bridegroom. 'That's a good one,' she stage-whispers so that those near can hear. 'Who's that guy she's marrying? What a schnook! Where'd she get that dress? This will never work!' I'm torn between laughter and anger. Kate is oblivious. No, Kate is not oblivious – she's feigning oblivion. Just as when she was small and the outside world made Kate turn to marble with quiet. 'You tell him, Jack. I want the strawberry licorice,' she whispered in confidence. The sun tattoo on her belly scorches through her wedding dress, which is fashioned from a halter top under the cape Sarah made ten years before for her home ec class. Furled laughter from Dolores. After the wedding, there is a cool and beautiful sunset. Kate and her bridegroom troop down to Lac La Jolie to have their wedding photograph taken, seated with a ginger-haired dog, their golden retriever, Mick Finn. They look young and healthy. Dolores is supposed to join them, they want to lead her to the reception at Kate's in-laws. They climb into the new husband's car and wait and wait for Dolores. Finally they see her approaching fast in her sports car. She slows down as if to stop. She waves at them, guns the engine, races past them into the sunset. Not to the sunset, Kate reminds me later. 'To the El Dorado!' A happening nightclub for middle-aged singles out somewhere on Highway 100. The image of her there is entwined forever with Kate's marriage, and I think of Dolores dancing that night with a stranger under a thousand stars, with skeins of wedding finery and a ginger dog in a dress. Nothing holds still in the clouds. She could have said to her dance partner, 'My daughter was married today. I wanted to be there, but I had important business elsewhere. I'm a CEO of a major food company, you know. Kate was the first of my children to be married, but it's not an institution I believe in anymore. And, boy, she had on some kind of peasant thing . . . it was so funny . . . In a wedding reception Polaroid photograph of Kate and Sarah and me, my mother has crayoned red rings around our heads, the little saints. Her progeny, her daughters, her targets.

Tough love was working. Her supplications started. 'Open House on Christmas Eve,' she wrote on an invitation in the mail. Her invitation contained a prayer and small picture of forest animals linked arm in arm, looking up at the star in the east. Also bribes: 'a coupon for a manicure and pedicure for the two of us at Gimbels. Signed, Mother and Dippy.' And suggestions: 'Christmas Open House: Do Your Gift Wrapping Early. Bring – the liver pate and cookies, wine, each other (You aren't Getting any Younger HOTshot). Pets stay @ Kate's.'

The next day it's a shepherd in the mail – maybe it's Jesus? – holding out a cake, and saying: *'Christmas Invitational to All! Nutty coffee will be served in English Rose of Tralee china breakfast cups – Pa Taylor's favorite! Nutty coffee is delicious! Entirely a different taste! Jacki, help yourself to the Scotch on the mantel! You don't have to make your bed! All is forgiven! Leave them laughing when you go!'*

Ohmomohmomohmom, a kind of rune with me. Where have you gone? Give me my mother back, I write in my head. Personals ad: 'One mother, missing in action. Wears tiara, doesn't eat, talks at ninety miles an hour. Believe it! Answers to the name of a department store. Steals dogs, cats, and horses.' I crumple the pages, toss them onto the floor at work. They land at my feet like popcorn balls. I miss the little things, of course. I want her to go shopping with me, I want her to bake me her cheesecake and not save a piece for Alfred. I want her to send me a box of Snappy Gingers and a crock of Peppercorn Butter, and not send me a bill. I want her to show up at my door with a smooth calm face like a butter pat and tranquil eyes, and say, 'All that crazy nonsense, that loony stuff I did when I was sick, wasn't it wild? Didn't I make you laugh? Crazy, huh?'

When my mother writes that she has heard me speaking in Italian on the radio, who is she hearing? What is in Sheba's mind, the avenging virago? When did the world take on such strange sounds and shapes, when did invisible marauders train secret bazookas on the walls of the house, when did curling irons become radioactive, frying pans become animate, children speak in the tongue of archangels? All of this in her imagination, a place brimming with evil. Her writings reflect a wild evil that has possessed her. Fantasizing of her former boyfriend: 'The child clung to his leg. "Not here!" He said. "Not here!"' There are more and more voices that only she can hear.

She is alone on Christmas Day, half buried in the packages she has shipped to herself. Kate has taken a peek in previous weeks, but she is sticking to our plan. Kate and her children and I hunker down in my Chicago apartment for Christmas. We imagine my mother rising before dawn to make coffee, waiting for the kettle to shriek. The rind of snow on Lake Puckawasay would look like a piece of old carpeting marked by the footprints of ice fishermen. In her fairy-tale cottage, Dolores excitedly runs back and forth, preparing for everyone's arrival. Her living room is transformed into a filigreed bandbox bursting with goodies, imaginary gifts from imaginary friends, daughters' gifts that she has sent herself: 'For the Best Mother in the World, Love Jacki,' my mother writes on a shiny red package. 'For the best little woman in the world, Love Always, Alfred,' says another. And a third: 'The Chamber of Commerce salutes you! Many happy holidays to Déjà Vu!' *Déjà vu.*

All these passing Christmases, and I am no closer to discovering the source of her fantasies, the banshee fairy who calls her past the shoals of safety. I am no closer than I have ever been to intercepting her between the first manic episode and the last crashing embers, the firestorm I can't stop. My mother parodies safety, the perfect family, the handsome and moneyed husband, and here we are teetering on the edge. My mother is isolated in her bungalow. We, her daughters, try to make *kruns kuchen* on the gas stove in my Chicago apartment. The simple cake burns in its pan, comes out soggy in alternate spots. Stupid stove. Stupid apartment. Stupid life. Eight years ago we had passed this night speculating, fantasizing. Was Dolores in a Vegas casino, the Parade of Roses, having her varicose veins stripped? Christmas Eve. Kate and I go to a Spanish Mass in a Puerto Rican church. Unreal, says Kate. We can't understand, incense as thick as sand coagulates in our nostrils. Christmas is a scent too pungent to inhale. I pick up the phone and call. My mother cries, Hello? Hello? And I hang up.

Tough love sucked. We had had enough, we hated it. Kate

decided to check on my mother on the evening of Christmas Day, breaking her tough love vow as she drove back to her own home in Wisconsin. When she reached Dolores's, she saw every light in the house ablaze. Dolores had also lit candles, rafts of them, and Kate could see that they'd been burning for hours, that the wax had overflowed and congealed into scurf on tables, floors, and shelves. Dolores had single-handedly laid out every plate, every piece of polished silver, arranged in borders and scrolls butter knives and pickle forks. She had burnished every wine glass and piece of leaded crystal, days of effort. She had made a feather centerpiece for the table, billowing up to look like frost trimmed with bubbles. The hours had passed, the day had passed. The salad greens had turned limp, the cranberry stuffing hardened like punctuation resting on each salad plate beside stale chunks of mashed potato. There was a roast in the oven, desiccated from overcooking, waiting all day. Her Christmas Open House. In case we came. She had taken a sedate scarf and wound it around her throat and pinned it with a cameo, an imitation of the picture in the cameo itself, her Victorian Aunt Martha. There were place cards for everyone, one for Alfred, others for us girls.

Dolores turns to Kate, her skin taut and translucent. Her collarbone pokes through her scarf like umbrella spokes. She gives Kate a look of stunning agony, shoulders sinking.

'You didn't come to eat, did you?' my mother mutters hoarsely. 'Nobody came to see me on Christmas Day. Nobody, all day. No phone calls. It was just me and Thorny.' Her face, ruined and labile, winks like the northern lights, from light to dark and dark to light, clouds racing over it. Her mouth crumples, eyes seal shut. Her forehead presses down on one of the chilly polished plates, and her hands clench and push to either side of her temples, and she cries a river for all that she has lost. Oh, tough, tough love.

Once I got into a fight with a man. I don't mean a kind of verbal fisticuffs, senseless and slashing, I mean a calculated fight we planned in unspoken agreement over dinner in Aleppo, Syria. We were war correspondents. I guess you would have to call us that because the Gulf War was on and we roamed Arab capitals and because wars were in his case a specialty and in mine something of an inner and natural dialogue. There are parts of the world that are settled, and call for a kind of civility and conformity to the rules or norm. And there are parts of the world that are unsettled, and call for self-invention on a daily basis. You make your own rules, and if you are scared or lonely it is best to let no one see that. Your first rule, always, is to get the story. In the lacunae of the day, you get each other's story because you are living on the surfeit of your own adrenaline and lust. After two bottles of Lebanese wine, Ksara red, mezze, kibbe, pigeons with raisins, he said, 'You know, Lyden, I'd like to know how tough you are, what drives you,' that sort of nonsense. It was just our nerves rattling around. I'd been talking about my stepfather. I can't think why, a part of the arid desert perhaps, or the blood color of the rock. 'You're tough!' the correspondent gibed at me. But in those days I was tough, or thought I was, or I would not have wound up in Aleppo in the middle of the night with a man who loved battles more than anything in the world, and made his own when they didn't exist. We drank more and more Ksara, and somewhere in the predawn hours he said something about my essentially loveless nature, or how else could I have treated my stepfather with such disregard?

'Creepo?' he said. A matter of transference: I lashed out. He pinned me so I couldn't move, but I could move, and I knew he wanted me to try. I kneed him in the groin as we rolled down off the bed and he was still then, half moaning. I ran and got another hotel room, bribing the management not to tell him where I was. I passed the night reliving old memories in my bathrobe in the strange room until he came to find me hours later and dragged me back upstairs.

'I bribed the management even more money than you,' he boasted. 'They asked if I wanted to find my wife. I said you bet I do.'

Beg pardon, you have a wife? I'm not it. I told him how tough I was.

He said, 'Take your best shot.'

I kicked him in the head, and he went down in a flash.

The next day he apologized and I apologized and believe I forgave him and he me, for always, and we shared a star-sized hangover and the leers of the Muhabarat as we rode down with two of them following us in the elevator.

'I consider last night doing my part against the Islamic movement in this country,' he whispered.

But we knew what we were doing as we did it – he was provoking, and I would therefore have to attack him. Provoke, attack, conflate. That was the underlying dynamic I felt with Sheba: when she provoked me, when she eluded me, it made me want to pounce on her all the harder. For a moment, for many such moments, I wanted to sink my teeth in her flesh, bind her and conquer her. I packed for Bab al-Hawa, Gate of the Winds.

Sheba, rising and hovering, mist off the lake like a winter evanescence, ice her shroud, assumes each dawn is the shape of a new destiny. Wherever you go, hey, that's where you belong. Whatever you believe, that's who you are. 'Come and get it, I'm out of gas!' my mother writes one morning in lipstick on the windshield of her car. That was back in the fall. Since then, the repo man's been on the case. The sporty Toyota and the cell phone disappear. My mother hauls her old bicycle out of the garage and takes to the winding back roads of Menomenee County as winter sets in. She rides the eight miles to Kate's house, her hair lacquered with wind and frost into an atomic shape, her feet pumping up and down like Ferris wheels.

'She wears all her antique jewelry when she rides that bike,' Kate reports to me. 'Her father's gold pen on a chain, Ray's antique stopwatch, pins and necklaces from when she was in high school. Cripes. Now she's gone and lost it all. Every day she comes over hollerin' and cryin' and sayin' another piece of her life is missin'.' Dolores has become the local pariah, the woman in the pink snowsuit on a bicycle, the woman caught stuffing hot dogs into her parka at the supermarket. Kate phones. 'Can'tcha come up, Jack, can'tcha come up?'

Kate's voice is a tourniquet being pulled taut. Kate implores. 'She don't eat anything I take over there. She's starvin', a bag of bones. You better come home.' From Kate's description, I know that Dolores's eyes are like rocket fire, her mind full of afterburn. She doesn't care about insolvency. 'I hope Menomenee County has a big tent,' my mother tells Kate flippantly. 'I hope when I lose this house they make a big space for Thorny and me in the poorhouse! And my business, of course! Creative Renaissance from the Clink!'

Time for me to come up. I haven't seen her in three months. I fly over the roads. She's modeling a bright yellow swing coat when I walk in early on a February Sunday afternoon. Pivot and turn, girls, pivot and turn. The coat blooms like a flower around her thin shoulders, flares and closes around her, vaginated, jack-in-the-pulpit. My mother, I remember her, inside this half-emaciated little woman. 'Like it?' she asks me. 'Like my coat?' The Christmas surprises that Kate saw weeks ago are still all over the house. A teacup dangles from a candlestick on the mantel, a teacup I bought for her in 1960 at Gimbels Schuster's Secret Santa Village. It was my first purchase, ever, from a special store for kids, a secret honeycomb of kid-sized things. An elf land is remembered here. My mother pivots and turns again. 'I made this coat,' she says. Perambulations, attempts to look pretty. 'Like it?' I do like it. It's my mother there underneath the reductions of mania, aged about twelve, trying to look so pretty. It's been so long since I've seen her. I move to embrace her, trace her ribs with my fingers, so bony, so much like a fish swimming upstream, and I place my fist in the cavelet below her collarbone, feel the current of blood below. I see the way her lips curl back from her gums and the puffy weal where they pull from the teeth, the brittle dullness of her hair. Her subcutaneous fat is gone, her breasts are flat, she suffers from vitamin deficiency. My hand rubs inside the back of her yellow coat collar, touches something familiar, a garment label, Gimbels Schuster. 'You didn't make this coat, Mom,' I say. 'You bought it.' Not that it matters, except that it's more money she doesn't have for a coat she doesn't need. I remark on this absently, trying to make conversation.

'So how'd you get it?' My voice is sharper than I wish it were.

'Shows what you know, Miss Voice of America,' she snaps, stepping back. She whops me so sharply on the side of the head that a contact pops out. I am on my knees, looking for the lens. 'I'm bored,' says my mother. 'Think I'll go for a ride.' She is frantic, thrumming with energy. She runs around the table, drops the lemon yellow coat from her shoulders.

'Wait, goddamit, will you?' I cry. I'm talking to an empty room.

She has on a jean jacket underneath her coat, and some gloves are in her pocket, but that's it. I'm blind and ambushed as she runs outside and I search for my lens. She gets a three-minute head start. The door she left open is refracted in my one good eye. Finding my lens, I plunge after her into the icy air. I catch up to her in my car on County Z, the narrow and zagging road to Menomenee, see her on her bicycle. My tires screech on ice. Wheels slide on each curve. My coming after her doesn't stop her. She pumps the bike up the hills, stands triumphant like a child, bangs her skinny butt on the seat going downhill. Eddying in the hardened snow. I slow down and open the window. 'Hey, get in the car, goddamit,' I yell. 'Get in the goddamn car!'

She ignores me. I'm blue from cursing, sky blue with the cold. I could run her into the ditch. I think hard about it. Satisfying, murderous. We ride on like this in the twists. I keep pace with her. Dolores is wind torched, Sheba implacable, the skin of her face as purple as a peeled beet from the cold and exertion. *Get in the goddamn car now!* I'm roaring. My throat is dry and sore. Blood vessels pulse like fireflies inside my head. I nose the car over, threatening to push her into the ditch. It's more difficult than you'd think, than in the movies. If I miss my aim and kill her, run her over, then what? Her bones are beneath the wheels, and I'm as murderous as she ever was. Daughter Flattens Lunatic Mother on County Back Roads. Two miles. Three. Past the little string of pearl lakes frozen hard, like the teeth in her manic smile. They are the lakes of my childhood, where my mother brought us swimming in that heady azure summer of freedom before she married the Doctor. Four miles. Five. There was a red waterwheel in one lake, Lake Ipesong, and if you climbed it and pitter-pattered it with your bare wet feet, slapping them down on moist black rubber, dripping and giddy, it was only a matter of time before you fell off into the waters of the waiting lake. Sinking beneath the shining surface, eyes open, searching for a mother going past on a bicycle in the twilight world rising to meet you. The red wooden waterwheel churning the bicycle wheels in the snow. The family up around the Christmas tree, the children tumbling end over end in the snow. Myself on a bike in the curves, trying to escape Creepo, to run away from home. Mabel, taking the S curves at sixty miles an hour. They took her license when she sped through that school zone beyond Wagner's. She was eighty-four. They should have done so. Still, it took the life out of her. All of us, the racing women.

My mother's child body goes up and down and up and down on the pedals, her feet two little waterwheels. Wagner's sanitarium is beside us, a hospice, not a hospital, now, its turrets all swags and banners and fetlocks of snow. People go there to die on their own terms. My mother ignores Wagner's, as always. The snowy fields are like rows of folded linen sheets. We go past the Gothic fish hatchery and limestone hops barns that the brewing companies built here in the last century. We are in a New World Bavarian bakeshop landscape of miniature lakes, skaters, and snow-dusted pines. 'Heygetinthegoddamncarthisveryinstant.' I lay on the horn, swerve, cut her off. She stops, bent over, breathing funnels of ragged air into her heaving accordion chest. She straightens and stands rapt before a magnificent stone portal that marks the turn into the brewery estate. Her bike lies half-buried in the snow.

'Creative Renaissance has a decorating job,' she croaks out. I hop out of the car and walk over to the mailbox where she's standing. It's Alfred's mailbox, as gaudy as a child's lunch bucket with smile stickers and pictures of cats, and cowboys wielding branding irons and springy butterflies, dozens and dozens of stickers, all colors, pink, green, and blue. She slips a letter inside the Alfred box. 'To Sir with Love,' it reads.

'I hope he likes it when he gets home from the French Riviera,' she mumbles, a look as concentrated as an artist at the easel. She fishes a roll of stickers from her pocket and peels off one or two with her teeth. She pastes them to the box. 'I do these one at a time,' my mother says, 'to get the best effect.' I am silent, hoisting the bike into the trunk, what they call enabling her.

Later, when we get home, the cloud enters her head. She perches on the couch and I watch while it envelops her. Her mouth opens and closes as she speaks silently, words I can't understand. Gutturals drip, water sounds, deep dribbles of gibberish, as if she'd been submerged. *Baba, ooooh. Kizma pro hizzim.* It's enough to make you think about spirit possession. I don't want to sleep here tonight, I think. I should, though. I should sleep here always. I should lie in front of the door as Sarah's husband did last summer in Denver. Sleep on the hall steps right where Dolores found Mabel as dead as a doornail. I call Kate. We'll both stand guard tonight, sleep over. My mother's eyes are open, but she sees nothing in this room nor in this world. Whom is she talking to? *Omneosis hiss gala hoa.* I can catch nothing. I think of Mabel, sitting there rocking in the shawl of twilight, the flayed skin of her hands like paint peeling in the sun. I think of the night she fell dead on the stairs, none of us there. Settle down. Cannot close my eyes. Stuck. Oh. Mabel. Dolores. Me.

A PETITION FOR GUARDIANSHIP
MENOMENEE COUNTY OFFICE OF THE GUARDIAN
JANUARY 5, 1989

A Memorandum Concerning the Mental Health of Dolores Gimbels, January 5, 1989, submitted by Jacki Lyden, in conjunction with Sarah Lyden and Kate Lyden

She has been sick now since late last June and has resisted all pleas for treatment. We love her very much but want her to be hospitalized because she is verging on homelessness and malnutrition, a result of the fact that she is completely and consistently delusional. She has no automobile and is riding a bike on hazardous rural roads in subfreezing temperatures. She has ardently and skillfully denied her need for treatment, and since being fired from her waitressing job last summer has spent more than fifty thousand dollars – all her life savings, all unprotected assets – and is currently living on seventy-two dollars a week unemployment. When challenged, she is extremely threatening and hostile. She is wholly resistant to the idea of treatment, as the County must be aware. Let me refer you to her complete mental history. (See attached, 1981 – commitment, Menomenee County.) Must we, or another unsuspecting person, wait for another murderous attack before the County intervenes?

The county sent a social worker out to see her. I liked her. Marcia. She was five months pregnant, cheerful and can-do. I didn't know if she could do my mother much good, but she was great for me and listened empathically when I rolled out long lists of complaints. We arranged for a secret rendezvous with Marcia, who would show up at Kate's for tea. My mother would be invited too, and Marcia could evaluate her. My mother didn't know she was a social worker, of course. On the appointed day, my mother wasn't dressed too oddly, behaved well. The idea, I hoped, was for Marcia to adjudge Dolores to be sick enough so that I could at least obtain a petition for guardianship to stop the hemorrhage of money. My mother sat down and opened up her new, handmade autobiography, in which she'd invented a revised matriarchy for her life. Over another hand-drawn picture of the Déjà Vu mam'selle, this time saying, 'Only the best, I'm not cheep!' and 'What can I do?' she'd pasted pictures of her father and mother and herself as a baby.

MY MOTHER MARTHA
by Dolores Gimbels
FOREWARD

I have known, and not known, many men. My mother Martha 'knew' only one, and that one was my father, Ray. To their dear memories are my memoirs written.

[Question: Has a book already been published with this title by Martha Mitchell's daughter?]

My Mother Martha is a hard-to-believe account of the

author's life. It relates events pulled from her mind after the passing of her mother, but which she can attest to as factual. Martha Gimbels was a small, timid woman . . . unmarried when I was born. Nothing is known to me at the present of her earlier life so I begin with what I can recall clearly and eerily.

I was bron! Where, I am not certain but in a house, delivered by a midwife, born out of wedlock, conceived in love.

I. Illegitimate

Martha Gimbels loved me! She loved me so much that she gave me up. Over and over it was drilled into me about the disgrace of being an illegitimate child. Almost nothing was more disgraceful, except when one party was already married and there could be no 'shotgun' wedding. Mabel, my adopted mother from the moment of conception's discovery, proudly pointed to her framed marriage certificate and to me, 'See – your brother was legitimate,' neglecting to mention that she had born a daughter herself out of wedlock when she was 14.

Martha Gimbels was a wealthy heiress and my father a handsome truck driver during the depression. I am not sure of all her names. When I am not sure I will say so. When I am proved wrong I can be truly sorry and apologize, but it is a fact I am involved in a complex lawsuit with the State of Wisconsin and more particularly Menomenee County as a direct result of the cover-up and Mabel's obsession. She would say, 'Dolores, if you only knew the truth,' and cry and wring her hands. In 1929 the headlines could have been: Wealthy Heiress: Sex. Scandal. Shame.

Marcia sat listening, leafing through twenty pages of the book, with pictures, conjectures, and purple prose. Dolores Gimbels painted in the middle of the book like a belladonna flower growing in a hidden glade. Secret poison. Naked lady. Marcia chatted with my mother, thanked her, and left.

'What a nice visit,' my mother said.

Afterward the social worker said to me sympathetically, 'Not much we can do. Her threats are too vague. Her judgment is impaired but shrewd. I'm afraid that means it's her choice. She's going to throw lots of things away.'

My petition for guardianship over her assets was denied. 'It's her choice,' Marcia repeated.

Her choice? Her choice is to be the CEO of a major Fortune 500 company, I say. Her choice is to send her armies into battle against the forces of Xerxes. Her choice is to send a cake shaped like a penis to her former boyfriend.

'Ain'tcha just toasted by all this, Jack,' says Kate. 'Dolores is such a liar. She just sat there in total denial. That book of total lies! At least at my meetings, we learn to take responsibility.'

'I am not part of this family,' says Sarah on the phone from Denver, when I tell her the latest. As if her sternness will change everything. 'What I like each week is to know exactly what I'm going to be doing at this time next week. I write it down in a book,' she says.

'You,' I say, 'were born on a different planet.'

The process server is waiting for Kate. He emerges like a fox from the bushes with a summons for her. A lawsuit has been filed. He knows Kate. 'I gotta ask you,' he says disapprovingly. 'What kind of daughter is sued by her own mother?'

Kate gives him a look, pulls the letter from its envelope and then the summons. She reads it and waves it in the process server's face. Dolores is suing to get back the car Kate bought from her.

'Yeah, well, what kind of mother writes her daughter as 'Kate

U. Bastard?' she asks the process server. The sun on her belly is a hard little star, shooting pointy rays.

My mother loves the law. She loves its weighty and stentorian tones, its thousand subclauses and findings of 'fact.' She loves its arcane legal language and references and all those dry case citings, the Code of Hammurabi. Legalese is something for her to transcribe with her shorthand, something for the windstorm of her brainpower. When she was first married, my mother was a legal secretary and learned to speak, write, and think like a lawyer. She worked for two Jewish brothers. It was as if she'd been sent to college after all, she said. She thought the brothers were fantastically kind and smart and funny and they sent baby gifts when I was born. How she cried, she said, when she realized she wouldn't be going back to work. And indeed she would have made a good attorney. I can see her as a trial lawyer, loving the fight, the confrontation. Thirty years after her first legal job, the law is still her ally, her only ally now, and on President's Day in February 1989 my mother sits writing briefs on yellow legal pads at her kitchen table. Sometimes my mother is the first to bring suit, more often she is countersuing. There are so many lawsuits of one sort or another that I keep track of only the most critical. She cites Abraham Lincoln and George Washington. She works on these suits and countersuits almost every day, for hours at a time. They keep her going like a dose of methedrine. First there is the bank, which is taking her to court over unpaid checks, eyeing the home loan with which she renovated Mabel's bungalow, her equity, eyeing the second property that Dolores owns for income. That's going to go, I can see it. We can't hang on to that any more than I could have saved her pension fund or her life insurance or mutual fund. She is suing them, and they are suing her.

'John,' says the banker's notes on the suit I have copied. 'I have the Dolores Gimbels brief here. It's taken us four hours to Xerox and I believe it will provide excellent testimony for our case. The woman is obviously completely deranged.' They're getting ready, closing in. Then there is the Menomenee County Hospital, where her countersuit over her refusal to pay has gone to the district appellate court. Her lawyer has quit now that she's ill again and sending him cookies instead of cash. But the jerk hasn't just quit: he's suing her for nonpayment, though he's collected thousands of dollars from my mother and watched while she has been forced to liquidate her assets to pay his bills, her impossible legal redemption. There are also two other lawsuits: one from the elderly couple she dinged in one of her car accidents, another from the cell phone company. In addition to the lawsuits, there's an avalanche of warning notices from creditors. Since she is in 'penury,' as she puts it, my mother decides that she will act as her own lawyer. And though sick, hallucinatory, her legal briefs work to the extent that they temporarily hold her attackers at bay. A giant B, giant R, giant I, giant E, giant F. These letters she arranges in a semicircle, like the epitaph on a tombstone on each brief she writes. It is a manic oratory, passing like a comet over memory and history, conflating both, spinning anew.

'Oh, you wise men of learning,' she writes in her scary Gothic handwriting in her Menomenee County appellate court brief on Presidents' Day. 'I am distressed that the legal system takes so long to correct such an injustice. Today, as we pay homage to our great presidents, I quote from Mr Lincoln's farewell message to his Springfield neighbors on Feb. 11, 1861.'

Here I have lived a quarter of a century, here I have passed from a young to an old man. Here my children are born, and one is buried. I now leave, not knowing when, or if ever, I may return, with a task before me greater than that which rested upon Washington. Without the assistance of that Divine Being, who ever attended him, I cannot succeed. With that assistance, I cannot fail. I feel that I too have been given this great task to do lest we forget our personal freedoms, a task I did not willingly assume, but now acknowledged – I cannot put aside. As I grow only older and deeper in debt – I will pursue this case to victory, with malice toward none – and charity toward all.

My family and I are estranged and my heart gets heavy, but my convictions as to the merits of this case press me on. It seems to me that if a BRIEF is limited to forty type-written pages this would approximate eighty hand-lettered pages. However, if six pages are read carefully there should be no need for addendums. Each case has its own uniqueness and therefore I cite no case law.

Quoting from the Church Manual by Mary Baker Eddy, Section 23. 'If a member of this church has a patient whom he does not heal, and whose case he cannot fully diagnose, he may consult with an MD on the anatomy involved. And it shall be the privilege of a Christian Scientist to confer with an MD on Ontology, or the Science of Being.'

Page 484:6–9 of the Christian Science textbook: Science and Health with a Key to the Scriptures:

Question: Does Christian Science, or metaphysical healing, include medication, material hygiene, mesmerism, hypnotism, theosophy, or spiritualism?

Answer: Not one of them is included in it.

Page 468:25–1

Question: What is life?

Answer: Life is Divine Principle, Mind, Soul, Spirit. Life is without beginning and without end. Eternity, not time, expresses the thought of Life, and time is no part of eternity. One ceases in proportion as the other is recognized. Time is finite, eternity is forever.

The Court will note, that appellant repeatedly acknowledged her religion; read daily from her Bible and Christian Science textbook; and on one occasion signed a 'Consent to Medication' under threats and duress, which she later withdrew. This case is a flagrant disregard for the fundamental principles of liberty upon which this country was established – by the very presidents we pay homage to today.

Signed, Dolores Gimbels, Esquire

My mother's a wraith, a poet, a magician. She is as destructive as Shiva's consort Durga, riding her tiger, slashing with eight or ten arms, a potent force of nature sheaving houses into sticks. She's a big bad wolf with long and pointed ears, a curly-headed little lady who appears each day in bizarre costume wearing badges of her previous existence at the courthouse in Big Bend, asking the clerk to notarize her lawsuits. ('I'm Dolores Taylor Gimbels Ballistreri. Will you please file this?') She's becoming anorexic, her breath is the breath of the damned. Once she was a mother who cut up old ball gowns to turn her daughters into Miss America contestants, but that was long ago in a country I shall call Then. This new time is out of time, irreal time. *'Irreal times,' says a female Iranian professor in Tehran taking her lipstick off to go out on the street. 'I've coined this word because our lives here are so irreal. I'm going out, so I take my makeup off.' She scrubs her lips.*

This new time is hallucination and mist. A cloud from the real world, like those I have entered myself.

Heart tight. October 23, 1994. Tel Aviv. Dizengoff Street. Breathing normal. Afternoon show filing time: 6 hours. First report from now for Morning Edition: 45 min. How many dead? What sort of explosive, how much? Where is the bus? Stop, record ambulance siren. Record man, broken English, blood-spattered. 'I sit in café over there and the bus come and I listen to the bomb. People, help me help me help me the back door.' 'You pulled the victims out of the back door?' 'Yes. I look, no head no arms no feet. I have problem looking. You go Jerusalem, bomb; you go Tel Aviv, bomb; wherever you go in Israel, bomb. Bibi, Bibi over here! This corner! Hang on, I'll do English in a minute. Gotcha. I told Mr Rabin repeatedly, Gaza has to be closed, and cleared. Cleared, I say, if they can't be contained. This is the direct responsibility of Yassir Arafat and the Labor Government. Miss, you're how old? 23? From New York? Yes. I was there at 9 o'clock in the morning. I saw decapitated bodies. The police weren't there. It was disgusting. Organs on the ground. The body without an arm and without a head right outside my store. And now I don't know. This thing, this terrorism, it's coming to my own home, where I live, where I live. It's coming to where I live.'

Oh, but the end of safety comes to us all. Right to where we live. My dear, someone once said, security is superstition. The fearful are caught as often as the bold. And only faith defends.

They see her every day, dressed in bright colors like a parrot, head cocked as if on a perch. My mother haunts the courthouse. She has become the avatar of her own illness. Florid painted lips, an exotic bird with a ribby cage of vertebrae. 'File this, please,' she insists to the clerk, her smile as hot as the burner on a stove.

FEBRUARY 22, 1989
COURT OF APPEALS IN WISCONSIN
DISTRICT NO. 2, STATE OF WISCONSIN, DEPARTMENT
OF HEALTH AND SOCIAL SERVICES
PLAINTIFF V. DOLORES GIMBELS N/K/A TAYLOR,
DEFENDANT

George Washington (in absentia)

It was Shakespeare who wrote:
There is nothing either good or bad
But thinking makes it so.

At times this mask which is my face is cold and hard. There is no warmth beneath its surface. The blood that courses through my veins is icy yet I am not dead. I ask myself, why not?

Why not? Kate and Sarah and I shriek on receiving our copies of the brief. Why not? W/o/w, aka Mom, that'd sure be easier on US!

It is a logical question. I have sunk to the dregs of desolation on prescription drugs, court-ordered. It was February 1980. I was finally out of Menomenee County Mental Hospital where I turned 50, an occasion marked only by the cessation of the menstrual cycle, and I attempted to rationalize what had happened to me. Tears did not flow then as they do now. My body was devoid of emotion, my nerves were paralyzed and I struggled to move facial muscles. If I had one friend, it was a neighbor. My meager monies were spent on pills. Pills for what? Pills that desensitized the senses to feel no sensation. No love, no hate, no joy, no sorrow, no fear. Out of the hospital, back to loneliness and desperation, I found a job eventually but not before one more suicide try. It was a good attempt. I swallowed all the pills with a large glass of alcohol. My daughter found me.

Kate found her. I was on the phone from Chicago. At work on a story. I could tell she was blacking out, her voice was melting. Rubbery. Stretched. I left the line open, called the sheriff from another extension. Called Kate. Kept her talking until they got there. I remembered Kate, age fourteen. How Dolores rushed her to the hospital to have her stomach pumped. Kate swallowed pills, my mother says to the Doctor, her husband. She swallowed every pill in the house. He never looks up from his newspaper.

Nobody likes me, my mother is sobbing on the telephone. Nobody likes me at all. I like you, I say. No, I don't always like you. But I love you.

The spring days and nights for my mother wink together like the lit windows of a passing train. In some windows the faces of her children appear. In others, the faces of scoundrels. Then the light blurs to chiaroscuro glowing from a tunnel. No one is there but she, no one is ever there but she. Somewhere at the other end of that tunnel is Alfred. Somewhere at the other end of that tunnel is everything, a catenation linking it all together. She is the scribe and witness, the lone star. Missives arrive from her that could be battle tracts from the Middle Kingdom or the religious writs of fourteenth-century Cathars. I can't make sense of her scribblings, I don't know where things are going. I am a traveler in Sheba's desert. Like me, my mother records what she sees. Like me, she sees what is there and only might be. Unlike me, she reports both the conscious and the unconscious. She sees the bomber, his motive, his fingerprints on the briefcase and what will come afterward. She inhabits their brains, becomes as evil. I send her yet another pleading letter, detailing our efforts on her 'behalf' with the county. Three pages, single-spaced, one question: 'Will you go for help? Think of all you missed. We want you back. Will you get help?' But you cannot help someone who speaks only to God.

WEDNESDAY, APRIL 17, 1989
LAKE PUCKAWASAY
WISCONSIN

Dear Jacki,

I have just finished reading your epic, and I thank you tremendously for the compliments you all paid me! You chose your 'word' very well.

I thought (as I was lost in thought) that I heard someone say your article needed editing. Personally – I always feel that is the writer's responsibility, and I think you agree.

Let me thank you again for your companionship, and all the groceries. So many profound things are occurring and from reading your rather lengthy article – I immediately made an important decision.

Surely Krist Gudnason must mean Christ, God's son. The wonderment is to be accepted, never taken for granted.

Love,
Mother
Laus Deo!

Who the hell is Krist Gudnason? I say to Kate.

Don't know, she says.

Christ's gonads? says Sarah, on the phone from Denver. Leave it, for pete's sake.

My mother is above and below my consciousness. I want her soul, but Sheba has gotten there before me and seized it without ransom and made my mother her hostage. It is late spring, and every day the postman brings another tract from the World of Mania.

'Oh, you Wise Men of Learning,' my mother writes in another of her briefs against the county hospital. As always, I scour it for clues.

Last year as I again looked over the files and records in this case, all that I had gathered, I burned. Etched in my memory is everything I need to remember. Much I want to forget. In my sparse sixteen pages I have tried to convey my deepest feelings. I do not know if I have done that well. As a child, I learned and said my bedtime prayers, and I learned the prayers of some of my little friends, especially 'Now I lay me down to sleep.' These days I make my petitions to God early, and I would like to share a prayer that I have written with you. How do we know if enough has been written to prevent the erosion of our civil liberties? I have been so engrossed in the life, love, and faith of one woman. Bit by bit the erosion wears away the shoreline. Those entrusted with the care of loved ones must have some basic theology. Menomenee County Mental Hospital attendants, nurses, and physicians had none, else we would not be trying this case. I am reminded of President Kennedy's words in June 1963, when he said, 'One hundred years of delay have passed.' In the 100 years I have been waiting for this case to be resolved, I have learned much. I take no credit – you have all pushed me relentlessly. To kindly pass over a friend or a foe, to share if we can the truths that we know. I wish I could look back on my life and say I have no regrets, but can any one of us do that? My silent prayers run deep – too moving to be audible. My thoughts fly as swiftly as time itself and are often lost the same way. Often I must remind myself to listen, lest my thoughts stray, but for as many times as I falter I know I will try again.

At times I am a very quiet person, at other times a childlike humor overtakes me. I chastise myself, but the medical men say it is good, right, and necessary. I love to laugh!

When I become angry for a just reason, I know that this too is my right. As I try to learn from you men of learning, I cannot help but wonder how you separate the shaft from the grain. It has been my own observation that I am not very good at it. But there are dedicated men and women so empowered, and I am grateful for that. I do not feel you do it without Divine Assistance.

Take what you want from what I say, but take only the best and forget the rest.

Signed,
Dolores 'Mafia Godmother' Gimbels

Give it a rest, will you? Sarah says when I get her on the phone. I like to do interpretive readings of Dolores's material. I do it with Kate and Sarah all the time. It's either that or go mad myself, better to do this than some terrible thing, to walk into the street raving, so I sing out the damn violins and paint a few more hearts and flowers. Gotten anything from Mom recently? I ask the girls, and they say, Oh, I got a pair of yellow men's bikini briefs meant for Alfred, stamped 'from me' and sent to 'Commander in Chief,' U.S. Military, Alfred—, Washington D.C.' 'Hey, I got a letter signed Mafia Godmother.' 'I got a poem for the whole family,' I tell them, with rhymes so thick they're blobs of syrup. Want to hear it? No, Jack, no. Shut up. Most definitely not. *No.*

I declaimed in a lowered voice:

> Speak softly when you speak to me
> speak clearly I when I do not see
> Your point is best expressed this day
> You should not argue anyway
> religion dwells within the heart
> To argue, may a friend depart!
> – Jack, you're hurting me. Stop.
> – damn. Helen Steiner Rice!
> – Put it on a greeting card, make a mint.
> – Make a million dollars.

— Speak softly when you speak to me,
or I'll sue you for everything you've got,
— Kate, U. Bastard!

I scrounge through the traces, peel off the shallow words,
catalogue the quirkiest symbols and the most annoying acts. I
have a file marked 'Rage,' one marked 'Raving,' another folder
called 'Benign.' Her poetry is in the Benign file. I am looking
for the chemical elements of the basic equation of mania. I am
looking for the source of the blue Nile. What often matters most
is this: Even when deluded, my mother hits back. She hits back,
and back, and back. And I have to admire her, even if she is
hitting me. Because she had nothing to hit with, because she did
it herself, with will, and will only. And a will not always her own.
'What will I pay you for your humiliation, Mr Administrator?' she
had written. 'Held in a jail cell? Handcuffed behind my back? A
drain for a toilet? Not one dime. Not one penny.' And indeed
she was right. Though she had been ill and our interventions
had saved her life, they were never something that she could feel
grateful for, nor accept or face with dignity. And she was willing
to sacrifice everything in her 'real' world to right the injustice of
her unreal one. To repudiate the unconscious world, she worked
like a dog, double shifts in the real world, selling the veal schnitzel
special or junior miss separates or spa diets or rooms with bath or
without bath, ankles puffing up over her shoes by day's end, all
to say, 'I was never sick, never crazy.' People have built temples
with less will. They have invaded other countries with the same
amount. The hospital administrator submitting testimony to the
Wisconsin Court of Appeals wrote of her 1980 commitment,
when the sheriff and stout matron had dragged her to court,

I am assuming here that she was brought in handcuffed
to our psychiatric unit. It is secure and locked. If the

patient willingly takes prescribed medication, a regimen is established. However, some, like Mrs Gimbels, resist medication until adjudication. She insisted she did not belong here and attempted to escape. In the process of returning her to the unit, the record reveals she threw a chair and turned over a table. To contain her, two male aides and a nurse were required. She was placed in seclusion. The seclusion room has only a mattress and no other amenities. Staff must accompany the patient out of seclusion to the bathroom when that is necessary. Eliminating on the floor is often a tactic a patient may use to express their displeasure at being in seclusion. Use of a bedpan or urinal is offered to patients while in seclusion. However, their co-operation in the use of it is necessary. The record does not contain information as to whether Mrs Gimbels did or did not use a bedpan. Adverse behavior such as urinating on the floor is generally charted.

I'd say 'piss on you' were it I. If I were the Queen of Sheba. If I had dandelion seeds stuck between my teeth, remembering that mist in the Wisconsin morning off Lake Puckawasay which hung like the veils of time itself outside my back door. I'd wear those veils like armor if they were all I had for raiment.

When Sheba claimed her, my mother devolved and decompensated. That is to say, she went plain stark, raving nuts. The past rose up for my mother like an invasion of sea monsters. Her thoughts turned ugly, her thoughts snaked fiercely alive and entwined her like a bound woman. Yet she wrote, she wrote all the time, day and night, and never slept except to fall in and out of blind trances. She wrote as if to say, If I get it down, if I leave a record of this life that is not life, of this siren song that sweeps me away, then perhaps my account will leave a trail to that subterranean cavern below. In the spring of 1988 when we couldn't be with her, we waited with dread for my mother to commit a murderous act. The sun came up and the sun went down on Dolores, alone and writing in her bungalow, totally mad. She called her writings, which I found later, 'The Evil Account.' She intended to file her account in court and chronicle the perfidies of her enemies before the judges, or, as she called them, the Wise Men of Learning. Her account was her guide and her companion, her Boswell. The house next door where her neighbor lived became The House Where He Cut Out His Child's Tongue and Ate It. Her ex-boy-friend colluded with her ex-husband in the Den of Iniquity inhabited by Opium Teachers. Her handwriting in 'The Evil Account' was an organic sporing, alive with what was wild, like something grown overnight after a heavy rain.

THE EVIL ACCOUNT

'Doc' came to see me regularly at Wagner's in 1966 and disagreed with the treatment program. Whenever they questioned me, he remained in the room. I never saw my doctor alone. I was feeling stronger and more lucid and asked Doc what he disagreed with – no answer. His expression was always sneering but one time he had a half smile and a big chrysanthemum he said was from his 'mother.' Could not have been true. Rather it was a pink and blue suggestion for the supposed pregnancy that never happened again for him. Dr Monster.

Last Saturday, April 22, Evil – my ex-husband and Slut – my ex-boyfriend, as they referred to themselves, told me they shot 'zingers' at me all over. I didn't know what that meant, I stupidly thought they meant a complimentary glance. They kept asking if I was tired and I said 'no.' Evil said, 'You should be, we shot you with as much as we use on a horse.'

I said, 'What?' He said, 'You are the evil one, Dolores, because you won't die. OK. We have to do it anyway.' I said, 'What?' Slut said, 'Search this place fast while Evil's new wife is down.' I feigned fatigue and followed them up to my bedroom and I said I would take a nap. Slut and Evil said, 'She's out like a light,' but I could hear them talking and searching my house. They didn't move anything but photographed my clothes, makeup, and hair combs. I heard Evil recording to someone on his Dictaphone he called 'Chief Indian' and said, 'This is where we should start. The KGB.' I moved in my bed so the zingers couldn't quite get me. He told Kate to 'stuff' what he had and Kate went into my bathroom. Evil took the poems he had written for me and ate the paper. He said, 'I can't hit her, Slut – you get her. The darts leave little marks and sores – some have vermin as the animals throwing the darts. They said they loaded my cat. They said I wouldn't be around long enough to remember. They would send someone else to finish me. SOMEONE does enter and leaves signs, daily, some signs are sent in by my grandchildren. I have been told I have 'no friends' and I do not know who to confide in. There is another plague judge, lawyers, all my doctors and clergy that seem to belong to the 'Club of Friends.' They seemed to have things stuffed in their clothes. Some of mine are missing. They referred to HER as a 'guy,' a 'gay old guy' and the Big Chief was waiting in the car. They were going to a 'stuffing party.' They said I had enough zingers so they could question me and asked where I kept my records. I told them! They know I know the names of their club members and I am 'marked.'

5:00 A.M. Read Adam and the Fallen Man! Good News Day! Alpha and Omega. Bank / Post Office / Shower (done)/ Self the beginning and the end.

Organize. Trash Out Day. Call the family!

> Jacki (done) 5:10 A.M.
> Kate
> Sarah

To finish the evil account. I state only that I found the cross and crown pin I knew to be mine — in Raymond L. ——— (my father's) dresser drawer, by snooping for it! Also in the drawer were pictures of mortals having sex with various animals in stone. The pin leads the Holy Purpose. It is for HIM. Amen, Alfred. After bearing the cross, ye receive the crown, and it is a light to the gentiles and all who love for: God is love. Write no more of the evil account. Go and tell others that I, God, am angry. Some have heard you and fear. But you Dolores are one of the chosen, you have nothing to fear, you are a writer. You are the Seventh Angel.

I am a writer who has nothing to fear. We are sitting at the Al Qadisseyah parade grounds in Baghdad, November 1990, a little jaded at the passing military parade. I have seen Saddam Hussein's megalomania in his architecture – the dun stone swords held aloft by crossed forearms said to be modeled on Saddam's, the sickeningly endless rows of Iranian helmets collected from dead fighters, now used as speed bumps on the road to the Tomb of the Unknown Soldier. I am at Saddam's parade, where a troupe of beleaguered Kurds, exploited by Saddam, dance in vivid color below the reviewing stand with a lambskin standard allegedly painted with their own blood. '*Bel rooh bel dam nifdeek ya Saddam, bel rooh bel dam nifdeek ya Saddam,*' they chant, pounding each syllable like a drum. 'In our blood and spirit we sacrifice our lives for Saddam, and the lives of our children's children for Saddam,' the sign translates. That was true, in more ways than one and almost surely not of their own choice. Amir, one of the translators and minders assigned by the Ministry of Information, tells me the blood is real. But I wonder. Amir is a pudgy marshmallow of a fellow who insists he holds a black belt in karate. Later, we are dancing in the black cave of a disco at the Sheraton Hotel with my friend Susan, who works for *Newsday*. She has already scored great rugs in the *souq* and has had intense conversations with her minder, Hassan, who is a student of existentialism. Susan and I are the only women gyrating. All the other guests at the disco are men who hulk together beyond the dance floor, smoldering in the shadow like lumps of coal. Susan and I tease each other with the titillation that Saddam's son Uday might show up, deliver himself of his pistol, and blow a few people away. Definitely it's happened, she claims, here at this very disco. An argument over a woman. A pistol shot could give us some news.

Sheba is here, I can sense it. At night in this realm I hear the drumbeats of dread, Saddam's drink-your-blood style threats, and reveille music as the Iraqi flag is hoisted on TV. I'm listening to the news. Amir translates. '*Sawfa n'hawil Kuwait ila hammaam m'n al dam, sawfa naja'l taboor altwaabeet yamtad m'n al Kuwait ila washinton, laatoon biakfanhim ma'hom.*' 'We will turn Kuwait into a bloodbath, we will let the line of coffins extend from Kuwait to Washington. Let each soldier bring with him his own body bag.' At the Al Rashid, the hotel's business cards boast: 'More than just a hotel.' How much more? We assume our phones are bugged, which makes me feel at home, as it is one of my mother's peculiar fantasies when she is sick that everything in the house is bugged. Amir says that in better times he was a sports journalist who covered international soccer matches for Baghdad. He went to Romania! To Poland! But now he's a jelly doughnut of a baby-sitter, glumly stuck on the minder beat with gawking journalists like me. One night he comes to my room at the Al Rashid with an open bottle of Scotch, a drop of it hanging from his mustache.

'Will you marry me?' he says half jokingly. He leans forward on the balls of his feet, as if peering out over a ledge. 'I want to get out of here.' He is not joking. Outside my room is a parking lot where the Shortat al-Najda riot police line up to drill each morning. It's no accident that they drill where we journalists can see them, raising dervishes of dust. No accident that the world's gone crazy, and real craziness is no crazier than this. I think of all the people who want to get out of there, who don't want to live in the presence of craziness. Five little words. *Get me out of here. Tal'eeni m'n hal jaheem.* Get me out of hell, the people I meet plead. I wrote those words in 'My Famous Book,' but I didn't call it hell. I called it home, just as they do. Amir is not getting out, either. I listen to the megalomaniac telling his Evil Account. I put on a dress and interview the British hostages, driving with them as far as the edge of a city, where, on pain of death, they remain inside the boundaries of the lunatic. We're in it together. I sit in their darkened parked cars, listening to John Coltrane on a tape player with the lights of Baghdad behind us, staring at the destiny out beyond the city's periphery.

'Good thoughts are an impervious armor,' my mother wrote, quoting Mary Baker Eddy in her 'Evil Account.' 'Clad therewith you are completely shielded from the attacks of error of every sort. And not only yourselves are safe but all whom your thoughts rest upon are thereby benefited.'

What if the opposite is true, I thought, reading her pages. What if you wished harm on someone and just by wishing it you could make it happen? Surely your thought would in some karmic way be the agent of your own destruction.

'Evil and Slut,' my mother wrote,

implicated Kate in parties and blowouts, they would get blown up with air in the garages, I found the tire pumps, and then blown out at parties exhibiting hatred and hostility by my neighbors to the South. Did Kate have a tripod machine gun aimed at me? Sarah had a Magnum, Jacki's finger stirred the wine and my doctor slipped her an extra vial of cyanide. There was a Red Circle Inn, a pool of blood on the burial grounds. Evil gave her pills and injections and the 'final shot' as he called it. Later the man remarried a woman who 'turned' into a man. They were pursuing me and then I was pursuing them. They kept changing places; I couldn't tell which sex they were. They said it was germ warfare. I said 'What?' He said, 'You know what that is Dolores, don't you?' 'Of course,' I said, 'but how does that fit into conversation?' 'Well, you know, just suppose someone came in here and released millions of germs and vermin, that would be germ warfare, right?' I was covered with zillions of little bumps all over, as he went on to say there was a black widow spider in the room but instead he got the spider bites and we all watched as he got smaller and smaller and horns grew where he had been standing.

Once I phoned my fiancé in New York from Cairo, the magazine editor who'd been present when my mother had last become ill. I had seen him in Egypt only the week before but wanted to say hello. It was the Sunday after Thanksgiving. The sweat was pouring off me. I'd just spent hours at a Cairo police station talking my way out of my third detention in as many days, explaining why I was talking to clamoring, rag-wrapped workers whose brethren were coming home from Iraq as stiff as sticks rattling in pine boxes. I talked until I got back my tape and tape recorder. President Bush was in Cairo, alliances were being formed, proclamations were being made. I was supposed to file, I needed a quick break. I phoned New York. A woman's voice answered. A voice I knew. It was ten A.M. on a Sunday at the fanciest hotel in Manhattan. You got the wrong room, he

insisted for days, but I didn't have the wrong room and he knew I
knew it. You're crazy, he said. The front desk told me I wasn't in
pointed tones of look-lady-we-can't-come-out-with-it-but-who-
you-gonna-believe-him-or-your-own-ears? I felt that I loved evil,
loved nothing but illusion and never would. I felt stunned and as
thick as a flightless bird wandering the Nile mud. Like my mother
when she is being swept away into insanity, betrayed by the loss
of power. The world as we know it shuts down as lights wink off,
one by one, the world waits, a loss of power you can almost feel
draining from the very pores of your skin. Waiting for missiles.
That's when Sheba comes.

After I hung up, I sat carefully on the bed and counted how
many nubby dots were in one square inch of the material: 168.
Four hours to file. I called the foreign editor and said I couldn't
do it. They said I could, I must, we know, we've been there, just
do it and fall apart later. I listened to my own breath exhale and
inhale, making the sound of human life, mingling with the car
horns and urine-scented dust and cardamom and sweat and fear
and gas exhaust and the crying in the streets over lottery tickets
and the knowledge that the Sphinx and the pyramids were out
there in the shrouded distance. Flesh glimmered in my brain
and there was a woman bound in bedsheets. Crush a dream to
see what's inside of it, grind it down to its various silicates and
trample it under the feet of all who've passed through your life.
Call it crazy. Without destruction, who is moved to act? Without
destruction, who is moved to conquer?

'President Bush,' I spoke into my tape recorder, 'said today
that Egypt . . . and Syria . . . and Jordan . . . stand against . . .'
and then I stopped to think of the point of all this and what it
had to do with my life. I'm sure I looked as though I was trying
to find the point all that afternoon. The call of the muezzin
said, This is another world, one hallowed five times a day in
incomprehensible sentences. I wrote and spoke my story and cut

my tape and made my deadline, but of course what I wrote was an illusion.

THE EVIL ACCOUNT CONTINUES

I want this continued harassment stopped. Elvin D, my neighbor, is a weak, wimpy ex-serviceman who always seems to do his wife's bidding. They both love driving stakes into my heart. Evil told me they both 'blow up' in the garage. I didn't know what that meant until I found 4–5 tire pumps etc. Elvin was trained to use the submachine guns for the arsenal. My other neighbor could use all the artillery and practiced martial arts. My house is between them. On April 30th, Elvin trained a submachine gun on my dinner table where I was getting ready for a party. I saw it and I saw him move. I moved first, right out of his range.

In the acid-yellow heat of August 1991 in Baghdad, the war is over, a memory dipped in the very real blood of those who'd been betrayed by the Americans. 'You left us with this butcher,' says a doctor at Mostashfa al-Kadhmiyaa Hospital, holding up what looks like a bound cat in swaddling but is, in fact, a dead baby. At Najaf in the shrines of Ali and Karbala, in the shrines of Hussein and Abbas, there are still bloodstains where the avenging Shiites were murdered after their U.S.-encouraged uprising. The holy shrines were where they took shelter from Saddam's bombs, where they were drawn and quartered and hung in the *bab al sahan*, the courtyards of the shrines. The *bab al sahan* ran with their blood, were littered with their smashed bodies. 'We don't know how many dead are there,' the soldiers tell the translators who tell us. 'They are dogs, not people.' The dead clogged the streets. At Basra we watch while the Tikriti governor, Latif Mahal, having murdered his dissident predecessor, places a feast of *quzi* lamb before us and talks of the coming famine, which Iraq's own government will ensure. The governor is dressed in military fatigues, striped shirt, a pistol on his hip. His eight-year-old son is dressed in exactly the same khakis and stripes and pistol. The governor claps his hands and his platter of half-eaten food, his *qus'a*, is removed to the floor. He claps again. His soldiers dive like dogs for the *qus'a*. You didn't come for us, the voices say. We were waiting. We took up arms, swords and pistols, and we died ungodly deaths, butchered stiff and grotesque in the iron-colored dust. You stood by and watched and never came. Can'tcha come up, Jack, can'tcha come up? *T'gder tji h'na, Amrika, t'gder tji h'na?*

One day to my driver, Quasm, I say, 'Let's play tempt-the-odds. Don't know when I'll be in El-Iraq in the near future. Going home to get married, so I believe. I want to photograph all the illegal things, all the statues of Saddam and the paintings of him, from resolute marsh Arab to resolute Kurdish mountaineer to resolute businessman in Italian suit to field marshal attire. God is everywhere, brother, and he sees what we are doing. And the phony family tree at the Saddam Art Gallery with Nebuchadnezzar at the head and Saddam his descendant and all the bridges and statues and bombed facilities. I want to break every rule. If they stop me, you tell them I'm the Queen of Sheba!'

Quasm laughs. He thinks I'm out of my mind. *Majnun*, crazy. He says it all the time. You're *majnun, sahafiya*. 'The Queen of Sheba! Yes, sir! Whatever you want, sir!'

And so we go. Another journalist, Walter, new here for one of the wires, says he wants to come along for he too is leaving Baghdad after this, his maiden voyage. I photograph the Standing Battle of a Million Men, the M'arakat al-Milyoon, where the statue of Saddam has his finger pointed toward the poisoned marshes of the Shatt-al-Arab waterway. Defeating the Iranians. The human waves, the mustard gas used by the Iraqis in the war.

I snap the camera openly, snap away. For Quasm it is an afternoon of adventure and mild hectoring, small bribes to each guard at each site. 'If the Americans can take pictures of us from the sky, brother, then what do we care if this schoolteacher snaps her photos?' he jokes in Arabic, referring to me. I am photographing the Fourteenth of July Bridge, the major Baghdad bridge named for the Ba'ath revolution, bombed early in the war. It is strictly off-limits and I know it; there's a military installation on the other side. When I see the Republican Guard coming I walk slowly back to the car. Never hurry. The Republican Guard. You can tell them by the red triangles on their olive drab. They're not stupid, not from the provinces. They went to school. One of my colleagues interviewed one of their victims in an internment camp, a man who tattooed his own name on his arm so his family could identify him after death. Quasm smiles nervously, but Walter melts down in the front seat of the car. I slide like a lady without a care in the world into the rear seat of the car, as if we're at Saks Fifth Avenue. There may be trouble. There may not be. 'Stay cool,' I say to Walter.

'*E'teeni 'l kaamira,*' says the guard, outside the window as his partner unslings his rifle, points it at the car, but lazily.

'*A'ilati,*' I say. '*Suwar 'a a'ilati.*' I make it clear that these are pictures of my family, and clutch the camera to my chest.

Quasm is silent. The guard is pointing a rifle at him, ordering him out of the car. It is he, as I well know, who will suffer the most.

'*Atfaali,*' I say, as the soldier gestures again for the film, all but stuffing it down my shirt. I've learned a little Arabic, just enough to get by. 'My children.' He looks like a bored brooder. I can't tell how it'll go, it doesn't seem that urgent. Quasm is smiling as if he's been doing it since the day he was born.

A scream unwinds like a curl of paper in a party blower. 'Aaaaaaaaaaaaah! Give him the goddamn film! Give him the goddamn film!' It's Walter, twisting around in the front seat, waggling with fear, and the guard and Quasm and I are all mesmerized by the fact that he's losing it. The hot car is dirty and stuffy. Walter's rage packs us in tight. His meltdown is more dangerous than anything, and I'm suddenly anxious, but my hands are moving. I am rewinding film as surreptitiously as I can in the back seat under my long skirt, thinking Walter's tantrum is a perfect cover, but rather risky. Maybe he's trying to help me. The attention's on him. But Walter reaches back and grabs my arm and tears the camera from my hand, knocking open the back and partly exposing the film as I try to bang the light guard shut. We exchange looks of malevolence as he waves the camera over my head and gives it triumphantly to the astonished guard.

The Republican Guard looks at me, then looks at Walter. He looks at Quasm, who is giving him the smile of a man stuck on a skewer. The guard's face isn't bored anymore, it is alive and complex, frittering with animation. He holds up the camera to the light and squints at us all again. I sputter with little jets of womanly indignation. 'My family, *a'ilati*,' I say again, thumping the air dramatically, impossibly ridiculous. 'My little daughter. *Binti el sagheera.*' The guard knows perfectly well that I'm a journalist and have about as many children as a nun. He knows perfectly well that I know that the Fourteenth of July Bridge is off-limits because everyone in Baghdad knows there's a military installation right behind it. Every journalist in Baghdad knows that the Iraqis hanged a guy who worked for the London *Observer*. They said he was a spy, but that guy was born in Iran. Well, just don't fool around. But we all fool around. The guard looks dead at Walter. He lifts his chin as if a speck of paper were stuck on his Adam's apple, he brushes his hand under his arched throat and simultaneously clicks his tongue against his teeth. The *a'fta*, the ultimate Arab gesture of disdain. The guard palms the camera back to me as though there might be something hot inside it.

In Arabic he says, '*Mo zawjha*,' 'He's not her husband, is he?' waving us on. I see him shrug his shoulders. Quasm crawls back into the car offering the guard necessary sycophantic apologies, practically embroidering them into the man's chest. Black silence from Walter in the front seat.

'Thanks, man,' I say. 'Without you, he probably would have kept the friggin' camera and all my film.'

'You're crazy,' he says.

'But I'm not gutless,' I say.

'*Majnun*,' says Quasm, whose safety I've risked. In his case I feel like a jerk. He will have to go in and make a report.

'You didn't tell him I was the Queen of Sheba,' I say to Quasm.

'*Malikat Sab'a, Balqees!*'

Later in Jordan when I developed the film, the partially exposed pictures had starbursts in them, phantoms in acetate, dappled as if with missile lights.

MAY 2, 1988

1:30 A.M.

LAKE PUCKAWASAY, WISCONSIN

Dear Judge MacGill:

I have reviewed my sworn testimony given yesterday and reiterate its truth – even as I go on, being interrupted only by my husband's phone call and my own safe return from serving our government. In which case, I know that may again be temporary, for I could not keep His Light from shining throughout the world. I have traveled through so many lands and spoken in so many voices.

Today, being my own Good News day, I will also remember the death of my mother, Mabel, who died on this day several years ago. As I wrote a former attorney of mine on

Good Friday, 'Only one time in my life did anyone earnestly tell me they were proud of me.' Today it brought a tear and a smile. That woman was my mother, a tormented woman. She was holding my arm as I took her to the wake of my father, a mafioso gentleman named Frank, and it was slippery and I slipped a little on the ice myself and she clutched my arm to keep me from falling, and said, 'Oh, Dolores, I am so proud of you.'

I was bewildered, of course, and thought she meant because I didn't fall on my ass in those high heels. So I said, 'Why?' Her reply was 'Just because of what you are!'

That compliment I give back to as many as have heard the Good News through Alfred, but especially to Him, and him, and all of you.

Love,
Dolores Gimbels

3:30 A.M.

This is the Second Day of May, for you Dolores have heard my Word and listened as I have warned, but the false ones, the Doctor and the—, have heard Me not and there is much to fear.

Wipe out the face of evil on the earth. I saw you tremble last night in fear. I am talking to you. Are you listening to me or goofing around out there? Fear is the beginning of knowledge. Change no mistake on this page. Save all the others for future generations. This is the New Testament of Truth in which good overcomes Evil. Rise early and avenge me on the scum of the earth.

You may also make some disparaging remarks about the Kangaroo Court.

Dolores Gimbels. Time, 5:30 A.M.

THE QUEEN OF SHEBA

SHEBA, ALONE in her bungalow, rises and hovers, flits through the past. Dolores is some stupid post, like a cenotaph. Sheba hates her. Sheba gathers each memory, the good ones, the persecutory, and constructs for herself her Book of the Dead. She draws the faces, gets it down on the page. Utters the speech, looks down on the testaments of the world spread out before her. There are blood signs on the pages that only she can see. There are maps and dioramas – an evil eye, an ant's progress of buried wonders. She dresses with her unguents and lotions, her perfumes and diamonds and rubies (some might call them old buttons). She adjusts the queenly tiara around her head (some might call it an old belt) and flattens herself against the wall to see if she can make herself into a shadow. Yes, the answer is that she can. Others have died in this house – the woman Mabel, the fisherman Louie, the Good Samaritan Eddie James Guenther, and Mrs Dolores Milquetoast. You may know her by several names, she was rather bovine, actually. Numerous animals have been slaughtered here; people who were meek and stood around waiting to inherit the earth. They got screwed instead. Sheba is as powerful and distant as the moon, and like a lunar entity she waxes and wanes. She can make herself as solid as fire-breathing Chimera in a nightmare or she can dissolve to translucence, growing so large that she *is* the light that Distorts other people's Eyes and Blinds them to the Truth.

Sheba gets in her car and drives to the – hospital and clinic in Menomenee. She passes Wagner's Hospice. She knew someone once who was dragged off there, a poorly understood young woman with a keen intelligence and several lovely children, shackled to an ogre who had dressed in the garments of a king. She enters the hospital, smells the vestigial ether, remembers that one of her daughters was born there, and asks for him by name. He comes out to meet her, so tall and white and changing shape all the time. Wouldn't you just know you couldn't even trust him to hold still, retain the same shape while she did what she had to do. Sheba would do what she had to do to this white demon thing that would *not listen*.

'There,' she cries. 'Take that, and that!'

In each hand she poises a piece of soft red chalk, a candlesized knob that children use to draw hopscotch squares. She drives the pieces into her ex-husband's white smock, right in front of the nurses and all the patients, crying, 'There!' and 'There!' and streaking his smock with long drools, like rusty blood veins in a piece of polished sandstone. It's her revenge. She has made the mark of an incision before the surgeon decides where to cut. 'I could have killed you,' Sheba cries to her ex-husband the Doctor, 'but I, God, have let you live so you can repent.' There he stands in the fatal world, his belly as large as the curve of a pregnant woman, marked over with red chalk. See how he likes it. Conception and delivery. Sheba glides like a shadow from the hospital and speeds her car through the S curves, sticks her tongue out at the flakes of the past, at Wagner's, at the great blue heron that shadows her onward, trumpeter for the regiments who will swell to her side.

In half an hour, she's at the Menomenee County Courthouse, where she is seated in court, as quiet as a communicant of the old school. She wears nothing on her head now but her invisible

Divine Light, the Light of Truth. There is Judge MacGill, her persecutor, her jailer. His corrupt law steals her money and houses and lands and gives them over to the hands of her enemies and locks her in the dungeon with a little drain for her bodily fluids. How would he like it, all that persecution and humiliation. Sheba is so full of thought, so powerful with it that she is weighted down as if by gold bullion bricks, measurable physical matter, all but immobilizing her. She sits so still that it might appear as if she's thinking of nothing at all, but really she is chuckling to herself, making her pact with God. She the Chosen, She the Anointed who has come to Save the World.

From deep in his chamber, Judge MacGill stands and eddies in his black robes, surging into the Menomenee County courtroom at Waupaca. The court reporter stares up at him through her thick glasses. The child's glasses should be removed, they're really too thick, Sheba has written of this somewhere. There is a hum in the courtroom, in each window the refracting midmorning light neatly cleaving the scene into little rectangles of faith as innocent as bars of soap lined up in a box. Everyone is respectful, everyone is orderly. You'd think you were in church.

Judge MacGill's bailiff turns to the courtroom. 'Would you all rise and face the bench?' he asks in the standard drone. Sheba stands and points an invisible zinger at him with her finger. *'What's the matter, do you all have an erection for Judge MacGill?'* she roars at all the sheep.

She rifles her accoutrements from her bag, a larger one than she usually carries. *'This is what we do to bad little boys,'* she cries, arms aloft like winged victory, brandishing a small paring knife and a cutting board. 'Come here and let me cut off your curlicue!!!'

Judge MacGill's face is as still as a fat humid morning before the rain. He could be remembering a worm he saw crawling on his tomato vine last night, or the carton of milk that his wife asked him to bring home from work that evening. He could not be where he is, in fact he must be anyplace but here, where the scene before him leaves him in wondrous suspense, touching infinity like a diver on a high platform. There is the powerful smell of her orchid perfume.

'Hey, buster, are you listening to me?' Sheba roars below his pulpit. She waves the knife like a conductor waving his baton. The people in the courtroom, the sheep, back away from her. Baaaa! to them too. Suddenly she drops her knife to the floor, whirls to the bench, snatches up the judge's brass nameplate, the one that tells him and the whole world exactly who is presiding over this kangaroo court. Sheba brandishes the nameplate over her shoulder like a flaming sword in a painting of Judgment Day and whops Judge MacGill straight on the head with his own damn name. See if he likes it, can remember who he is, the humiliation. It all happens somehow in the cusp of an instant. A shutter snapping, more quickly than the bailiff, half slumbering at the back of the room, really knows. But now he has her, has surrounded my mother in a half nelson and wrestles her to the floor.

She spits a Certs that she has under her tongue straight into the bailiff's face. She will not be dallied with. 'I will have *you* arrested,' she says. 'I am making a citizen's arrest right this very minute! All of you!'

And then it's over. Everyone who's been stock-still is moving, fluent in anxiety, feet pummeling by above her head. She remembers when they lived in a basement, she can still see the feet. Sheba raises up her wrists from where she lies on the floor reaching for the manacles, knowing that whatever they do to her now, they'll never think of her as powerless again.

Sheba in the bin, Sheba on the dock. The parable of the Queen of Sheba, come to conquer. This time I felt that after twenty-five years, perhaps I had her, that I was prepared. She could not escape us, but neither would we mistreat her. They led her off to the county hospital, but there were no restraints beyond hand-cuffs, no straitjacket, no closed observation doors with a slot for a meal tray. The county acted with patience and caution, probably because after two years of litigation at obvious cost to herself, my mother's was not a routine case. And I think the passage of time had engendered more progressive methods, gave at least encouragement to a minimum of restraint with the mentally ill. The social worker promised me that they'd treat her as delicately as possible. She hadn't hurt Judge MacGill, other than whacking him one in his dignity. Later he would tell me, a gentle man with forbearance, 'Your mother had an amazing ability to write extraordinary legal briefs, even when she was clearly very sick, and I came to admire her spunk and fight. Of course, I never expected her to attack me in my own courtroom, but she was one of my most interesting cases and I had empathy for her.'

On the locked ward, Sheba sits waiting. Forty-eight hours until her commitment hearing. Avenged. Her notebook is open.

I, the Lord Your God, am a jealous God and ye shall have no other Gods before me. THANK YOU FOR LISTENING. Glenn the psych aide is tearing out my pages as fast as I can write them. Menomenee Hospital says Dolores's suicide records read: she was a patient of Dr ———. Wrong! D, wrong, alcohol? I'm not sure. Many discrepancies. Someone is stealing my jewels. Dolores insisted on some furniture for herself and the children as she had owned home and furniture at time of marriage. Was Koehn, my former boyfriend, a Russian spy? Cain, you killed your brother. Cane, Kane, Cain. He worked for the KGB. Take vitamin E oil. It will keep your skin looking young and supple. Whisper something sweet in a loved one's ear. Hold hands. If you don't smoke your pipe, and just wear it in your mouth, it's like jewelry!

In Marcia the social worker's opinion, the courtroom spectacle was 'for the best. I think this is a cry for help. She could have really hurt someone in there, but she used her imagination.' Yes, I said on the phone, it's for the best, thinking of all the 1,001 near misses, the interstices of threat and suspension of threat. A relief to think only of the physical world in connection with Dolores, flooded with her stacks of bills and threatened legal actions, which I'd started to photocopy and keep at the office. The night before her court hearing I drove home to Menomenee, and the next day Kate and I sat while yet another judge, not MacGill, questioned my mother. Her language by then was unbroken surf, ladyfinger waves, captured only when she wrote things down, and it was clear to me why she wasn't talking much at the hospital: she couldn't answer the questions. She'd lost the sequences of speech. Whole paragraphs of her thought dissolved into a hypnotic and unrepeatable riff of babble, labials and hisses and murmuring diphthongs, quite untranslatable. As if the Queen of Sheba, cornered, had come rushing out in dreamspeak not understood by real-world people. Real-world people can't hear the timbrels and glockenspiels that the Shebas of our moment dream into our existence. Sheba braves reality with nothing more than blobs of paint and whole vaults of imagination, and, when her dream world turns dark and full of rage, we await her reality with our own speechlessness. It's the same in war zones, where you wait for the irrational to reign, to invade.

My mother's head bobbed up and down as she sat at her hearing, her eyes seamed shut, her chin tilted toward the ceiling. When she did open her eyes, she had trouble fixing on the human beings in the room before her. 'Ohzenor rata bizza hum,' my mother spoke under her breath, as her eyes closed. 'Brew ola, ta deum orso,' clacked her laughing tongue. Her smile screwed itself so tightly to her face that it reminded me of the grins of petrified heads. Even her hair seemed rusty, not her own. And as I have been before in her presence, I am oddly admiring and drawn to her. There is no denying that I am absurdly proud. She is so ill, so gone, so bravely lunatic and indefatigable. And I wonder, will we ever get her back, back from that Wide Sargasso Sea in which she swam and sailed and drifted beyond the realm of mortal thought?

You may recall the fairy tale of Elsa and the swans. Elsa wove the jackets of stinging nettles for her six brothers, young men whom an evil sorceress had turned into swans. She wove the jackets at night in secret, her hands bleeding, not bending from her task. Transformative jackets she made after her day's labor when she thought no one was looking, and her stepmother the sorceress chided her for her raw hands, never knowing that Elsa was weaving the jackets of her undoing. Elsa had seven years to reverse the spell before the enchantment became permanent, and during that time her brothers the swans circled the earth. They saw much human vagary. They saw humanity's lusts and betrayals, its wars and famines, and also the sweet defining moments of tranquillity and victory. As men, they had no power to travel the earth with omniscience, but as swans, the sky was their orbit. When Elsa finally threw the jackets over them, rimpling all but the arm of the sixth brother back to manhood, their journey was complete.

I think of their journey as a parallel world, like the trajectory of my mother's mental illness. To turn Sheba back into Dolores, to turn a swan back into a human being, my sisters and I had to make an invisible net without her knowing it. Call it a strait-jacket, the fabric of our reality. Some of its strands were our stories, the mundane family ones that filled in human memory, and other strands were the spinning narratives of testimony on behalf of the insane, the jokes we told one another and tales remembered back to my mother even when she couldn't understand our language. I would put into this tightly woven fabric the things we told the judge in court, our testimonies of her previous life in the real world. Instead of nettles that stung our hands, we had lithium. Dolores had never been given lithium. Lithium is the stinging nettle of our modern reality, the sorcerer's brewing green liquid that banishes evil spells. My mother doesn't especially like taking lithium – she sometimes complains that it makes her left hand tremble – but she takes it, every day, three times a day.

Her transformation back to reality was as gradual as the lengthening of the late spring days and as I imagine the swan's return to human form would be. First you recognized a shape – an arm, belonging to the general universe of human limbs, then a hand, your own hand in the particular. Then fingers, and fingernails with half-moons surfacing beneath them. As Elsa's brothers returned to human form, the days passed, yours to name and know, and you would once again understand the concept of tomorrow. Yet as you looked at your hands and thought of your days, you would remember that you had once lived in realms that other humans could never imagine, that you had had for a time an inhuman body. You had been inhabited. You would see the feathers beneath your fingernails or at least imagine them there in that white delicate trace of half-moon like a broken wafer. You would see that you had had wings that once made silhouettes against the moon.

When my mother was committed after attacking Judge MacGill, I would visit her at the Menomenee County Hospital and we'd walk. We'd walk over the broad green lawns and see where the violets were stabbing into the aprons below the oak trees. We'd see where the grass was the deepest, truest shade of emerald. At first my mother always gazed into the distance and often pointed to the horizon. 'See that big black dog out there with a duck in its mouth?' she might say. But there would be no big black dog with a duck in its mouth. Nor did I ever see the stranger she was sure was following behind us. I never saw the invisible tent in which men with secret zinger pistols fanned poison darts at us as we walked into the shadows of the early summer twilight. The staff, this time, did not appear to be literally wrestling her into submission, nor was there any such need. She did not attack them, grabbing tables, chairs, anything sharp. She took her medication, went to group therapy, and when she had an 'evil' thought, she'd write it down in her notebook, her palimpsest, as my mother tried to edit out the winged and astonishing parts of her speech, those that struck their own rhythms, rushed ahead in her mouth, squawking and honking in place of her own voice. The people who'd figured so mightily in her fantasies began to reassemble into normal color, size, shape, and human dimensions. The Judge. The Lawyer. The Neighbor. The former boyfriend. The ex-husband. Her daughters. Alfred – she was embarrassed to death over her fantasies about that man and sent a note via the sheriff apologizing. But when she was in the hospital, it was a long time before she could separate her visions from her human memory. She might say, 'Jacki, didn't —— have a gun in his pocket when he came to see me? Didn't so-and-so threaten me at knifepoint? I'm sure he had a gun. I can see the gun, I can tell you what it looks like.'

No, I'd say, and no and *no*. No one had a gun. No one harmed you. She thought at last about her brain, with its chambers and synapses and endorphins waving in a wind of passion like curtains in a tempest, and the rooms inside her brain, furnished with a million transcendent scenes that flickered as she walked from chamber to chamber. 'The doctor says it's just a condition,' she said of her bipolar diagnosis, 'like diabetes or high blood pressure. I just have to take the lithium for it, like people take medication for their hearts.' Yes, I said, yes and yes. Forever. Forever, my mother said, sounding sad. And more than sad: mortal and finite. I think it was the first moment that my mother ever accepted mental illness as a condition of her life, and it came after so many seasons of insanity. Yet each time she thought the craziness would never come again, that Sheba was gone forever, kept out by good intentions and reams of effort. And each time, she remembered very little of what had been done or said when she was sick. Which I regret. She doesn't remember in any specific way the costumes and speeches and strange migrations, the visit to bail out a prisoner or attempts to steal a horse or set a feast for Mary Baker Eddy. What she remembers is the feeling that she could set the world on fire, that she could paint what people were thinking and feeling, that she had the physical prowess of three – that she felt wonderful. That she was brilliant. That's what she remembers.

'When I was sick I knew I could walk for miles without getting tired,' my mother has told me. 'I knew I could ride a horse as fast as the wind. When I was in the hospital I could play Ping-Pong and never, ever miss the ball!' She remembers the sense of omniscience that made her feel as though she could walk through fire. That is why she has saved, as I have, the notebooks and writings, drawings and files, which are the cryptography of that other life. They are her canon, her psalms.

The day my mother came home from the hospital, after a month or so, was a big day, a day of cooking and cleaning and getting ready for reentrance into family society, and when she came in with Kate, we put our arms around her. She had gained weight but was still so thin that I thought of the rhyme 'Step on a crack, break your mother's back.' She was a person whom strong emotion would buffet, with a fragile face that had in it the expectation of bruising. But she looked all around her, touched the objects of her home, a few of which I left as I found them because I wanted to remind her. They appeared to have lifted and resettled into place as if by gusts of wind: a doll's teacup hanging from a candlestick, a cross with a cameo necklace twisted over the crucifix.

'I'm home,' she said, 'I'm home. I'm home after what seems like such a long, long time.' Her eyes were clear, her face composed. Our mother was back. It had been nearly a year since I came home to find Marie Antoinette seated before her vanity, dressed in bustier and garters. Sheba would be out there somewhere on the road, blazing proud. I realized, not for the first time, that I'd very much miss her. I've never wanted her back, with her echo chamber voice and her claws, but I miss her power, her redemption of the mundane, and there are moments when I close my eyes and, thinking of her magnificent transmutations, feel that Sheba has never left.

It was hard, of course. After the earthquake, the story begins, after the tidal wave scours the beach, after the fire. After the war ends, the memory of war begins and never ends. My mother lost the second house she owned and most of her life savings, including what she'd saved for retirement. She was bankrupt, and the bank could have foreclosed on Mabel's bungalow, on which my mother had taken out a home improvement loan. I argued with the bank – in a small town, after forty-odd years of residence, this is still a personal conversation. They held off taking Dolores to court, and eventually, she paid or settled what she could on most of her debts. I wrote to each and every bill collector, exactly three dozen of them, and offered fifty cents on the dollar when I could or how-dare-you-sell-a-crazy-woman-a-car-type letters when that seemed more appropriate. Miraculously, almost every creditor was willing to accept some money rather than nothing at all. It was seven years before my mother ever got another credit card, and she still treats it as though it were breakable.

People forgave her. My mother was so clearly desperate to get a job. She started waitressing again immediately when she got well, and kept that as her night job, working sixty hours a week when most people think of retiring, until a couple years ago. During the days she got another job, and because in her well life she is a charming and amazing force of nature, she got a good one: assistant to the executive of a software company. She's become responsible for getting flagpoles painted and parking lots cleared of snow and checks mailed out and she can find things in the office that other people have lost. She dressed as a man last Halloween, she wins raffles. She gets up at five A.M. to do her face and hair and exercise, is at her desk by eight o'clock, and never leaves before five, filling the vending machines, renting out office space, organizing her boss's life as efficiently as she once sewed up her own in costumes of fantasy. She has collected all the crazy recipes she'd made when she was ill and tried them again, sane. Pretty good! Could she really have made a go of it with Déjà Vu Foods? 'I can cook well even when I'm sick,' my mother maintains, and with the exception of anchovy cookies I'd say that is true. My mother and I take our coffee out to the deck of the Dolores-Mabel bungalow and sip from what is left of the Think About Me cups. We think about her. She started over, right where she'd begun on Lake Puckawasay, and it is Menomenee County that changes around her, sold to the highest bidder, transforming lakes and forests and farms into an uninspired, multiplexed, strip-mall suburban welter. Only my mother's small town survives as a reminder of the past, and just one of the farms remains from her days as a young bride, when the fertile reaches of so much farmland threatened to bury her alive.

My mother still sits before her vanity and dons her costumes, big frilled skirts the size of rainbows and pantaloons with can-can ruffles and turquoise concoctions with lace trims and those puffy-sleeved off-the-shoulder blouses, trimmed in ribbons. It's her Dolly Parton square dance look. She square-dances three or four times a week. I went with her once recently on a rainy night to a local primary school and watched her promenading around the room with the Swinging Stars and the Hoedowners, the Dudes and Dolls, the Taws and Paws, the Boots and Slippers. The Wisconsin Square Dance motto this year is 'For unmatched comfort and fun, dance and mix in ninety-six.' The room was full of elderly children, Dolores among the very youngest of them, hooting and skipping, laughing a lot, doing the allemandes and spin-the-bottles and banner-stealing. The caller addresses them as 'girls and boys,' when they are not 'ladies and gents,' and tells them to 'make a wave down the middle.' They do so, and there is Dolores. She is concentrating on her skips, letting the breeze from the floor fans ruffle her auburn hair, flirting with one of the Dudes, whose wife stands impatiently waiting for him to finish sashaying my mother around the dance floor, her turquoise skirt doing a full-circumference sail. Kate and Sarah, home on a visit, stand with me as we watch our mother. In the square dances that her group performs, there are sixty-eight main steps and a plus set of twenty-seven, and our mother knows them all. She twirls in front of us while we sit on the sidelines.

'Isn't this fun?' she calls out, laughing. 'Why can't we do it?' we say. She whirls the span of the equator. She has the energy of someone I have seen before. She has the memory of that energy that can do anything.

I still dream of Sheba. For me the need to know more of her lies beyond tomorrow; burns and calls. For a long time after my mother's last confinement, I would still see them all, the girl in the well, the beckoning hand with its long pointed nails, the veil in the mist. I traveled within months of my mother's recovery to India, and then was briefly based in London, and went eventually to Jordan, where I fell in love with the Middle East. I arrived in Jordan a few days after Saddam Hussein invaded Kuwait, and tourists were fleeing west on the airline I was boarding to go east. Women in bronze face masks and inky black veils sailed by, and the sky was the blue of lapis lazuli, the moment the Persian poet Bijan Jalili calls happiness, a blue sky with a few clouds. Time suspended and has never been the same again. I felt the power of someone returning home after a long, long trip, in the desert. I loved the camaraderie of my colleagues, some of whom were scoundrels who had been out there way too long, and some of whom had grown up in the countries that were now being held hostage by other nations, and others who spoke three or four languages because that's what had come of going to Oxford. Some of my colleagues were so utterly charming that King Hussein and Queen Noor would have them quietly to dinner, and I lived as the person who sat at the Mad Hatter's Tea Party and entertained my friends as we waited in long shadows for coming annihilation with stories of what had happened in the twilight worlds in which I had tried to discover the Queen of Sheba.

And that is where I am now. Somewhere else. I fall in love with strange places and strangers, many of whom become my friends, and I know when I think of them and my mother and my past, and even the air on which we share our stories, that as in Walt Whitman's words, I contradict myself. *Do I contradict myself? Very well then I contradict myself. I am large, I contain multitudes.* My mother contained multitudes in our small town. I never doubted it.

I have written most of this book in Canada, and will probably finish it in my grandfather's ancestral town in Ireland, but I remember starting it in a garden in London and showing it to a friend in 1990 in Baghdad. It was just scraps of memory then, Sheba, my souvenir stubs, passport stamps from the trip. And it's time to pack up now and put things away. Soon I will be saying good-bye to one of the more tender traveling companions in my life, whom I met in Tehran, to which he will return. Though I can tell you where I am going next, I do not know where I will call home, where I will settle, and I don't know who I shall ever share a home with, though in recent months, or is it just recent days, it seems that I could do that, given the right city on our spinning globe, crowded with its ballerinas and despots and incantations and explosions. A city I would have to love because it is eccentric and strange and full of the kind of people who would say, 'Ah, your mother thought she was the Queen of Sheba? *Tant pis*. Mine thought she was the Queen of the Universe!'

My mother, the 1950s housewife, never asks me to settle down. I am as content as any traveler deducing that she has everything she needs for the road. I have my books, and I have my friends, I have my incarnations of what is holy in a slew of religions and I have my letters and my need for speech. Like my mother I can look into the future and see a thousand stories waiting there. And maybe a home defined by that shared and sacred space with which we redeem our lives.

But when I think of the word *home*, and I think of the word *mother*, I see our small house at the edge of the pasture, the one my father helped to build. I see Kate and Sarah and me running through long grass to settle in the afternoon on our mother's bed, where she sat before her vanity and held up first one bauble and then another to her ears or throat, a goddess brushing hair that gushed like a flume down her back.

'Always remember,' my mother is saying, as the brush descends, 'that you are the most beautiful woman in the room,' and I think of myself waiting the world over, waiting, waiting for the children of Londonderry or the body counts in Tel Aviv or the shouts of Death to America to die away in Iran, waiting for the snow to stop so the ferry can come to take us for a glass of wine, over Lake Ontario, waiting for comfort and for change. And I think that no matter where I wait I have something no one else has. I have carried a framed photograph of my mother with me in all these places. In the picture she is dining out, wearing the satin brocade sheath made just for her on the Kowloon Road in Hong Kong in 1960, an exquisite dress with embossed pagodas and Chinese characters and plumed peacocks. She is in her midthirties in the picture, dark-haired and dark-eyed and glowing, younger than I am now. I wear her dress with its matching bolero for special occasions. I wore it for my thirty-fifth birthday in Hong Kong. For my thirty-seventh birthday with Geraldine and Tony and Renee in London. For my fortieth birthday with all of them and more in Washington. Perhaps I will wear it the next time I fall in love. I do not know where I will be, but I do know that wherever I go, and whatever I intend, I will carry the photograph of my mother in this dress. Sheba lurks behind the smile of the woman in this picture, perhaps in the darkness next to her, present, a threat who could emerge, should emerge, but who in more than half a decade has not. Lithium, pray to God, keeps her at bay. Her powers remain, however, her maps and territories, her songs and poems, her history and the tiny ways in which she curls her hair and paints her lips. As a daughter I have exhumed her and studied the arch of her eyebrows, the cleft in her throat. I have tried to fix her on these pages, so that wherever I go I can say to her, 'I had you there, then. I caught you, forever.' What I know of her resides in the calcium of my bones, the rose quartz of my heart, is stuck beneath my teeth.

'Always remember you are the most beautiful woman in the room,' my mother is saying in my head. I look at her photograph, right now this minute, and she is. She looks a lot like the daughter of the Queen of Sheba, who is, like Sheba, at last at peace.